CONTENTS

Chasing the Nomadic Dream	1
Introduction	3
Mattapoisett, MA to Gloucester Point, VA	8
Gloucester Point, VA to Beaufort, NC	34
Beaufort, North Carolina	66
Beaufort to The Bahamas	73
Spanish Wells	135
Eleuthera	148
Hatchet Bay	153
The Exumas	172
Return to Hatchet Bay	224
The Southern Abacos	257
The Northwestern Abacos	316
Well's Bay to St Augustine	358
Epilogue	382
Acknowledgements	385
Books By This Author	387

CHASING THE NOMADIC DREAM

By

Paul Trammell

Copyright 2020

PAUL TRAMMELL

Freedom to roam
On a floating home
Might make me smile
For a little while
If the deep blue sea
Were kind to me
I would follow the wind
Wherever it may send
I would follow the stars
No noise from cars
Sunset and sunrise
Multicolored skies
Whatever the weather
For worse or for better
Nature by my side
My only bride

INTRODUCTION

To live our best life, we must let go of our fears and chase our dreams, and in order to have dreams worth chasing, we have to dream big and dream often.

Life is a series of decisions and resulting actions. We are often encountered by situations that require decisions in the moment, but we are also encountered by ideas that require long thought before making decisions based on these ideas. While we always have the option of not deciding and instead following the path of least resistance, this rarely leads to anything noteworthy, and never to greatness. It is the decisions and plans we make and the actions leading to their fruition that make life interesting.

For as long as I can remember, I've dreamed about living deep within nature, living off the land and removed from society. While I used to think it would happen in the mountains and forests, or perhaps a tropical jungle, the dream eventually specified sailing. On a sailboat, I could not only live deep within nature, but I could also be nomadic and dip in and out of society whenever I chose.

It took me a long time and a lot of thinking to figure out how to make this dream into reality, but I eventually found the pieces of the puzzle. Step by step, I walked toward the dream, and away from my old life.

In October of 2019, having sold my house in Florida and divesting myself of nearly all of my possessions, I drove to Massachusetts, with everything I owned in my Suburban and a U-Haul trailer, where my new boat waited for me. She wasn't a new boat at all, rather she was built in 1972. *Windflower* was a Cartwright 40, also known as the Bluewater 40, designed by Jerry Cartwright and built right there in Buzzards Bay, Massachusetts. She lived in Mattapoisett her whole life, coming out of the water every winter.

While she was well cared for, she was also getting old and many of her parts were ready for replacement. I didn't have the time to do everything I wanted to do to her, not by a longshot, so I focused on the bare necessities for sailing her south and away from the coming New England winter. I worked on her without pause as the weather got colder and stormier. Being from Florida, I did not relish the idea of sailing in the North Atlantic that late in the year.

I was a solo sailor, and intended to remain one, but *Windflower* was a heavily built 40' cutter, 10' longer and three times the weight of my previous boat, a 30' Dufour Arpege. I did not have enough confidence in my ability to sail her alone on a multi-day passage, so I recruited help, and Cristina and Albert came to help me sail south.

I met Albert a few months prior in Maine. He and I both showed up at the same time to look at a boat for sale, a beautiful Yankee 38. He was a pleasant gentleman, older than me, and I learned that he was a delivery captain. I logged him in my mind as a potential crew to help me move whatever boat I bought south.

Cristina is a friend from all the way back in high school, and she sailed with me once before, from Miami to Jacksonville, on my previous boat, *Sobrius*.

My intentions were to sail her to the Chesapeake Bay and spend another month working on her, then sail to the Caribbean for the winter. This was to be the start of my cruising life. I hoped to be retired as a carpenter for good, and to simply sail to interesting places and write about them.

I craved adventure. I craved solitude. I craved communion with nature. All could be found on the ocean, and I intended to find them and delve deep within.

I almost sank *Windflower* with a hose on our first day together. I was filling up the water tanks, which the listing advertised as having a 100-gallon capacity, and in my naivety, I thought it would overflow out the deck-fill when the tanks were full. Instead, it overflowed into the bilge and eventually floated the floorboards. I was shocked that this was even possible, but, like many things on *Windflower*, the water tanks needed some attention, as did the bilge pump.

In my three weeks in Mattapoisett, I worked all day every day on *Windflower*. I tried my best to waterproof all the leaking deck hardware. I didn't feel that I had the time to re-bed everything, so I just caulked around nearly everything on deck with heavy-duty marine caulk (3M 5200). I took apart, cleaned, and lubricated all the seacocks, and replaced most of the drain hoses, as well as the exhaust hose. I installed an AIS transmitter (a device that uses VHF radio frequency to broadcast and receive from other boats information such as location, speed, and heading, all in order to avoid collisions). I had the engine worked on to fix an oil leak, did a multitude of minor repairs, and I spent a lot of time cleaning and organizing the interior.

I also took her out sailing a few times to get to know my new boat, on days when the weather was nice, but the weather was always on my mind. I watched the wind forecasts daily, looking for a good weather window to sail south to the Chesapeake Bay, where I intended to stay for a month and continue working on *Windflower* before heading to the Caribbean. This would be a three or four-day trip. But four consecutive days of reasonable weather was a rare occurrence. Nor'easters formed and terrorized the ocean every week, sometimes twice a week. One storm, while I was there, was so strong that it produced sustained winds over 50 knots for over a day. This worried me. Under no circumstances did I want to be out in such conditions.

Eventually a reasonable weather window appeared, and Cristina and Albert showed up to help me sail.

Cristina, Albert and I sailed *Windflower* in the bay on the day before departure. We practiced man-overboard drills, maneuvered through all points of sail, and checked over everything we could think of. In the evening, we sat down to a nice dinner, and decided to leave before sunrise to catch the outgoing tide.

Windflower *at the Mattapoisett Boatyard*

MATTAPOISETT, MA TO GLOUCESTER POINT, VA

Liquid earth
All around
Covering all in sight
Bright blue, dark blue, green
Grey or black at night
Calm, flat and serene
Rolling swell or windblown chop
Misty white with fog
Quiet
Thunderous and howling mad
Bountiful and giving
All encompassing
Hungry and devouring
Liquid earth
All around
Many faces
Many moods
Indifferent to man
Awe inspiring
Never tiring
Life started here
Liquid earth all around
Many creatures to be found

Beneath its dynamic surface
Things of beauty
Things of fear
Creatures unseen
Creatures dear
Some to eat
Some to eat us
Respect inducing
Desire producing
Liquid Earth
All around
No greater world
Shall be found

The high-pitched beeping of an alarm wakes me in the night, and it takes me a moment to realize that I'm on a boat. A few uncomfortable moments pass before I understand what the offensive and somewhat distressing sound is, and I slowly get up, carefully make my way through the cabin, and shut it off.

"It's just the gale alarm on the barometer," I say to Albert, who looks at me from inside his sleeping bag nestled in the quarterberth opposite the navigation table, as if this might be a reassuring fact. Without another word, I creep back to the V-berth and crawl under the warm blankets.

Time passes, I fall back asleep, and the confounded thing sounds again, waking me a second time, and I repeat the process. The gale alarm doesn't worry me, since I've been watching the forecast and don't expect any strong winds. But I can't say for the other two crew. I imagine it unsettles them a bit.

A much less frightening alarm wakes me at 3:30 in the morning and I get up, get dressed, and make coffee. I consult the barometer and record that inside the boat is 61 degrees, the humidity is 88%, and the pressure 1007 hPa. It is October 23rd and finally time to begin sailing south.

At 4:00am, Albert is standing in the dark at the bow and casting off the mooring lines while I stand at the helm, peering into the nothingness of a dark and foggy night. As we slowly motor forward, Albert shines the spotlight on moorings and I steer around them.

I can scarcely see one boat length ahead, but the spotlight Albert holds constantly shines on highly-reflective mooring balls. I turn to port, then to starboard, zig zagging across the bay in the relentless and disorienting fog.

I notice one light flashing in the sky, illuminating the fog directly behind us, and wonder what it might be. Clearly it's a lighthouse, but the Mattapoisett lighthouse is on my left and still ahead of us, it can't be behind us already.

I experience a moment of disorientation.

Look at the chartplotter, you fool!

The little boat on my chartplotter is heading for the rocks. *Is that me?* According to the instrument, shallow water is getting close, but my own firm sense of direction does not accept what the chartplotter is trying to tell me. I look ahead at Albert. No moorings are in my way. I need a moment to think.

What's to think about, you fool, trust the chartplotter and turn around.

Of course, I need to look at the chartplotter and not Albert. Generally speaking, what I see overrules the chartplotter, but when there is nothing to see but fog, the chartplotter rules. The fog is confusing me. I fix my tired eyes on the chartplotter and swing us around 120 degrees to port, putting us back on course. I want to do this gradually, so as not to alert Albert and Cristina to my mistake, but I abandon that plan and just turn hard. Later Albert tells me he knew we were heading toward land, but he figured I knew what I was doing. He was wrong.

Eventually, we pass by the final mooring, the bay widens, and the fog starts to lift. A dark and featureless world is revealed. The surrounding land at the edges of the black Mattapoisett Harbor become dark monoliths, barely visible as black silhouettes against a slightly less black sky. There is almost nothing to see. The darkness is broken as a light illuminates the sky every six seconds. Now the lighthouse *is* behind us, and this time it sits in the right place.

I give the helm to Albert and go below to check the 47-year-old stuffing box. This is the seal on the propeller shaft that separates the inside of the boat from the ocean. It is not dripping (it should be dripping about once a minute) and is quite warm. I pour water over it and determine to do so every 22 minutes. The countdown timer on my watch is already set to 22 minutes, as this is what I use to sleep when singlehanding. I actually sleep for 20 minutes and the other two are for checking the instruments and scanning the horizon. Any more than 20 minutes would dramatically increase the chances of colliding with a ship just over the horizon.

I retake the helm and a sense of relief washes over me as I steer us across the wide water while a red lighted buoy flashes in the distance like an electronic friend waving goodbye. We raise the mainsail, unfurl the yankee, and shut off the rumbling engine. Suddenly I can hear the gentle gurgle of water moving past the hull, the breeze accelerating past the sails, and the metallic creaking of the rigging. The night is otherwise silent and the contrast to the previous cacophony is dramatic in its understatement.

The faint smell of seaweed and low tide is in the air, as well as the strange but identifiable aroma of coming rain. The drizzle starts just before the sun rises over Cape Cod to our left and I put on my big yellow rain slicker, one that I pulled from a dumpster at the marina where I lived in Florida before I left. None of us mention that it is raining, we just keep on sailing. When it's raining and the ship has no bimini for cover, a sailor has three options: get wet, put on foul weather gear, or go below. I am at the helm, so I put on foul weather gear, but water finds its way through my clothing and I get wet anyway. Waterproof is a relative term.

At 8:00am, the wind is a perfect 12.6 knots and we sail on a close reach, into the wind, at 5.8 knots. *Windflower* cuts through the little waves with authority, as if challenging the ocean to throw more her way. *Windflower* wants to run across the ocean and slice a long furrow through the water for hundreds of miles. The open ocean lies ahead and we will soon be there. She is ready for an ocean passage, I can feel it through the cockpit sole in my feet and through the wheel in my hands. I melt into the vessel and become one with her while clenching my teeth in an uncontainable smile. Adventure is here and now and it is only increasing.

We tack twice before rounding the last obstacle, a rocky shoal off Cuttyhunk Island, and I point our bow 218 degrees, straight for the Chesapeake Bay. *Windflower* heels to about 15 degrees and accelerates to 6.5 knots and all is as it should be.

The ocean's energy is no longer attenuated by land and my vessel rises to the occasion, slicing through the endless advance of 6' swell, rising and falling, leaning over and pressing forward. I hold the wheel in both hands, standing at the helm in the light rain and saltwater misting from the bow. This is why I am here, this is why I sold my house. This is my now and this is my future, only I hope the future will be warmer and drier.

An hour later, I give Albert the helm and go below to check all the through-hull fittings for leaks. To my great pleasure, no seawater is finding its way in. However, a different problem comes to my attention at the navigation table. The batteries are already low, with the voltmeter reading 12.2, and this worries me. I start the engine to charge them and let it run for an hour. The batteries are back up to 12.6 when I shut the engine off.

"What do you think, should we sail into Long Island Sound and go through New York City?" Albert asks, in a suggestive manner.

Cristina looks at me as if supporting the suggestion. I don't understand why they would suggest such a thing, unless they have not been paying attention to the weather, which is likely, since they are crew and do not share the responsibility of the ship and everyone's safety, as I do.

"There's no good reason to do that," I say. "We would have to sail upwind all day in Long Island Sound, directly into the wind, in fact, we'd have to motor. It would add at least a day to the trip, and that would put us in danger of being out in very bad weather Sunday as we approach the Chesapeake Bay. The forecast shows 25-30 knots straight out of the south for Sunday. We'd probably get stuck anchoring at Sandy Hook for three days. No. That's a bad idea."

They acquiesce, but something doesn't seem right. Wasn't this obviously a bad idea? It certainly seems that way to me. Perhaps Albert is unsure about *Windflower's* ability to safely get us to our destination. [After the passage, Cristina told me that this was indeed the case.] Cristina used to live in New York City and might have in mind trying to catch some friends or at least wave to them as we motor down the East River.

"If we go through New York City, maybe we could have the woman who designed your tablecloth aboard for dinner. She's very influential, you know. It could be good for your writing career." A year ago, Cristina gave me a tablecloth with a coral reef print designed by a woman in New York City.

This sounds rather absurd to me, and I give the short reply "We have to let the weather determine our course."

The crew are perplexing me. I don't understand why we would do anything but continue sailing directly toward our destination. Although the ride is lively, upwind in the 6' seas, *Windflower* was made for much more challenging conditions and she sails quite well in these. Her full keel cuts through the waves without any hint of slamming and tracks straight and true. She is smooth but excited, like a horse galloping across the plains after a season in the corral.

Block Island comes into view, and its big offshore wind turbines rise like white sentinels from the deep blue water. We all stand transfixed by the spinning behemoths and I wonder how they are secured to the seafloor.

The wind is now blowing 20 knots and we cut through the waves at 7. *Windflower* is heeled about 20 degrees and moving with authority through 6-7' swells with full main and yankee flying. But the leeward rail dips very close to the water-line, and I take this as a sure sign that a reef is called for. While Albert steers, I lower the main and secure the first reef. *Windflower* rights herself noticeably and slows to 6.5 knots.

I check the voltmeter, and again, the batteries are down to 12.3 volts. This is not right, but all I can do is run the engine if they need to be charged. I watch the voltmeter, and an hour later I start the engine again.

Albert is at the helm and I go below to change into dry clothes. When I come back up, Albert says to me "Why don't we sail behind Block Island, find a calm stretch, and have lunch?" Cristina looks at me for an answer, as if backing up Albert.

What an absurd idea, I think. Detour half a day in order to go behind Block Island? For lunch? I don't understand *at all* what these two are getting at, but I suspect it's another ploy to get us to go through Long Island Sound.

"If you two would like lunch, I'll gladly make something to eat. What would you like?" They ask for peanut butter and jelly sandwiches and five minutes later I come up with two. I don't make one for myself, because peanuts sometimes upset my stomach when I am offshore.

"I have good friends in New York City, Paul, and you need to get people interested in your journeys. Sailing through the city would generate interest. You can't be a writer in a vacuum, you know."

I feel like throwing my arms in the air and groaning out loud, but I maintain relative control. Again, I mention the headwinds we would face today in the sound, and the foul weather coming Sunday. I end with "We'd probably end up anchored at Sandy Hook for a few days waiting out the bad weather, probably in very uncomfortable condition. None of us want that, do we?" I feel like I'm fighting a battle to keep us on course, not with the weather or my vessel, but with the crew.

But the crew are not finished yet.

The wind turbines get closer and have us all fixated on them when Albert turns *Windflower* towards them and says "Well, it seems we're all interested, so why don't we get closer for a better look?"

"Please don't Albert. Just keep us on course." I look at Navionics on my phone for our heading. "217 degrees, please." We have already lost a degree.

I begin to wonder if I shouldn't have done this passage solo. I feel my crew are conspiring against me now.

As the three of us sit in the cockpit, something hits me in the head, and then the arm. I reach down and pick up the shackle from the first reef block on the clew of the mainsail. It worked its way loose and fell. [I installed blocks (pulleys) on the clew and tack of the two reefs in order to reduce friction while using the single-line reefing. Months later, I removed the blocks because they chafed the sail too much.] The sail noisily shakes in the wind while I go below and fish around the hardware drawer for a replacement, as only the "U" part of the shackle remains. Although I have many, I cannot find one the right size. Back in the cockpit, I untie the reefing line from the boom and run it through the clew without a shackle, tie it off to the boom, pull the line tight, and the reef is again secure.

"It'll work just as good like that," I assure my silent crew.

I go below and lay down for a nap, but I hear the unmistakable sound of the sails being trimmed tighter, and I feel

Windflower alter course just a bit to starboard. Good grief, I think, Albert is turning us toward shore, but I don't have the energy to continue the battle and I shut my eyes and quickly fall asleep.

The ride is lively when I wake, and the boat is a bit hard to get around in down below. Luckily, Jerry Cartwright designed her with handholds all over the interior, so no matter where one is below, a handhold is always in reach, and there's always another to grab along the way to wherever one is going. I make my way to the cockpit with all four appendages and emerge into the cool air, which seems impatient to get to wherever it is going. I take the helm and Albert goes down for some rest.

An hour later, Cristina comes up.

"Albert's not feeling well," she says.

Before I can respond, Albert emerges from the companionway, leans over the side, vomits, and goes below without a word. He continues to get worse as the day wears on, and I am stuck at the helm.

At 4:30pm, we are 15nm (nautical miles (1nm = 1.1 miles)) south and slightly west of Block Island.

Cristina comes into the cockpit from below. "Albert is very ill. I've been checking his pulse, which is normal, but I'm afraid he is getting dehydrated. He won't take any food or fluids, and is refusing to take medication. He asks if we can sail into the lee of Long Island, for calmer water."

I consider the request. "The wind is blowing from the east-northeast, and is forecast to veer, which would allow us to sail there. If I turn now, we'll have to motor upwind. I'll change course as soon as the wind allows."

I don't want to motor all the way there, into the waves and wind, in fact, I don't want to go there at all. I want to continue sailing at 7 knots toward our destination. While Albert is paid crew, here specifically to help me sail to Chesapeake Bay, and has a responsibility to do so, I, as the captain, have a responsibility to keep Albert from getting worse. I weigh the two conflicting responsibilities in my head.

Albert remains seriously ill and Cristina, who is a physician, keeps watch over him, checks his pulse, tries to get him to drink fluids, and offers medication, which he continues to refuse. He asks if we are going to Long Island, and I say that I think the wind will veer any minute now. I'm watching the forecast on my phone, which somehow still has service.

40.7361° N, 71.7674° W, 21nm south of Montauk Point, NY

The wind never changes direction, and at 7:30pm I am asked again to head to Long Island. Although it is very difficult for me, since I am ready to be in the Chesapeake Bay, which I imagine to be a much warmer climate than that of Mattapoisett, Massachusetts, I tack and start the engine. We motor-sail for the rest of the day and into the night, no longer heading toward our destination, but instead away from it, while Albert comes up and vomits every so often, then collapses in his berth. I stay at the helm as the sun sets and the temperature plummets.

At 11:00pm we are 2nm off Long Island and the water is indeed calm. I turn, cut the engine, and begin sailing along the coast, just outside the "Fish Trap Area" labeled on the charts.

I've been at the helm for nearly 12 hours and I begin to mentally prepare myself for an all-nighter. Cristina, who weighs 95 pounds and is acclimated to South Florida, is in the early stages of hypothermia and completely immobile, wearing her foul-weather gear and curled up under blankets down below. [She later tells me that she wanted to help steer, but was literally unable to move her limbs. This is a sign of entering the second stage of hypothermia, as she explains.] Albert is either sleeping or vomiting over the side. I am cold and tired, but resigned to do what I have to do. At least the night is peaceful and we are sailing; it really is beautiful.

The stars shine above, reflect off the gently moving ocean, and the peace is only occasionally broken by short one-sided conversations on the VHF radio. While musing at the dark and serene setting, a voice in a thick New York City accent belts out of the VHF "How about f--- you buddy?" and the serenity is replaced by incredulity that someone would say such a thing on the VHF, although I laugh at the quote.

40.9701° N, 72.0021° W, 2.5nm southeast of Napeague Harbor, NY, Day 2

To my great pleasure, Albert comes up and relieves me around midnight. He says he is still queasy, but is smiling and ready for a turn at the helm. I thank him, wish him good evening, and go below. I set my countdown timer and sleep for 22 minutes, after which I go up, check on Albert, and go back to sleep. Two more times, I get up after 22 minutes and check on him, and both times he says I can get some more rest, which is a great relief. I take the helm around 1:30 in the morning and steer for about two hours before Albert relieves me again.

In the morning, as I steer my ship and enjoy the warm rays of sunlight, notice the wind is much calmer than before, and check the weather forecast. Two calm and nearly windless days in a row are on order. While the autopilot steers, I take the reef out of the mainsail, hoist the staysail, then point us toward the Chesapeake Bay.

When Albert and Cristina come up, I declare that the weather is to be calm for two days, long enough for us to motor all the way to the Delaware Bay, and perhaps the Chesapeake. Our new course is 134 degrees. I do not ask their opinions and go below for a nap. I sense a bit of a turn to starboard, but fall asleep anyway.

When I wake up much later, Albert is still at the helm, Cristina has on long pink rubber gloves and is doing dishes. Albert reports that the stuffing box is no longer hot. I check it and even though it is not dripping, it is quite cool.

Albert still has not eaten anything since yesterday, but

he doesn't look so bad anymore.

By mid-afternoon, the sun is out and the temperature is a pleasant 67. The breeze is 7 knots straight on the nose and we motor with the sails down. Since I have not eaten a solid meal yet, I am famished. I leave Cristina at the helm and tell her I'll make us something to eat. I go below and step into the galley.

The situation calls for something familiar and delicious, and I decide on an old favorite from my time living at the marina in Jacksonville. Into a bowl I put salsa, avocado, garlic stuffed olives, and canned salmon. The ingredients are not mixed, but rather sit, for the most part, in their own spaces. Cristina and I eat the concoction with tortilla chips seated in the cockpit while the Raymarine wheel pilot steers. The simple pleasure of a good meal is magnified by the deep ocean setting, and the fact that my body demands nutrition after a day of nearly fasting.

The stuffing box is on my mind, and I check it after lunch. It's much cooler than the ambient temperature, although I still see no water dripping, as I should. I'll have to continue to monitor it for the duration of the passage.

At 6:00pm I get up from a nap. Albert, at the helm, sees me, smiles, and says "What's for dinner?"

"Albert's back!"

Cristina and I rejoice at his recovery. She was worried, especially the day before, that he would become severely dehydrated and require medical attention. This was another argument used in the attempt to get me to turn toward shore the previous day. Perhaps the early rumblings of seasickness were part of the reason Albert persisted in urging the detour to begin with, Cristina later speculates.

I make a big pot of clam chowder, or rather I heat up three cans, and we all eat it in the cockpit with crackers while the sun shines down on us. I marvel at how calm the Atlantic Ocean is. Here we are, in the North Atlantic in October, north of Cape Hatteras, and the ocean is as calm as can be. Not only that, but the sun is out and the air is warm. It all seems so unlikely, and wonderful.

A small black speck on the horizon grows and flaps jet-black wings. I notice each wing has a bright red circle. It flies next to us and then lands on the lifeline for a rest. It's a red-wing blackbird. What a blessing it is to provide a bit of solid ground for a migrating bird to rest as it flies the shortest route between two faraway places, taking the little songbird out over the ocean. The majestic bird repositions and sits for a while on the coiled up and hanging spinnaker halyard. Without saying goodbye, or even looking back at us, the bird leaps into the air and disappears ahead.

"That was a good omen," I declare.

At 10:00pm, 30nm east of Surf City, NJ, I wake from a long nap, put on some warm clothes, and check on Albert. He's ready for a break, so I make coffee and then take the helm at 10:30. "Sleep as long as you want," I tell Albert.

I wasn't cold when I was down below, nor when I emerged from the cabin, but after sitting still at the helm for just a few minutes, the true nature of the temperature dawns on me, and I wish I'd put on another layer, or perhaps the black fuzzy neck warmer. I imagine how nice the synthetic fleece would feel on my neck, all bunched up under my chin, holding in all the heat that is currently radiating away from me out of my cold neck.

Luckily, I have a cup of hot coffee in an insulated, spill-proof mug, and I sip it in the cockpit while we motor south through the dark but starry night. With no bimini above my head, all the night's sky is in view.

Without warning, the stationary sky is streaked by a thin green line that appears in an instant and fades in a second. I look up as much as I can, leaning back to do so. A few more shooting stars decorate the sky with streaks of yellow-green light and I smile at my luck. I must have done something good in this life in order to be able to be here, on this fine vessel, out on the ocean at night, looking up at the stars and seeing little meteors as they burn up after travelling through vast unknown reaches of deep space, perhaps for millennia.

Sailing at night is literally otherworldly, for this is a world that few ever experience. While millions of people are within one hundred miles of us, none are within eyesight, and none share this view of the sky, which is free of light pollution and therefore glorious in its abundance of visible stars.

After a long spell of stargazing, my coffee mug is empty and I fancy a snack. I turn on the autopilot, go below and fetch a chocolate chip muffin. I bought these at the Mattapoisett Diner, as an impulse-buy after a decadent breakfast. The muffins are such wonderful treats, and bringing eight of them along was a fine decision indeed. I refill my coffee and return to the wheel, smiling and full of chocolate muffin.

Late at night, I sit at the helm, steering towards a particular star and monitoring the white numbers that depict our heading on the dark screen of the chartplotter. I occasionally repeat the phrase "bigger numbers to the right" to remind myself which way to steer. I'm trying to keep the number at 209, heading for the red buoy at Smith Island Shoal, which is about 12nm offshore just north of the Chesapeake Bay.

12:18am, 39.4467° N, 73.7964° W, 25.7nm east of Brigantine, NJ, Day 3

Boats are constantly in view and I use the AIS to check on all of them. It's not only useful, but also fun to learn their names, sizes, speeds, countries of registration, etc. It's amazing to see a little light on the horizon, and then find out it is a Dutch ship 350 meters long moving at 21 knots. Installing this piece of equipment was a high priority before leaving Mattapoisett and is invaluable when other boats are around. I'm happy to have crew, because with so many other boats out here, I would not be able to sleep much if I was alone.

A red light appears in the sky, grows brighter, about two hand-widths above the horizon, then it disappears. I've seen a few shooting stars tonight, but I don't know what this light was. I think I saw two airplanes fly through the same airspace only moments before. Could it have been a military exercise, a rocket or a flare from an airplane? I'm perplexed. I'm also cold and tired and my mind is working slowly.

I see another one. *It's an emergency flare!*

It must be a flare, what else could it be. But the light never rose, as I expect a flare to. Should I steer towards it? It seems very far away. I get out the binoculars and peer in the direction of the flare. I'm not sure what I saw, but it might have been a flare. What is protocol in this situation, I wonder.

I turn on the autopilot, pick up the VHF, and call the Coast Guard. I report the possible flare to them, give my position, and answer a few questions. Now, with my conscience clear, I feel like I've done the right thing.

After about ten minutes, the Coast Guard calls back and asks more questions, which I answer. I wait and listen afterwards, but they never issue a call for ships to be on the lookout for a vessel in distress, which I often hear them do when a possible flare is reported. This makes me think that they confirmed it was a military exercise.

Later in the evening, Cristina comes up and sits with me for the second half of my watch, and the company is appreciated as we admire the spectacular night sky. I tell her about seeing the flares and calling the Coast Guard. She tells me she heard me on the radio, but wasn't sure what I was talking about. Albert relieves me at six in the morning and I give up the helm, but stay in the cockpit for a while, enjoying the scenery and the relaxation that comes from not having to steer.

How wonderful it is to be travelling south after spending a month in New England with winter coming soon.

We soon pass by Atlantic City, and I think back to the time I stayed at a casino hotel there with an old girlfriend, many years ago. I decided I'd gamble only once, and I chose a slot machine. I looked for a coin slot but instead found only a place to insert a bill. I was further dismayed to find that five dollars was the minimum bet, but I was in at this point, my mind was made up to gamble, and I was determined to do so. I fished a five out of my wallet and slipped it into the hungry machine.

I tried to pull the arm, but the arm was fake and stationary, and there was only a disappointing button to press. I reluctantly pressed the big rectangular button. No numbers rolled, no sound was made. Only a digital screen told me I had lost. It was quite anticlimactic and the entertainment of it was not at all worth five dollars, not even one, for that matter.

Albert comes up late in the evening and relieves me, and I fall asleep without delay. Later, I wake to the sound of the robot voice on the VHF reciting the weather. I fall back asleep, but wake again to the same voice. I assume Albert must be listening to the weather on the radio, for a second time.

"Good morning Albert," I say as I emerge from the companionway into the twilight.

"Good morning.

"How was your shift?"

"Oh, it was fine, but now I can't see the chartplotter. It just got darker and darker as the sky brightened."

"Did you adjust the backlight as it got lighter out?" I ask.

"I didn't want to touch it," he says.

I look at it and can't see anything on the screen, so it's impossible to adjust the backlight. I end up draping a coat over the instrument, and in the resulting darkness, I am able to see the screen and turn the backlight back up to its daylight setting.

Although Albert clearly has a lot of sailing experience, I begin to think that he has never used a chartplotter before. He clearly does not want to touch it, like he might break it if he presses the wrong buttons. I used to feel the same way about computers before I got used to them.

Albert tells me that the VHF switched itself to the weather during the night. How strange, I think, for the radio to do such a thing. But later in the day while I am at the helm, a loud voice reciting the weather startles me, and I have to switch the radio back to 16.

The sun comes up over the horizon in a truly magnificent display of colors, a red and orange band separating grey ocean from grey sky. The water reflects the colors on the waves, as does the sky in its clouds, which are also water in a different state. Three of us stare east and are silent. There are no words to be spoken among ourselves in the presence of such beauty; our senses are completely occupied by the spectacle.

While staring at the colors on the horizon, little dark shapes rise into view and sit on the horizon to the south. We are 30nm southeast of Ocean City, NJ. As we slowly move across the calm surface of the ocean, the shapes slowly turn into trawlers and sportfishers. Eventually, as we get closer, we can see that they are not moving, which the AIS confirms, and we all wonder what they are doing. Then we hear a gunshot.

"Maybe it's a fishing tournament and that was the starting gun," I say.

I've never been in a fishing tournament, but this is what I imagine one looks like, a dense cluster of power boats sitting still.

We slowly pass the fleet, giving them plenty of room so as not to disturb the competition, should it be one. Each boat is adorned with fishing rods, some with so many that they look like porcupines sitting on the water. The rising sun is bright and backlights the fleet so they all look like silhouettes. Slowly, the fleet fades into the distance behind us, and the ocean again seems lonely and still.

The empty horizon spawns two more ships, but these are big ones, and one is ahead and coming directly at us. I look it up on the AIS and see that its name is *Everladen*, apparently a poor hardworking ship that never gets a rest. I call the captain on the VHF radio and we agree to pass starboard to starboard. After it passes, I realize that I was looking at the wrong vessel. *Everladen* and *Windflower* passed four miles apart going in opposite directions, so it was quite obvious that we would pass starboard to starboard. The boat I though was *Everladen* was a cargo ship anchored way offshore. This illustrates how polite ships' captains are and how we should never feel awkward about asking how to pass. Even though I called and asked a ridiculous question with a very obvious answer, the captain of *Everladen* was polite and professional in giving me the answer.

The evening comes and with it fog. The breeze is only 5 knots and the ocean looks like glass. Darkness is complete as the clouds obscure the stars while the moon is above the other side of the Earth.

The fog on the water sometimes elicits the impression that we are going backwards. It hangs over the smooth and reflective, yet dark, surface of the ocean and renders impossible any sense of distance or proportion. A faraway light illuminates a patch of fog and draws my eye to it. I find it hard not to steer towards the fuzzy light. I have to concentrate, the fog is distracting me and confusing my sense of direction for the second time on this journey.

Albert relieves me around midnight, and I sleep for two hours before taking the helm for two hours, and the night is a blur of sleeping and taking the helm.

In the morning, when I relieve Albert, he tells me of altering course twice to avoid ships. I ask if he used the AIS. Of course, he says no, he just read their lights and watched their bearing to decide how to proceed, "As I've always done," he says. He truly is an old-school holdout of a sailor.

I check the tides on my phone. I use an application on my phone, which, through some magic trick of technology, does not need phone or internet connection to work, but knows what the tides will be just about anywhere in the world. I discover that we will be entering the marina tomorrow around low tide. Navionics shows seven feet as the shallowest depth at the marina, so we should be fine as long as I pay attention and stay in the deep part of the channel. *Windflower* draws six feet.

Albert suggests checking the fluid levels, so I shut off the engine and go below. The oil and coolant are both a bit low, so I top them off. The transmission oil is fine. I return to the cockpit, start the engine back up, and continue motoring towards our destination, thinking about a hamburger and a hot shower.

At 1:30pm, we are 20nm east of the Delaware/Maryland state line, the breeze has come back, and when it becomes strong enough to move us along, we hoist the sails and cut the engine. We make 5.5 knots in 8 knots of breeze and my mood lightens with the beauty and quiet brought on by the natural propulsion.

Throughout the day, we pass lots of shipping traffic and sportfishers of all sizes, as we have the entire journey. I'm thankful again for the AIS and for not being alone out here. Singlehanding can be a wonderful experience, but constant traffic makes it stressful and exhausting, as I can't allow myself to sleep when I'm alone and traffic is around.

The wind dies in the evening and I take the sails down and start the engine. The batteries are low again. They need to be charged about every six hours, and this is just from running the instruments and navigation lights, which are all LED. Something must be wrong with the batteries or the charging system. I thought I worked this out in Mattapoisett, but obviously I have not yet fixed the problem. I wish I bought new batteries there, and I almost did. If the batteries die out here, we will be sailing without navigation lights, instruments, or the ability to start the engine. The crew hasn't brought this up, but it worries me a bit.

The air is still as the sun sets on a hazy horizon, and

soon all is dark. The surface of the ocean is like a giant sheet of perfectly smooth black glass, across which we efortlessly glide. The only sound is that of the engine and the barely-perceptible gurgling of the water through which we pass. There are no stars out tonight, nor moon to shed light on the otherworldly scene, of which there is little to see.

I only pass one boat on my night watch. It's quiet out here. My mind wanders from place to place, making up little stories, having conversations with people who are not here. I try to think of something useful, but the dark night has its way with my thoughts. In the absence of sensory input, my mind creates its own scenes and stories to fill the empty space. I can see how a person might go mad if kept in darkness and silence for any length of time.

12:15am, 37.5921° N, 75.1892° W, 20nm east of Cedar Island, VA, Day4

I'm cold, and I can't help but think about how nice it might be at the marina we sail towards. I'll be able to plug in the space heater, take a hot shower, and eat hot meals. I think there is a restaurant there, and I'll order a hamburger.

Albert relives me well before I go mad, and I sleep for three hours, which is an incredible luxury, before relieving him and retaking the helm.

I watch the eastern horizon for signs of light. I know it will come on so slowly as to be hard to notice. But it does come and the black horizon turns grey, and the dark purple comes next. An hour later the warm reds, yellows and oranges cover the sky, then a vivid magenta, a color rare in nature, fills out the scene. But as quickly as they come, the warm colors fade, and the sky becomes a soft blue-grey screen.

At 6:30am we finally pass Smith Island Shoal, a feature that exists on the chart, but is not seen with the eye. The temperature is a pleasant 70 and the sun has found its way from behind the clouds. It's a beautiful day and everyone is happy when we turn to starboard and point at the bay.

As we approach the Chesapeake Bay Bridge and the tunnel over which we shall pass, I notice a white boat slowly moving back and forth across the opening, like a sentinel pacing before a gate. I wonder if it is the Coast Guard or some other military craft guarding the entrance to the bay.

At 10:30 we pass over the tunnel and enter Chesapeake Bay proper. The "sentinel" is just a chartered fishing boat. We are almost there and success is immanent as we slowly sail north. A marked channel leads us to the York River, where we turn to port and follow the red and green buoys upstream.

We motor into Sarah Creek, off the York River, on the sunny and warm Saturday afternoon. I can see the red and green channel markers, but they veer way off to the left and appear to lead to a house on the shore instead of the marina, which is further to the right. I can picture in my head where the channel should be, and a fictional representation creates itself in my tired mind, in the center of the creek, not at all where the markers show. *This is where it must be*, I am sure. I call the York River Yacht Haven office on channel 9.

"York River Yacht Haven, York River Yacht Haven, *Windflower*."

"Go ahead *Windflower*."

"It seems like the last red marker is too close to shore, do I need to honor that one?"

"You most certainly do."

"The one that's right in front of the white house?"

"Yes, keep it to starboard."

"Keeping it to starboard, thank you."

As we pass the last red marker, between it and the rocky shore, the water is deep and it all makes sense as we cruise by. I feel quite foolish for doubting its position.

As we near the marina, Albert stands on the bow looking for obstacles and right away points at the water ahead and tells me to turn to starboard. Foolishly and obstinately, I ask what I am avoiding instead of quickly heeding his warning. He repeats with urgency to turn to starboard hard, so I do. "Shallow water, I can see the bottom clearly" he says. Sure enough, as we pass by I see sand just a foot below the dark green water, as well a white stick marking the shoal.

I have to turn 180 degrees to go around the shoal and into B dock, at which point my stern is aimed at my slip, so I make the decision to back in. This is my first time backing into a slip, and I proceed with trepidation. Much to my surprise and delight, the maneuver is a success. Two young men wait on the dock and take our lines. I step ashore with a huge grin and feeling like a king.

Two older men, smiling and carrying drinks, walk up to us to say hello. John and Carry introduce themselves to me and Cristina. They rent a cabin on shore that looks out over the entrance to the marina and they tell us they watched us come in, listened to us on the radio, and monitored us on the AIS. They jovially share with us us how shallow the channel is, how to avoid the sandbars, and where the deep water is. Everything they say is delivered with great enthusiasm and big smiles, as if they are describing some wonderful entertainment, and their joy spills over into Cristina and me and it's a fine welcome to Virginia.

My slip is the last one on the dock before the T at the end, where sits a large white boat that appears to be a schooner without masts. It has a big flat deck, a long wooden bowsprit, and a large raised pilothouse. Its name is carved into the wood below the bowsprit, *Oystercatcher*.

I smile at the wonder of having arrived at my first destination on *Windflower*. I have achieved a major goal and a weight has been lifted off my shoulders. Stress melts away. No longer am I under pressure to get out of Mattapoisett before winter sets in. No longer need I watch for a weather window (at least not until I am ready to head further south).

I treat the crew to dinner at the restaurant, which is fantastic. Even though it is cold, Cristina wants to sit outside, to stay away from the noise inside, the incessant babbling of the television and all the people. She wants to preserve the peace we experienced offshore, and I understand this. Albert goes back to the boat for a coat and I ask him to bring me a hat.

the crew, braving the cold

Windflower *leaving her home of 47 years*

Approaching the York River Yacht Haven in Gloucester Point, Virginia.
Oystercatcher *is the boat on the left with the big pilothouse.*

GLOUCESTER POINT, VA TO BEAUFORT, NC

Give me the sun and degrees
I'm done with the cold
Warm water if you please
For I am getting old
Fish on coral reef
I'll sail there today
Islands and palm trees
If I can only find the way

Bright morning light and bitter cold air greet me as I emerge from the companionway at 7:30am on December 19, 2019, and have a look around. The 23-degree air stings my throat as I breathe it into my lungs. It's the coldest day yet, as if my resolve to live deep within nature is being tested by the Mother.

A big white house looks back at me from shore and I imagine the family inside. The parents are sipping coffee and the children hot chocolate. A Christmas tree stands in the living room and brightly colored presents are stacked underneath. They all wear pajamas and slippers and a fire burns in the fireplace.

What am I doing out here? I think to myself. It's too cold to be outside.

I too am drinking hot coffee, yet I stand in a cold boat wearing an enormous bright orange Mustang one-piece suit, tall insulated rubber boots, sock liners and wool socks, long underwear, three shirts and a wool sweater, my neck warmer, and the Mad Bomber hat. I look like the snowmobilers in photos I remember from my childhood in North Dakota. Nothing on *Windflower* suggests Christmas or family. Everything about her suggests one man is about to head to sea alone.

The mainsail cover was removed yesterday, the staysail is unbagged and its sheets run to their winches. I switch on the instruments and we are ready to get underway. Finally, it is time to sail south.

For the past two months, I worked on *Windflower* at the York River Yacht Haven in Gloucester Point, VA, preparing her for the next phase of the passage south. I installed a solar panel arch and two 175 watt panels, new batteries, a new anchor, new hatches, a new main halyard, rope clutches, a bimini, a third reef, jacklines and cleats, preventers, a below-deck autopilot, a new headstay. I raised the boom to clear my head and the new bimini, I raised the roller furler to clear the anchor, and made various other additions and improvements.

I waited about two weeks for a weather window to allow passage to the Caribbean, but decided to take a three-day window and sail to Beaufort, NC, out and around Cape Hatteras.

Yesterday, I left the marina and anchored just outside in the York River. Bernard Moitessier (one of my favorite authors) said that one should anchor out the night before a passage to "renew one's contract with the sea," and while I agree with his words, I'm also here because I couldn't have gotten out of the marina at low tide this morning. Like Moitessier, I am alone and will be for the foreseeable future.

With gloved hands, I grasp the halyard, lean back and pull hard, raising the mainsail halfway, where it flutters in the cold breeze. I turn the dial on the binnacles and lock the wheel to center. At the bow, I sit down and pull up the anchor while *Windflower* tries to sail forward. Even though I am wearing neoprene gloves, the cold wet chain makes my fingers go numb almost immediately. She tacks three times and on the third I get the anchor all the way up. After dipping it in the water twice to get the mud off, I return to the cockpit and steer us into deeper water. The mainsail slowly rises as I crank on the winch, and by the time I get it to the top of the mast I have to open up my suit to cool off. A wisp of steam rises from my chest, but the chill is back within moments.

I open the rope clutch on the port rail and the furling line runs out as I pull in on the jib sheet. The yankee leaps out and springs to life like the wing of a gull. The staysail rises to attention at the pull of the halyard and *Windflower* responds by accelerating and heeling. Yorktown is disappearing behind us while the Chesapeake Bay emerges from the cold grey fog ahead.

By 8:36am we (*Windflower* and I) are making 5 knots in 7.5 knots of cold breeze under full main, yankee and staysail. The sun is shining in the blue sky, but does little to warm the air, which is still in the twenties. Two small pieces of ice slip off the mainsail, land in the cockpit, and shatter. My breath crystalizes into little clouds with each cold exhale. We sail upwind and *Windflower* heels to starboard as I hang on to the wheel. I know it's going to be a cold day and a colder night, but I smile at the realization that we are finally making progress south. I don't care about the cold, not yet.

The wind picks up as we near the mouth of the York River and enter the Chesapeake Bay, too wide to see across. *Windflower* accelerates and the leeward rail inches closer to the dark water while the bow splits the bay with ease and authority. I reef the main from the cockpit and congratulate myself for the properly-working reefing system. We now make 7.5 knots in 14 knots of breeze, and although this is the speed at which one might carefully maneuver a car in a parking lot, it feels positively fast from the helm of a 40' sailboat.

We continue to heel and accelerate, and I remind myself that I should be taking it easy on the old girl. There is no hurry today. I have a good three-day window to make it to Beaufort, and the journey should take only two. I ease the mainsheet, take in a bit of topping lift, then drop the halyard to the second-reef mark, pull in the blue second reef line, release the topping lift, and finally sheet back in. The process takes about two minutes and now the mainsail has two reefs. I luff the yankee and pull in on the furling line, and *Windflower* is balanced. She slows to 6.5 knots, heals ten degrees less, and the ride is much nicer.

By 10:00am the temperature has risen to 30 degrees and the sun is still shining bright. The wind, however, is both inescapable and frigid, and I need every bit of the cold-weather clothing I own to stay reasonably warm.

I remember my days as a carpenter, when I occasionally had to work in temperatures like this, and try to muster some strength from the memory. But I was rarely in the wind, and I was always active and working. It's quite another thing to be sitting at the helm, fully exposed to the weather, and requires a lot more clothing to stay relatively warm. The day is making it clear that I am not at all acclimated to these conditions, and I hope that it warms up soon.

As we progress towards the mouth of the bay, we turn more downwind, and the headsails become blanketed by the main. The preventer holds the main firmly in position, and I decide to leave it alone. I furl the yankee all the way in and then release the staysail halyard and pull on the downhaul. But the downhaul does not move and the sail remains up. I'm already tethered to the jackline, and I creep up on deck and make my way to the inner forestay as the blue-grey water rushes by. The downhaul is wrapped around the lever that releases the inner forestay, and as I unwrap it I make a mental note to keep the downhaul tensioned and cleated instead of leaving it slack when the sail is up.

Back in the cockpit, I pull on the downhaul and the sail drops quickly to the deck, held taught by the sheet and ready for raising whenever I determine the need for it.

At 11:30am we are going almost straight downwind under the full main making 5.5 knots in 14 knots of breeze. The preventer holds the boom firmly to port and has already justified itself. I'd be scared without it.

Something unusual about the mainsail catches my eye, and as I look up, I see the lower batten is poking out of its slot. I watch it for a while, monitoring it, trying to determine if it is making progress in its attempt at escape. It's not long before I can see that it clearly desires to be free, but I wonder if I can just ignore it. No, it will eventually snag a shroud and break, possibly tearing the mainsail. I have to remove it.

I lower the mainsail enough to reach the batten, step up on deck and slip all ten feet of it out of the sail, then toss it below. I'll find a good place for it later. It tried to work its way free on the passage from Mattapoisett, I recall. Albert pointed it out and we removed it before it liberated itself by leaping into the ocean.

Comfortably seated in the cockpit again, I look up at the mainsail to see if the missing batten has caused any problem with the sail. There's a slight flutter in the roach of the sail at the empty batten pocket, so I tension the first reef line just a bit and the sail stiffens and quiets. There we go, nothing I couldn't take care of. *Windflower* sails on without further complaint.

The tunnel comes into view, or rather the gap in the highway above the tunnel, which marks the entrance into the bay. It was here that I felt the joy of the successful completion of the first passage south on *Windflower* a month and a half ago. Cristina and Albert shared the moment with me. Now I am heading out to face the Atlantic Ocean, Cape Hatteras, and

Cape Lookout alone. *Windflower* feels like a different boat now, but it also feels like a different season. It was a beautiful and warm day when we sailed in, a fine autumn day, but today is a bitter cold and menacing winter day.

At 12:45pm we sail over the tunnel and I marvel at all the cars that must be passing underneath. Hundreds of people are moving below us at 60 miles an hour, in both directions, going to work, or going shopping, or rushing to visit relatives for Christmas. Some of the cars hold only one person, and some of them are lonely and sad, while others are content and comfortable in their solitude. Other cars contain entire families, and some are noisy and full of bickering, others are singing Christmas carols, and in others the passengers are completely absorbed into their electronic devices.

I have my own electronic devices, and I check one, which tells me that we travel at 5 knots in 14 knots of breeze, the depth is 61 feet and we head at 140 degrees. We are leaving the protected waters of the bay and entering the mighty and unpredictable Atlantic Ocean. But the ocean and I are old friends and I feel welcome here. We sail downwind at a casual pace and all is as it should be.

I should check for leaks, I think to myself. As often as the bilge-pump runs, there surely is water coming from somewhere, and as we are heading out into the ocean, I can't let any leaks go unattended. I set the autopilot, go below, grab a flashlight and stick my head into the space under the cockpit.

I really expect to see everything dry and in order, but this is not so. A continuous stream of water dribbles from one of the many drain hoses. I replaced all but one of these hoses in Mattapoisett, and it is quite distressing to see something I worked on not functioning properly, suggesting the work was a wasted effort and perhaps I should have just left it as it was. But I console myself with the notion that new hose applications need the hose-clamps tightened after a short time.

I crawl out and return with a screwdriver while the autopilot steers. I tighten both hose-clamps on the leaking seacock while *Windflower*, and the tiny space beneath the cockpit, bounce and roll. But the stream flowing from the hose is only reduced to an aggressive drip. I crawl out and return with a hose-clamp and put it on the very base of the hose, beneath the other two, and tighten it down as much as I can. The leak stops. I check all the other hose clamps within reach, and find many can be tightened a bit.

At 2:00pm I try flying the yankee, but it is blanketed by the main and does me no good, so I furl it. The wind has reduced to 12 knots and we sail at only 4 knots against an incoming tide.

It is becoming more obvious that I am not acclimated to the cold air, especially when I sit in it all day. My shoulders are tight and hunched up in effort to keep my neck warm. My body shivers, even though I have on ample clothing. I remember the HotHands. This is exactly what I bought them for and I have some right next to me in the lazarette. I fish them out and put HotHands in both my boots and my gloves. I'm wearing ski gloves and the Muck boots, both the warmest I have, and they are adequate, but the HotHands are a luxury, warming my blood as it passes through the veins in my hands and feet.

At 2:37pm, I check the bilge and am elated to see no water.

At 2:40, I release the preventer, sheet the main all the way in, tension the preventer on a winch but don't cleat it off, and gybe. I use the preventer on the winch to control the mainsail as it moves across, then I attach the other preventer before letting the mainsheet out, tension the new preventer on a winch, and cleat it off.

Our speed is up to 5.5 knots, so I assume we might have escaped the tidal current. My hands are very warm in the ski gloves, too warm, I think, so I change to lighter gloves. I don't want to perspire in any of my gear.

I listen to the weather forecast on the VHF radio. Tonight: wind NW 10-15 becoming 5-10 after midnight, seas 4-5' at 7 seconds becoming 2-3' at 7 seconds. Friday, north winds

5-10, seas 2', Friday night NE winds 10-15, seas 2', Saturday NE winds 5-10, Sunday NE winds 5-10.

I like the forecast, it's gentle and pleasant. We will be graced with following breeze the whole way, just strong enough to sail, and nothing threatening is reported. I smile at the thought of a care-free journey.

At 3:30pm, we get passed by a submarine, which, as far as I know, is a first for me. The captain's voice comes through on the VHF warning everyone to stay 500 yards away and not to cross their bow. The tower and a bit of the hull are out of the water when they pass by to starboard. It doesn't look like any sort of boat at all, but rather like a small building moving vertically through the water.

Something falls from the rigging, hits the deck, and bounces into the water. I catch a glimpse of it before it disappears and see that it is small and black, but I'm not sure what it is. Perhaps *Windflower* is shedding unnecessary parts, yes, that must be it.

I look up at the mainsail and see that the next batten is working its way loose. It must have been the batten cover plate I saw bouncing off the deck. *Windflower*, are you sure you don't need that?

At 4:00pm, I take my first 20-minute nap, laying down in the relative warmth of the cabin, but I don't sleep at all. I'm kept awake by a banging noise coming from up front, perhaps from a locker door swinging with the ship. I think it must be coming from the V-berth, but the V-berth is packed full of stuff and the suspect doors are inaccessible. I'll just have to deal with it, I tell myself, it's just one of the many noises on the boat. Just another noise.

At 6:00pm it is 39 degrees inside the boat and very cold outside. The wind is less than 10 knots but somehow we make 6 knots. Perhaps a current is with us. I go below and am comforted by the relative warmth and lack of wind. I make a pot of tea and pour some in a cup and the rest in the thermos. The banging continues but I try to ignore it.

Later, after a brief stint at the cold helm, I make a pot of chicken and rice soup, which is fabulous and warms me immensely. I take off my boots and move the HotHands from the backs of my feet to under my toes, which is a big improvement.

I emerge with a full belly and a cup of hot tea in hand and look up at the stars. Fantastic! The sky is black and countless millions of bright points in the sky tell tales of stars unknown lightyears away. Their beauty is overwhelming and I stare up at them until my neck is sore, but the cold is shocking. Even in all my gear the cold air penetrates and my body tensions in response. How do people deal with this, I wonder. How do people live in weather like this, and why?

I notice lights on the horizon that are not stars. I check the AIS and see that *Grandeur of the Seas* is the ship and she is 918' long with a beam of 121'. I assume she is heading into the bay. The banging from up front continues to annoy me.

At 10:00pm we make 5 knots at 160 degrees. It's still 39 degrees inside *Windflower*. She is used to these temperatures, but I am not. Soon I will introduce her to the relatively easy ways of the tropics. There is no need to be cold when one is nomadic. I'm reminded of Muddy Waters' lyrics "goin' where the weather suits my clothes."

I try to get some rest and take two naps in a row, but I don't sleep much. I'm still not in the rhythm of napping 20 minutes at a time, but I know that if I just go through the motions, the rhythm will come. For now, the banging keeps my mind anchored in this world, and sleep eludes me.

After my fruitless nap, I pour a cup of hot tea from the thermos and take bites directly from the chocolate cake from the Farmer's Daughter, a store in Gloucester Point. The cake is delicious and my mouth continues reaching for more as if it has its own directive to eat as much cake as it can, as quickly as it can, but the cake so rich that I have to be careful not to eat too much. I know it will upset my stomach if I don't muster up some self-control. *Stop eating cake, stop eating cake!* says my conscious mind. *Eat more cake! Eat more cake!* says my mouth.

The banging from the V-berth continues and I can take it no longer. Investigation reveals two locker doors are swinging with the motion of the boat and one is colliding with the bulkhead. Unfortunately, I piled so much stuff in the V-berth that the doors will be hard to get to. I do what I can and get an old pair of jeans between the door and the bulkhead that it bangs into. It's a temporary fix at best, but for the moment the incessant banging has ceased.

At 11:45pm, I start the engine. The sails have been slatting and banging around and I'm sure that this is bad for both them and the standing rigging. Running the engine annoys me, but I have not the patience to sit still on a windless ocean. I'm cold and I want to get to our destination as quickly as possible, and the engine will make it warmer inside the cabin, a little.

The Navionics app on my phone is not working. I like to look at the phone when I'm down below, checking our position and heading, looking at what is ahead of us, etc. But the app thinks we are back at the marina in Gloucester Point, which is very disappointing. I expected to be able to both navigate and monitor the AIS with the phone from inside the boat.

At 1:38am, we are 15nm east of Kittyhawk, NC, it has warmed to 41 degrees inside the boat, and it feels a little warmer outside than it was earlier. We must be sailing across water warmed by the Gulf Stream, and I welcome the few degrees and hope for more.

A check of the AIS reveals that a fishing vessel, *Hope and Sydney,* is coming up behind me. I like knowing the names of boats around me. It seems familiar, like we are all friends out here on the ocean. I want them all to know my name too, and I imagine the skipper of *Hope and Sydney* reading *Windflower's* name on his AIS and thinking, at least for a moment, that we are friends.

A military vessel, which is transmitting on the AIS, passes on the horizon heading north. The military vessels I've seen in the past have not transmitted their presence on the AIS, so this surprises me. As we pass, another light appears next to it on the horizon, not showing up on the AIS. I assume they are related, the two vessels.

The other light grows quickly, like it's approaching fast. My heartrate increases. I check the AIS again, and the mysterious boat is still not showing up. It continues coming right at me. The light changes, grows, then a cloud moves in front of it. *How can a cloud move in front of a ship, is this some new military trick?* The light becomes enormous and bright like a heavenly body, and finally my heartrate peaks, then slows, and I realize that It's not a ship at all, but rather the rising moon, and I laugh at myself for mistaking the moon for a boat.

For the next few minutes, I stare at the rising moon and take in the unusual and starkly beautiful sight of a massive glowing body rising above the otherwise dark horizon.

Navionics is still not working, or maybe the GPS on my phone isn't working. This illustrates why we should have backups for everything important. I'm very thankful not to be relying on the phone as my only source of navigation. In addition to the chartplotter and the phone, I have paper charts. My Garmin InReach and two handheld VHF radios display our GPS coordinates.

It's dark out, the sky is clear, and the lights of Virginia are faint on the western horizon. The stars are shining bright and I stare up at them in awe while steering. I love to steer this way, keeping a particular star lined up with some part of the boat. Tonight, I have a star trapped within the triangle made by the capshroud, the mast, and the starboard spreader. I can keep it inside if I focus hard enough, and when I do, *Windlfower* sails a straight course. This sort of steering is meditative and beautiful and I feel lucky to be out here, alone and at peace with the world.

A big shooting star streaks across the sky like a missile in a celestial video game. It leaves a long misty trail that glows yellow-green after the meteor burns up and disappears, and it occurs to me that this is the sort of thing that most people don't get to see, a meteor in the night sky surrounded by countless stars. I weep for the hundreds of thousands of people on shore, not far away at all, who just missed the spectacle, and those living in urban areas full of light pollution that can't see the night sky at all. Even though I am cold, I am happy because I get to see the glory and feel the blessing of nature.

At 1:57am, like a homecoming, Navionics is back! I can now look at my phone and see a map of the ocean with my little boat sailing across it.

I check the bilge at 2:30am and am shocked and dismayed to see that again, it is full of water. I check the bilge-pump switch and find that somehow I must have left it turned off, *again*. I switch it on and the bilge empties, but I still don't know where all the water is coming from.

I check the rudderpost and see a tiny drip. But what scares me is behind the rudderpost. Water, a lot of it, is seeping in through the bulkhead separating the propane locker from the rest of the boat.

I return to the cockpit and empty out all the gear in the aft lazarette/propane locker: big hose, small hose, old halyard, drogue, spare gas stove, small gas cylinders, dock lines... At the bottom is about a foot of water. Laying on my stomach and reaching down deep with a fruit juice container with the top cut off, the sort with a handle, I bail out as much as I can. As I get near the bottom, I can see water coming in faster than I can bail it out. It's welling up from the center. I can bail almost to the bottom, but not quite. I can see it's a hole, like a drain, not a ragged hole, but one that someone installed on purpose. How absurd, I think, for there to be an open drain below the waterline.

The softwood plugs are in the bottom drawer under the steps, and I fish out the smallest one I can find. It is still too big, so I whittle it down, then sand it smooth and return to the scene of the crime. I can't reach the bottom of the propane locker, but I remember seeing a reaching and grabbing tool in one of the lockers, the sort of tool that might be used to retrieve a dropped nut from underneath the engine, or some other inaccessible place, of which there are a few in this boat. I dig around until I find it. With the reaching and grabbing tool, I hold the plug and try to place it in the drain. It still doesn't fit, so I sand it some more, try it, sand it... Finally, it fits and I tap it in firmly with a 2-pound sledge hammer. I'm happy to have found the leak, but I suspect there are more.

*Dressed for the bitter cold.
When you put on your harness, make sure your
tether is clipped to both D-rings,
not just one, like in this photo.*

At 5:23am, it is 46 degrees inside, which feels considerably warmer than the 23 we started the journey with. But still, as I sit at the helm in all my gear and wrapped in two blankets, I am cold. Please can we go to the Caribbean? I want to be warm. I can imagine the feeling of warmth and the bright sun on my skin, and the blue water, warm enough to swim in without a wetsuit.

Unfortunately, I cannot sail there today. A big storm is coming and *Windflower* and I must settle for a safe harbor in North Carolina.

I sit at the helm, dressed in all my warm gear and two blankets, one over my legs and one around my body, trying to stay warm by thinking of the tropics. The eastern sky brightens ever so slightly, promising the warmth of the sun, which hides just over the horizon. I dream of the warmth the sun will bring, but sunrise is a long slow process. An hour later it is still not up, but the sky is colored magenta and orange, and the clouds are outlined in vibrant yellow. Further west the sky is grey and black, but accented in purple.

I turn to 190 degrees and see Scripts Lighted Buoy on the chart, but I can't see the buoy on the ocean. *Windflower* aims at the Diamond Shoals Lighted Buoy 12. I check my phone, and Navionics thinks I am at the York River Yacht Haven, which is disappointing and almost makes me angry.

Finally, the sun breaks free of the horizon and rises quickly, a giant ball of light and heat, too bright to look at. I can feel its warm rays on the skin of my face, the only skin I have exposed. But as soon as it is up, the sun hides behind a cloud and the warmth it brought is taken back.

At 6:36am, we are 7nm east of Rodanthe, NC. My stomach is now acclimated to sailing and I've the hunger of one who hasn't eaten enough, so I make coffee and an omelet. While standing in the galley, the portlights are at eye level and I look outside while cooking. Suddenly a big ship nearly fills the view, passing to port going the other way. I quickly climb to the cockpit and check the AIS to find out why the alarm didn't go off.

The instrument identifies *Zin Vancouver* as the ship, which is 4.5nm away, much further than it looks. It's so hard to judge distance on the ocean, especially with big ships. Their size is so out of proportion to any other vessels that it is nearly impossible to tell how far away they are, or how fast they are moving, and when these ships are close, their size defies logic.

After breakfast, with the sun shining bright, I change out of the big orange suit, which has become slightly damp with perspiration. It feels positively liberating to get into more normal clothes. The suit is plenty warm, but it is also the biggest and bulkiest thing I have ever worn.

White birds sit in the water spaced far apart, covering a large area. This seems odd so far offshore, but what do I know about the ways of seabirds? When we get closer, I can tell they are northern gannets, sleek and bright white with long necks and black on the underside of their wingtips. They sit way out here as comfortably as someone might sit on their couch watching the television while a fire burns in the fireplace. Family is all around them, and the sun warms their white feathers. The birds that we sail close to take flight, while others remain unbothered by our presence.

I've seen northern gannets while surfing in Florida. They hunt like pelicans, but dive from higher up and further from the beach. The gannets fold back their wings and drop like missiles into the water. They can even swim further down if they need to in order to reach their prey, using their wings in the water much like they do in the air.

We sail very slowly in the early morning, peacefully and quietly. I thoroughly enjoy the sensation of my home slowly moving across the Atlantic Ocean as if she is meant to be here, and she is, but my patience comes to an end when the sails start slatting. I take them down and start the engine.

The breeze is only 6 knots, from behind. We motor at 6.5 knots at 187 degrees, I can see low clouds over the Gulf Stream to the east and I think of the warm water that must be causing the clouds to form above.

We've been sailing 24 hours now and I check the Garmin InReach, which tells me we have covered 130 miles.

At 9:11am, we are 10nm east of Avon, NC, and it is all of 52 degrees inside, which is positively warm compared to yesterday. I'm thankful for every one of these degrees, and that the clouds are clearing out and allowing more sun to spill through.

The wind is still less than 10 knots from behind. I see something brown in the water ahead and I swerve to starboard to avoid it. It dives when we get close, probably a sea turtle.

At 10:00am, I cut off the engine and we are sailing again, downwind with the main only. I can make out something on the horizon, a tower perhaps, at Diamond Shoals,

10nm ahead. The sun has made more progress in its war with the clouds, and the color of the water is changing from dark grey to dark blue. My mood follows suit and I feel a small sense of joy beating down the grimace of cold and grey.

At 11:00am, I make lunch courtesy of the Farmer's Daughter: a bagel with jalapeno jelly, jalapeno cheese, diced fresh jalapenos, olives, and carrots. The chocolate pound cake is still making its rounds, and is as good as ever. I eat it with reckless abandon now. Apparently, I've been burning a lot of calories, and my body demands nourishment.

At 11:52am, we are sailing against a 2-knot current, as indicated by the difference between speed over ground and boat speed. We are 2nm from Diamond Shoals, and only making 3 knots. I start the engine again.

The tower comes into view and it looks like a mini oil rig, like a steel house on long and rusting steel legs, perched high above the blue water. As we get closer I can see the remnants of an old steel spiral staircase running up one of the legs. Only one section of the stairs remains. There is a lower level consisting of a catwalk around the outside, then a flat building on the main level, and a tower in one corner with a light on top. Two letters, "ON" remain on the side while others have obviously fallen into the ocean. It appears that the light has not been on for years.

At 12:45pm, I shut off the engine, turn into the wind, and round the shoal. On the other side of the lighthouse are the letters "A" and "N." I take more pictures as it all fades into the background. I have now sailed around Cape Hatteras, and a feeling of accomplishment runs through me like a warm shiver.

The old Diamond Shoals Lighthouse, now retired but still standing proud

At 1:05pm we get passed by the cargo ship *Cosco Vietnam*, 334 meters long and moving at an impressive 20 knots. I picture it full of toilet paper, Tupperware, and plastic bracelets.

We are now 70nm from Cape Lookout. I can feel it cooling off outside and I put a blanket over my legs. It's sure to be another cold night, but we should be anchored safely by mid-morning and my first solo passage aboard *Windflower* will be complete. We will be in a safe harbor and I'll be eating a hot bowl of chili in the cockpit while smiling at the world. Bob Marley will be playing on the tiny sound system, and I'll be contemplating a trip ashore in *Little Flower*, the dinghy.

I feel tired and I look all around. Diamond shoals is behind us, *Cosco Vietnam* is well past, and shore is 15nm away. There is nothing I might run into, and so I should nap. I go below, set the countdown timer on my watch, which has been set at 22 minutes since I bought the watch in St Petersburg, Florida, in 2016. I lay down and the feeling is glorious. A sailor's body is never relaxed unless laying down. Even when sitting the core is working to keep balance as the boat constantly moves. This makes laying down an unexpectedly wonderful feeling.

I fall asleep and dream, then feel a buzz on my arm and the dream evaporates. I'm on a boat, and the boat is moving across the ocean with nobody at the helm. I have to get up!

I poke my head out of the companionway and all is ocean and water and sky, *Windflower*, and nothing else. I check the chartplotter and we still proceed in the same direction we did 20 minutes ago. The AIS shows no ships within its range of 24 miles, and so I lay down again. The countdown timer resets and restarts itself, so I need not do anything to the watch. I fall asleep again. I dream. I awake to the buzzing on my left wrist. Again, I get up quickly, hold on to a post to assist my drowsy balance, then slowly and carefully make my way up the steps. I take two more naps, checking the horizon and the instruments between each.

After my final nap, I clip my tether to the large padeye outside the companionway before stepping out into the cockpit. I've read that sailors sometimes fall overboard when moving between cockpit and companionway, since their center of gravity is high. Should something unexpected happen, this is a vulnerable position and one should just go ahead and clip in before making the transition. That's why I installed the two large padeyes on either side of the companionway. Both are through-bolted and reinforced with matching backing plates on the inside.

While sitting at the helm, once again in control of my vessel, I try to remember how many naps I just took, but they all blur together. I look at the time, trying to remember when I laid down for the first one. It's all a mystery, and inconsequential.

A look at the chartplotter tells me that we have rounded all of Cape Hatteras. Diamond Shoals was just the beginning, but now the cape has been rounded, and I acknowledge the achievement for a second time, why not?

Enjoying the helm between Cape Hatteras and Cape Lookout

The breeze comes up throughout the day and by 6:00pm we make 6 knots in 18 knots of breeze under one reef and staysail. The following wind and the sunset make for a magical setting. It's not nearly as cold as it was yesterday, and for that I am thankful. But even though I took four naps in a row, I am still tired and my mind is foggy. While they may sound restful, 20-minute naps are a pale substitute for a good night's sleep and it takes time to get used to the program.

At 8:00pm, I am experimenting with the radar, adjusting its three settings and learning about the differences they make. I'm absorbed in the electronic device when the mainsail goes aback with a bang and *Windflower* swings abruptly to starboard. I hear the metallic ping of something as it hits the deck and bounces, a small piece of hardware probably. I'll have to check on that later, but not right now.

The boom stays in place, held firmly by the preventer, thank God, but we turn into the wind whether I want to or not. I go with it and steer to port, and *Windflower* faces the wind, tacks, and comes back around to the original course, a full 360 degrees. I tell myself to be more careful. I don't want to do that again; it's both embarrassing and dangerous, both for me and *Windflower*, as evidenced by the unknown part she shed. I picture my father following my tracker online and wondering why I just made a small loop. I need to step up my game. Sailing downwind is no joke.

At 10:00pm, the wind is blowing harder, up to 20 knots, and we sail on a deep broad reach with one reef and staysail, but *Windflower* is not balanced. She has a lot of weather helm, trying to turn herself into the wind, and steering is difficult and takes both strength and focus. I've probably got the wrong sail combination up, but it's dark and cold, so I don't have the gumption to change the sailplan.

As soon as she gets off course a little, she tries hard to turn into the wind, and the wheel must be turned hard to get her back on course. When the autopilot is on, I can hear it working hard too. I wonder if I should just have the headsail up. [In retrospect, I should have been sailing with the headsail only, not the main.]

We make 6-7 knots, and I feel like the second reef is called for. It's a dark night and I can't see any of the lines I need to work with, so I go below and turn on the spreader lights. When I emerge from the companionway, the entire boat is lit up and I wonder why I don't turn on the spreader lights more often. I can see *everything*.

I begin the process of putting in the second reef, but while pulling in the blue reefing line, it gets caught on the mast cleat, the one I have already been thinking of removing.

I mentally raise it up on the priority list and vow to remove it in Beaufort, but for now, I have to go to the mast and unhook the line. However, the deck is brightly-lit, and this makes going forward feel safer.

At 11:00pm, we are 15nm east of Cape Lookout. I get the reef in, shut off the very bright spreader lights, and see that we make just over 6 knots. The wind is still 15-20 knots, and *Windflower* is much easier to steer.

It's getting colder, so I go below and come back out with two blankets. One I drape across my legs and the other I wrap around my torso. I wish I still had the big orange suit on, but I can't talk myself into changing into it. The irrational fear of being cold while changing outweighs the rational need of warmer clothes.

HotHands, that's what I need. I open up the lazarette and pull out the big ziplock bag full of cold-weather gear. I take off my gloves and open up two HotHands. I put one in the left-hand glove and put the glove on. But when I try to put the other glove on, my thumb can't find its place, and I realize that this is also a left glove. Somehow I have two left gloves here. I search all around in the dark. Aha, I found it. I slip the HotHand into the glove and try to put it on. No! It can't be, *but it is*, another left glove. How can this be? *How can there be three left gloves in the cockpit and no right gloves?* It's like I've slipped into the Twilight Zone. I was wearing a pair of gloves only moments ago. *My kingdom for the right glove!*

The mainsail backwinds as I search for the missing glove, and the preventer again saves the day. In this wind, an unintentional gybe could destroy the rig. I must be more careful.

I get us back on course, set the autopilot, and stand up. I shake out the blankets and still cannot find the right glove. My right hand is getting cold now. I go below and come back up with a headlamp, and find the missing glove right away, on the cockpit sole in plain view. I must be getting delirious. Now, where is the other HotHand?

The saga repeats itself.

By midnight I have both gloves on and HotHands in each. It was a lot of work, the seemingly simple task of putting glove warmers inside gloves, but the warmth in my cold hands was well worth the effort.

As we near Cape Lookout in the cold and dark night, I zoom in on the chartplotter. We are heading for a point that I chose when we rounded Cape Hatteras, and at the time, this seemed logical. But with the chart zoomed in, I see that we will cross shoals on this course. The seas are running at about 8 feet, and the shallowest shoals on the chart are 30 feet deep. We could probably just continue on and sail across, but I'm not comfortable with this.

We have been following another boat, and I can see it crossing the shoals in the distance, at the same point we aim for, but I don't know what the draft of that boat is, or if the captain has local knowledge, or if he is simply making a brazen mistake. I also know that sandbars shift and grow, and the chart shows but a historical picture. I decide to change course. I don't want to get to the Beaufort Inlet before sunrise anyway. I have time to kill, and sailing the long way around the cape is the right way to kill it.

I need to gybe. We sail on a course nearly straight downwind, but I need to be on a broad reach on the other tack. I don't want to gybe in 20 knots, so I turn into the wind, sheet in, tack, switch the preventers, and keep turning until we are on the desired broad reach. This is what I call a chicken gybe. It's the safe thing to do in a breeze strong enough to make me not want to gybe. We now steer for the outside of the cape, taking the safer course.

The swell is now abeam and we roll with it. The ride is much livelier now and in the dark, the waves reflect no light. I can't see them coming at all, so each one is a surprise.

The night is dark and cold, but having the wind behind us keeps the chill down. The stars are out in full force, and I am thankful to be nearing our destination. I look forward to a good night's sleep, and a hot meal tomorrow. It should be warmer here than it was in Gloucester Point, where every time I checked the weather in Beaufort, it was nearly ten degrees warmer.

At 2:00am, I turn us downwind and we finally round Cape Lookout. The night is dark, but a few stars peek through the gaps between invisible clouds. With the breeze and waves behind me, the ride is smooth, and I'm not particularly cold.

A half hour later, we've rounded the cape and it's time to change course and aim for Beaufort Inlet. I release the preventer and clip it to the rail, forgetting to pull in the slack, sheet *Windflower* in, turn us to starboard, and sheet in some more. The cold wind hits me in the face and my whole body feels its chill.

Suddenly, I am very cold, and I realize that I'm underdressed for the weather. If I needed the orange suit before, I certainly need it now. A wave hits the bow as we accelerate into the wind and cold spray mists everything in its path, including me. What was a calm motion moments ago is now aggressive and intense. The sea is no longer simply a dark undulating mass, but rather a leaping web of white lines that slam into the bow and send cold white mists of water flying into me.

Windflower heels to port, her bow rises and falls, splitting the seas like she was designed to do, but still the spray flies. I try to wrap up in the blankets to keep warm, again wishing that I was wearing the orange suit. I could go below and put it on, but I don't want to go through all that, especially while sailing upwind. Besides, we are close now, I think. I feel like we are almost there.

But we are not almost there, and we continue in these conditions for another four hours.

By 5:00am I am miserable, cold, wet, and exhausted. The batteries are low, so I don't want to run the autopilot. We are only 5nm from the first lighted buoy of Beaufort Inlet, and I will strike the sails and start the engine when we get there. Just one more hour of this. I can take it. *How tough are you?* I ask myself. I can take it.

At 5:30am I can see the light of the first buoy in the otherwise dark night, and I can feel the relief coming. We'll motor slowly through the buoys and the sun will begin to illuminate this side of the world before we enter the inlet. It will be warm. Once inside, the protected waters will be calm. I'll anchor, eat a hot bowl of soup, take a nap, and wake up warm and vibrant. We are going to win!

At 6:00am it is still completely dark. I turn *Windflower* to face the wind and start the engine, letting it idle in neutral. I'm so glad to be here. The wind and spray in my face have ceased and I feel better already. I'm fatigued, but the close proximity to the end of the voyage, and thus the end of the cold, has me energized. Still, I proceed with caution and I try to move slowly, thinking about my actions before I do anything.

I release the staysail halyard and pull on the downhaul, but it catches on something again. Carefully I walk to the bow, dragging my tether along the jackline, and unhook the downhaul from an obstacle in the rigging. As *Windflower* rolls in the waves, I creep back to the cockpit, pull the staysail the rest of the way down, and slip the downhaul line into the cam cleat.

I release the main halyard and pull in on all three reefing lines. As the sail comes down, *Windflower* rocks back and forth in the waves, no longer stabilized by the big mainsail. The sail flogs in the wind and lines are flapping all over. I sheet the main all the way in, then go up on deck, and lose my balance. I fall backwards and grab a lazyjack. I'm tethered, but I still could have fallen in. *I've got to be more careful*, I tell myself. I *must* be more careful.

I pull the mainsail the rest of the way down, holding on tight as I do. I get two sail-ties on it and figure that will do for tonight.

I put the engine in gear as we slowly drift downwind, then something terrible happens. The engine groans, I reach for the gear shift to put her in neutral, but it's too late, the engine quits. The rumbling of the engine ceases and the sound of the wind again dominates the cold and dark night. We are drifting downwind, away from land and any obstacles, and I take a moment to assess the situation.

I look over the port rail, nothing. I look over the starboard rail, and see the preventer line, pulled taught, leading down from the bow into the water, pointed right at the propeller, as if saying *now look what you've done, you idiot*. I grab the line and pull, but it is bar-tight.

I've really done it now. I've committed a terrible sailing sin and allowed a line to get caught in the propeller. I forgot to check for lines in the water before I started the engine, and again before I put her in gear. All the while, the excess of the preventer line was hanging submerged just waiting for the propeller to start spinning and catch it. I should have pulled in the excess hours ago when I unclipped the preventer from the boom.

Now I have no choice but to put the sails back up. But something within stirs me to another course of action. My stomach churns and my bowels roll. Something in me wants out, *now*. I go below and undo my PFD, drop it to the floor and step out of the leg straps as quickly as I can. There's no time. I unzip my jacket. I have to get the bibs off before I can sit on the head, but the shoulder straps are under the jacket. There's not enough time! How can this be happening right now? I need to put the sails up. We are drifting downwind. I can't do this now.

Another terrible thing happens and I have to spend some time on cleanup and damage control, all the while drifting downwind, back out into the dark and windy ocean.

Humbled twice, I get back to the cockpit and go to work. We are facing straight downwind in 20 knots of breeze, so I put the staysail up first. This allows me to turn *Windflower* onto a reach, and I begin cranking the mainsail up. I can't get us to face the wind all the way, so the sail is under a lot of pressure. I have to grind hard on the winch the whole way up, but I leave one reef in. At 6:40am, we are once again making progress toward land. In 40 minutes, we drifted about ¾ of a mile.

We now sail at about 50 degrees off the channel, aiming for the beach to the south. I am lucky that the wind comes from shore. This way I can anchor off the beach and try to fix the problem.

It occurs to me that I might be able to spin the propeller shaft by hand, or with the large Channel Locks, and undo the line while underway. I go below and give it a try while the auto-pilot steers. No luck. I get another idea and start the engine. I ease her into reverse, but again no luck. I shut the engine off. I didn't fix the problem, but I am relieved to see that the engine still runs.

While screwing around with these ideas, *Windflower's* sails become aback, and we switch to port tack. No problem, I think, we'll just go to the beaches on the north side of the inlet. I continue on in the new northerly direction, as if I meant to tack. I'm very tired.

As we cross through the buoys of the channel, the sun is rising and I feel some of its warmth. I am exhausted and badly in need of a nap. We have crossed the channel and are still a few miles offshore, so I set the alarm and lay down in the cockpit. I get up ten minutes later and look around. I can see fishing boats along the shore and a ship far out coming in. I can't nap anymore, but the ten minutes down has me feeling better.

When we get near enough to see the beach, I am dismayed to see a whole fleet of shrimp boats dragging nets all along the shore on the north side of the inlet, where I want to anchor. I want to anchor close to the inlet, because there's a chance I'll need to get towed in.

Off in the distance ahead, I see the little harbor on Cape Lookout and its stately but quaint lighthouse on the beach. My friend Eddie recommended this as a potential place to anchor. *Why not?* I think.

The last shrimp boat turns around as I continue sailing up the beach, and the coast is all mine. Good, I need room to maneuver, as I have no use of my engine. I sail us in close to shore, just inside the inlet to the Cape Lookout anchorage, but not all the way in. I don't want to get trapped. It's shallow in there anyway.

I slow down, point into the wind, drop the staysail, furl the yankee that was only partially out, and release the main halyard. I carefully creep to the bow in a low crouch and send the anchor to the bottom. I hold the chain and let the anchor position itself before slowly letting out rode (anchor line and/or chain). We are in 20' of water, so I let out 125'. When it feels good and set, I take the main the rest of the way down and strap on some sail ties.

Location: 34º 38.13' N, 76º 32.66' W

The air is cold and the water is sure to be ice-cold; I'm going to need relief as soon as I get out, so I go below and put a kettle of water on the stove to boil.

I put on my heaviest wetsuit, the O'Neil Mutant 4/3 with the built-in hood, as well as booties and gloves. I put tools in a bag and lower it over the side so I can access them from the water. The bag contains a razor knife, channel locks, needle-nose pliers, a rigging knife, a large flathead screwdriver, a long Phillips screwdriver, and a small hammer. I tie a fender to a line and toss it over the stern, in case an unexpected current pulls me away from my ship. I put out the new ladder for the first time and step down into the water.

I can't tell how cold the water is until I'm all the way in and feel it on my face, and then as it slowly seeps into the wet-suit. The water is shockingly cold and in my already-tired state I know I've only got a couple of minutes before hypothermia sets in and I won't be able to control my hands.

The water is blue and clear, and I can easily see the boat when I dive below. The problem looks neat, just line twisted around the shaft. I pull on it, but it doesn't move. Back at the surface I breathe and reach into the bag for the razor knife. The line is easy to cut, and I go right to work unwrapping it. It comes off easier than I imagined it would. I surface and breath, go back down and unwrap some more. It's still coming off easily. I'm going to win!

I surface and breathe one more time, then dive and take the rest of the line off. I've won!

I get out of the water, raise my arms in the air in victory, but no one is there to see except two horses on the beach.

The wetsuit comes off on deck and the cold air assaults me, but redemption waits for me below. The hot water is on the stove and I pour it into a bucket, to which I add an equal amount of room-temperature water. Back in the cockpit, I dump the warm water over myself and the feeling is glorious. It's not the hot shower I hoped for last night, but it is fine indeed.

My brand-new preventer line, already cut

the Cape Lookout Lighthouse

wild horses on the Shackleford Banks

Considering all I have been through in the last twelve

hours, and my meager ten minutes of sleep, I should be exceedingly tired, but the cold water has given me a burst of adrenaline and now I am wide awake and in fine spirits. I make a big celebratory omelet with onions, tomatoes, canned smoked oysters, and jalapeno cheese. When I am finished, I lay down and read about five pages of "Two Years in the Klondike and Alaskan Gold Fields" by William Haskell, before falling asleep. I like this book because the experiences of the characters in Alaska put the mild cold I experience into perspective. At least it's not -60 outside.

I sleep for four hours. Before laying down, I reminded myself of where I was and that we were safely anchored, so that I might not wake up in a panic thinking we are sailing or drifting, as is often the case with me after the first sleep after a passage.

It works. I wake up feeling calm and rested, and happy that the line is no longer around the propeller shaft.

I learned a few lessons on this passage:

1) Dress warmer than you think necessary
2) Have easy access to warm gear
3) Have a headlamp available at all times
4) Keep lines organized and in the boat at all times
5) Check for lines in the water before starting the engine
6) Check for lines in the water before putting the engine in gear
7) Always keep a balanced sail plan
8) Study the charts ahead of time and have plans for rounding capes
9) Spend more time securing everything inside before a passage
10) Sleep all you can before approaching land since you can't sleep on the approach
11) Coffee is great to stay awake for a few hours, but it will bring on a hard crash later, so it's no good for a single-

hander on a passage
12) When sailing downwind, sail under the headsails, not the main
13) Put on warmer clothes before turning into the wind

Winners:

HotHands; Mustang Anti-Exposure One Piece Floatation Worksuit; preventers (the preventers prevented five unintentional gybes on this passage. I can't stress enough how important it is to have a good preventer setup.); Garhauer carabiners, rope clutches, and blocks; single line reefing; Stanley thermos; ski gloves; Muck boots; sock liners; Turtlefur neck warmer; hot tea; test plugs for blocking the dorade vents (I bought these for heavy weather, but they also keep out cold drafts); blankets in the cockpit; headlamp; abundance of tools; Mad Bomber hat; my new ladder; Under Armor long underwear; LaCroix in the lazarette; Grundens Sou'wester hat; Pelagic Autopilot

Losers:

Seat cushions (they are always too wet to sit on and the one on the high side always slips off when I step on it); Navionics on my phone (or perhaps it was the iPhone's GPS not functioning); AIS alarm (the "siren" activated by the B&G chartplotter never worked); mainsail battens (3 out of four came out of their sleeves and had to be removed),
Things I need:

A replacement for the Mad Bomber; whisker pole; new headlanp; 5/4 wetsuit; windvane self-steering rig

BEAUFORT, NORTH CAROLINA

A home at sea
A calm safe harbor
A friendly small town
For my Windflower

A beach to surf
And reef to swim
No land nor turf
Nor curious whim

Could take me back
To previous sands
For our next tack
Leads to more islands

Sunday, Dec 22

CHASING THE NOMADIC DREAM

E ven after my four-hour nap, I sleep soundly from 8:00pm to 5:00am. When I wake up, I am as hungry as I've ever been, and I make another big omelet, much like the one the day before, and the repetition does not diminish my enjoyment of the meal in the slightest.

One good thing about the cold weather is that food keeps without refrigeration, so I still have good eggs, cheese, and vegetables. I make a pot of coffee and eat the omelet with fruit juice on the side. My body craves the food and it goes down quickly and with a smile. To finally be on my way, making progress south, even if it is still cold, feels like winning. My dream is coming within reach, in fact, it is already happening.

Even though technically I'm living the dream, it's very cold in the boat. I have an electric heater, and the boat has an inverter, so why not try plugging it in? I dig out the little space heater that warmed me for two months in Gloucester Point (while plugged in to shore power) and plug it in to the inverter. I hope this works.

I turn it on and the little heater starts up with a whir, but immediately quits, and on top of that, the green light on the inverter goes out. My heart sinks.

I have a pretty good idea what I have done, so I take the inverter off the wall (it was mounted under the navigation table) and look at it. Of course that didn't work, *you fool*. The inverter is rated at 350 watts, and the heater draws 1500. It must have just blown a fuse, I think to myself.

I take it apart, figuring I can't break what's already broken. Inside the device, I quickly find two 20 amp fuses, just like the fuses in cars. The one in front blocks access to the one behind it, so, even though it does not look like it's blown, I try to pry it out, but does not budge. I keep increasing my effort and the severity of my tool until it pops out. Actually, some of it pops out, and some of it stays in place. It appears to have been soldered to the circuit board, and I broke it apart, so I broke the inverter twice.

I let the inverter project rest on the navigation table and consider taking *Little Flower* out for a sail. The anchorage inside the cape looks perfect for sailing the dinghy around, and I might find surf on the other side of the island. But the wind is cold and strong, and I know how cold the water is already. I opt to stay safe.

I figure I should try again to fix the inverter, so I test the wires feeding it, and they have juice. I cut and strip a piece of 16g wire and wrap it around the two posts of the fuse I broke, connecting them.

I put the inverter back together, mount it to its place under the navigation table, and turn it on. To my great surprise, its little green light illuminates, as if saying *I'm back, you fixed me!* I test the wires on the outlet and find 118 volts A/C. It is alive! Even though I broke it twice, I declare to myself that I fixed it.

I stay inside and make coffee mid-day, communicate with friends, study charts of Beaufort and The Bahamas, and read Ralph Waldo Emerson. His words pique my interest and I take notes. The world needs more of what he preached. We need to look upon nature as our savior, not as a resource to mine and destroy, nor as a plaything.

> *"A life in harmony with nature, the love of truth and virtue, will purge the eyes to understand her text. By degrees we may come to know the primitive sense of the permanent objects of nature so that the world to us may be an open book, and every form significant in its hidden life and final cause."*

Ralph Waldo Emerson

Emerson was telling us that the more we come to know

nature, the more nature will teach us. The more we live in harmony with nature, the more we live in harmony with truth and virtue. Everything, living or inanimate, within nature, has a meaning and a story. To live in harmony with nature is to learn the meaning and hear the story.

This is what I seek in my sailboat on the ocean. I want to live deep within nature, and the sailboat is my means to do so. In *Windflower*, I plan to live in harmony with nature as best I can, or at least take a large step in that direction.

The following day, I wait until noon to pull up the anchor, so I can catch the incoming tide in the inlet. The cool air is dense and wet, and I can barely see the beach through the fog as I motor up the coast. We enter the inlet and turn right towards Beaufort. Eddie suggested an anchorage near Town Creek Marina, and I plan to give it a look and buy fuel at the marina.

I am a bit nervous about navigating the narrow channel between the inlet and the marina, but even though it looks tiny on the charts, it is wide enough, well-marked, and plenty deep. I rather enjoy the still water and the quiet surroundings after having spent two days in the windy and cold anchorage at Cape Lookout.

I pull *Windflower* very slowly into a slip at Town Creek Marina. I meet Carol on the dock, who, even though it is raining, is ready to take my lines and help me fuel up. The floating docks are new and the wood that makes up the docks is still golden brown, not yet weathered to grey. It is a beautiful marina and I am happy to be here; I think I'll stay.

I figure I needed about 15 gallons, and I pump the diesel into the tank slowly so as not to overfill. After pumping for five or ten minutes, Carol comes over to ask if everything is alright. I say it is, and she goes on to tell me that I have only pumped a little over one gallon so far. I suppose I am in a slow and careful mood. I speed up the pump, and *Windflower* takes 13.5 gallons after motoring 14.75 hours, for 0.92 gallon per hour.

Christmas is coming soon and so is a windstorm. A strong low is moving up the coast, and this is why I had to pull into Beaufort instead of sailing all the way to The Bahamas from the Chesapeake Bay. I am unfamiliar with the area, and feel like I should play it safe, so instead of anchoring, I decided to treat myself and *Windflower* to a couple nights in the slip. I think a hot shower will do me good, as will some grocery shopping.

After fueling up *Windflower*, I take the courtesy car to the grocery store. What a wonderful perk a courtesy car is! The office closes soon after I get back, and that is the last I see any employees of the marina. The office is closed for Christmas Eve, Christmas Day, and Boxing Day.

After all is done, I find the men's showers, switch on the lights, turn on the hot water, undress, and step into the most wonderful warmth I might have ever experienced. After having been so cold for so long, the hot water and the steam are like heaven, and since I am the only person in the marina, as far as I can tell, I see no reason not to stand under the hot water for as long as I please. I stand for an eternity, occasionally turning around, but mostly just standing still with the water hitting me in the head. This is certainly one of the best showers ever, in fact it might be the highlight of the trip. There is nothing so wonderful as a hot shower after having endured cold, especially wet and cold simultaneously. The shower is absolutely luxurious and makes staying at the marina worth every penny.

There are many chores to do on Christmas Eve. While most of America is wrapping presents, entertaining family, going to church, singing Christmas carols, drinking eggnog, and sitting by fireplaces, I plug the propane-locker drain.

The hole needs to be clean and dry for any sealant to stick, so I dry it with a torch, then clean it with a round file. I fill it with 3M 5200 and cap it with a custom wooden plug. I then cut the excess off the running backstays, add blocks to reef clews 1 and 3, fill two old bolt holes in the salon hatch with epoxy (still trying to fix the leak). I also walk to town and buy two books: "Dharma Bums" by Jack Kerouac, and "American Gods" by Neil Gaiman. You can't have too many good books onboard.

I check the unused water tank and am dismayed and surprised to find it nearly half-full of water. Luckily it is fresh water, clean fresh water. Somehow water from the other tank found its way into this tank. I pump out about 7 gallons. Eventually, I come to understand that it must be the vents. Both tanks share a vent, and when the boat heels, water from the full tank must flow through the vent and siphon into the unused tank. Luckily, I wrapped all the food I stored down there in plastic bags, and I only stored canned food. Most of the space is taken up by fruit juice bottles. I intend to drink the juice, then fill them with water and store them down there again.

I try to "activate the siren" on the chartplotter so the AIS alarm would sound inside the boat, but I fail. I am sure the siren worked back in Gloucester Point, but I can't get it to sound again.

Christmas day is just another day for me. I spend it preparing for departure, which is looking immanent for tomorrow. No storms are predicted in the Atlantic, and forecasted winds are 20 or less. Most days I should be sailing upwind, but it all looks manageable. By the time we get there, I'll probably have dreadlocks from the wind blowing and twisting up my hair, I think.

I bring the 12' surfboard inside and strap it to the starboard berths. Since we will be sailing upwind, we should have much better performance with the surfboard inside. I climb the mast and install the windex on top. This takes a while because I have to drill into the masthead so I can bolt it in place. I also inspect the rigging while up there, and all the shining stainless-steel looks good to me, even though it is 17 years old. While on the mast, I also plug any holes I find with butyl tape, to keep water out. Every time it rains, water streams down the mast inside the boat.

BEAUFORT TO THE BAHAMAS

The passage of time occurs without measure
Becomes irrelevant like some esoteric science
Goes on behind the scene of our conscious
The sky is either light or dark
Or in between
Blue or black or painted in warm colors
Sun and moon and stars
Decorate the heavens and reflect off the sea
Sleep, the usual marker of days
Broken into multiple events
Fragmented
Was that yesterday, or the day before?
Or three days prior?
The question is moot
It was simply then

Dec 26

Yesterday was the biggest day of the year in most American households, but today is the big day for me. This is the day I've been working towards for the last three months. This is the day I've dreamed about and longed for. This is the day I sail my new boat to the tropics. I'm finally leaving the cold north and sailing to one of my favorite of all places, The Bahamas.

This morning there is no rush to leave early, because I want to catch the outgoing tide and high tide at the inlet is not until 7:35am. I make a big omelet with the last four eggs, a pot of coffee, and enjoy my last breakfast while tied to land. Today begins a long journey and there will be no omelets aboard *Windflower* in the tropics, since I have no refrigeration.

I take off the big blue mainsail cover and untie the sail ties. The staysail is bagged, so I free it of its bondage and run its green sheets through the cars to the cockpit.

The wind is very light this morning, which is good, since I will have very little room to maneuver when backing out of the slip. All of the docklines are doubled, so I untie the redundant lines first. I start the engine and switch on all the instruments at the panel: AIS, VHF, Radar, Sailing Instruments, Autopilot. I put on my Spinlock Deckvest PFD with its two harnesses. The temperature this morning is a pleasant 55 degrees, so much nicer than the frigid departure from Gloucester Point.

The couple from a boat anchored in the creek pull up in their dinghy.

"Would you like help casting off?"

"That would be great, thanks!"

"Where are you headed?"

"The Bahamas."

"Oh, us too. We're leaving for Spanish Wells this morning. We're just going to get more coffee. I'm afraid of running out. We were going to leave yesterday, but we have an 11-year-old boy on board, and he was upset about leaving on Christmas day."

"I'm headed for Spanish Wells too! I think today is a better day to leave, the Gulf Stream will be calmer today. What's the name of your boat?"

"*Traveller.*"

"I'll keep an eye out for you. I'm *Windflower.*"

It is 8:00am when I untie all but the short midship line and hand it to my new friend, who holds on until *Windflower* starts backing out. My vessel is 40 feet long, and the space between me and the boats behind looks like it's about 41 feet. The sportfishers facing my stern probably have chairs that cost more than my boat.

Windflower doesn't have much propwalk, but regardless, she also doesn't steer worth a hoot in reverse. It takes moving forward and backwards, barely turning with each shift of gears, 10, maybe 15 times, to get *Windflower* to turn 90 degrees to port so I can motor out of the marina.

Finally I am able to clear the dock and we are underway! The Bahamas, here we come! This is the big moment I've been waiting so long for. I stand proud at the helm and steer past *Traveller*, under the power lines where a bridge used to be, past a fleet of fishing boats, around Pivers Island with its marine biological station, and past another marina full of shallow-draft motor vessels. I wave to a fisherman on the shore. He pauses as if wondering whether or not I am waving at him, then waves back without enthusiasm. It's just another day to him, fishing at his usual spot, and I am just another boat passing by. But to me the day is momentous. I am chasing my dream, and I intend to find it in The Bahamas.

Looking at the buoys that mark the channel, I repeat to myself "red left on the way out," my converse to "red right return," so as not to make a terrible mistake while daydreaming about clear water, warm sun, colorful fish, and transparent waves. "Red left on the way out," I repeat again, and I can almost taste the lobster.

The wind is just noticeable, but still too light for sailing as we exit the inlet and enter the Atlantic Ocean. The motor pushes us along at 6 knots. The sun is out and the air is warm and clear. It is so very much nicer out here than it was on the day I came in when it was cold and misty and windy.

At 9:50am, the wind is up to 6.5 knots, so I hoist the sails and shut off the engine. There is no rush this morning, and I want to start this passage under sail. Motoring is no fun at all, but sailing in a light breeze is always pleasant. We make 3 knots, a casual walking pace. Our movement across the water is silent and smooth and the warm sun shines on my smiling face. I take off the big yellow bibs, which requires first taking off the PFD and jacket, then I put the jacket and the PFD back on. This is starting out to be a very good day.

Windflower under full sail with Little
Flower *strapped to the deck*

At 10:10am, the wind dies. I reluctantly start the noisy engine and we rumble on, putting the Beaufort Inlet, civilization, hot showers, and grocery stores further behind us. Twenty minutes later the breeze comes back at 9 knots and I shut the engine off again. We make 5 knots in glorious silence. Eleuthera is 550nm away at 192 degrees, just west of south. But I cannot take a direct route there.

First, we must cross the mighty Gulf Stream at a 90-degree angle. This current moves from SSW to NNE at up to 3 knots and is 60-100nm wide. When the wind blows against the current, dangerous, steep, short-period waves quickly build up. The warm water in the stream also creates its own thunderstorms. It's best to cross it in benign conditions and to cross it as quickly as possible.

We sail all day on a close reach making 6 knots on a course of 140 degrees, aiming just south of a 90-degree angle across the Gulf Stream, since it will carry us northeast while we are in its grip. If we get lucky, we might find ourselves in an eddy on the other side, a counter-current taking us towards our destination.

On the other side, the water temperature, and thus the air temperature, is much greater than over here on the west side of the stream. The feeling of the warm air on my skin lives in my mind like a dream. I've been cold for three months and I've had enough of it. I can't relax in the cold air, always tense or even shivering, my shoulders hunched and my toes numb. I want to wear shorts and nothing else and get hot at mid-day then cool off in the clear water while looking at colorful fish swimming about strange coral formations.

In the early afternoon I note there are neither ships in sight nor on the AIS, and the conditions are benign, and all this suggests I take a nap, since I can. I lay down in the cockpit and close my eyes. Whether I actually sleep or not is of no consequence, I simply must go through the process. Sleep will come automatically later. But as I stare up at the sky with closed eyes, the sun warms my face and my mind wanders off.

I wake up after 20 minutes, realize that I fell asleep, sit up, and look around. All is blue sea and blue sky, a few clouds, and no sign of mankind anywhere beyond my ship. I am at peace, the world around me is at peace, and I lay back down and fall asleep immediately.

My stomach is speaking to me when I awake, telling me about an avocado, which stirs up the image of a jar of salsa. I go below and make guacamole out of the two and enjoy it in the cockpit with tortilla chips as the autopilot steers. My stomach approves.

This is the good life: easy sailing offshore, out of sight of land, out of the reach of modern society and pop culture, completely out of the rat race, guacamole and a sailboat, peace and quiet, nothing but my own world and my own thoughts to keep me company. I am in my element, and the element is good.

At 4:15pm, the temperature is 68 and the sails suddenly become limp. A sudden calm is sometimes a harbinger of a change for the worse in the weather. I take the staysail down, reef the main, and start the engine.

I remember a sudden calm on my way to The Bahamas the last time I sailed there. I was crossing the Gulf Stream at night just east of Fort Lauderdale. The sailing was fine and *Sobrius*, my 30' Dufour Arpege, was making good headway on a beam reach in a SSE breeze. The wind was blowing the same direction as the current and the sea was peacefully calm. I was sailing to The Bahamas solo for the first time, and all was right in the world. Then the breeze died, the air felt strangely warm all of a sudden, and I cocked my head to the side wondering what was up. The stars disappeared and the night became very dark. Moments later, the wind came on hard and fast from the East, and with it came rain, hard angry rain in big drops that wanted to pummel me. *Sobrius* was overpowered, and I was blind. The rain, propelled by the wind, was not heavy enough to pummel me, so it satisfied itself by blinding and thoroughly soaking me. I had only time to grab my big yellow rain slicker and then close off the companionway, shutting myself off from the instruments. No matter, I couldn't see them anyway. But I was concerned not to have the AIS, since I couldn't see through the rain.

I steered by feel, pinching into the wind to take the power out of the sails, using the heeling angle of the boat to steer. There was nothing to do but sit there and take it, and my only consolation was the thought that it couldn't last forever. It was over within an hour, but it still tested my endurance.

This memory is fresh in my mind and this is why I reef the main and take the staysail down. A sudden calm is reason enough to reef, especially when singlehanded, I reason.

But this time there is no squall, and the wind remains very light. I take in some of the yankee, sheet the rest of it tight, and continue motoring at 135 degrees. Although we still point 145, the current is taking us north, so our course over ground, as measured by the GPS, is ten degrees less than the magnetic compass bearing.

Perhaps I should check the bilge, I think to myself. It's something that should be checked at least daily, in case water is finding its way in, and should the automatic bilge pump not be working, an unlikely case. I go below and lift the central floorboard, exposing the propeller shaft and the low point of the bilge below.

I am horrified to see water up over the sump and covering the diesel tank just below the propeller shaft. The bilge pump should have turned on a long time ago; its float valve should have lifted and activated the pump well before this level of water was reached, and where is all this water coming from?

This is exactly what I didn't want to see.

I turn on the pump manually with the switch at the base of the steps and the bilge empties quickly. If the float valve is really not working, I will have to monitor the bilge frequently, and for the entire passage. This does not give me a feeling of security, and yet again, I'm glad there is no one else aboard to whom I would have to explain the situation.

On to the next question: where is the water coming from? A dry boat gives me peace of mind, a leaking boat, especially when offshore, is disturbing. I crawl under the cockpit, where six through-hulls and seacocks live, and one in the way back, the starboard cockpit seat drain, is dripping just a bit, but not so much as to have caused the leak that filled the bilge. This is the one seacock I neglected to service back in Mattapoisett, and so it still has the old hose and hose-clamps. I decide it's not worth messing with.

I picture, in my head, turning one of the screws on one of its two hose-clamps and the clamp breaking and the hose splitting. I try to close the seacock and the 47-year-old through-hull breaks and a flood of water pours in while I scurry out backwards to get a softwood plug and a hammer. No, let's just let that alone. The water is coming from somewhere else, but where?

I take two more naps before the sun sets. I have to remind myself to sleep in the day. It's not natural, but it becomes easy as the passage progresses. Now I am still on a diurnal schedule, sleeping at night and awake when the sun is out, and I never nap in the day unless I'm sailing offshore.

At 7:00pm, I check the bilge again, and there is no water to be seen. The mystery is still strong. Surely this lack of water is a clue, but I can't put it together. *Windflower* holds a few mysteries, and I'm confident I will solve them all eventually. I just hope the bilge remains dry for the rest of the passage. Again, I find myself thankful that I have no passengers. Would it be ethical to continue the passage if I were responsible for someone else's safety?

I'm perfectly willing to risk my own skin; I've been doing that all my life. I risk my life to surf, to freedive, on long mountain-biking excursions alone in the woods, at work on top of roofs and ladders, and simply driving to work every morning. I am fine with that, I live life on my own terms.

Having crew, on the other hand, adds a whole different element to sailing, and one that I am not at all familiar with. At what point does a technical difficulty, like an unknown source of water in the bilge, constitute an unacceptable amount risk to which I could expose my crew? I have no idea. So, I find myself at peace with my solitude. No crew means much less responsibility and much easier decision making.

Of course we will continue the journey. I will fix whatever needs fixing along the way, and should my beloved sink to the bottom of the ocean, I will await rescue in the life-raft while eating Cliff Bars and reading my Kindle. If I die, I die doing what I love, having lived exactly the life I chose. This thought reminds me that I neglected to write a will before I left.

The sun has journeyed over the horizon to warm the other side of the earth, leaving this side to darken and cool until its return. The gentle breeze is 6 knots directly on the nose and the surface of the ocean is as still as a sleeping child. We motor across a giant pane of dark glass, yet it seems we sit still in a featureless world.

At 7:30pm I take the mainsail down and the evening becomes even more quiet without its flapping about.

The Navionics app on my phone thinks we are at Gloucester Point, which is terribly disappointing. I stare at the icon representing our position and expect it to move, yet it does not. I want to be able to sit inside, at the navigation table, and see where we are, what our course is, how fast we travel, and what boats are around us. Even if the GPS isn't working, why would it think we are at Gloucester Point? Now I have three things that are not right: the bilge pump, the unknown leak, and the lack of GPS position on my phone. Three things on the first day - no problem, we still make headway and we float just fine. Almost all is well.

It's dark now, and I remember it's time to switch on the masthead tricolor, yet when I look up, I see no light. Perhaps the masthead is blocking the light, it protrudes aft a good bit. I step up on deck and look up from abeam, but still see no light. I go below and turn on the anchor light, and it comes on. I try the tricolor again, and it does not come on, and I frown.

I add a fourth problem to the growing list, then turn on the bow and stern lights. They are wired together with the steaming light, and that's fine for now, since we are under power, but I'll have to figure out how to disconnect the steaming light when we are sailing at night. A long screw terminal is mounted at the base of the mast, and I'm sure it has to be one of the many wires connected there.

I take another nap and fall asleep right away. It's easier when it's dark, and all four of my new problems fade away as sleep takes over.

At 11:00pm, the temperature is 71 and I can feel redemption from the previous three months of relentless and unforgiving cold. I no longer need to pile on the winter-weather gear just to sit in the cockpit and I can even lie down out here for a nap. Sleeping in the cockpit provides quick access to the helm should action be called for, the more pleasant sounds of the wind and the water, and the fresh air. It's both convenient and comfortable, and at night, I only need open my eyes to see the stars.

But for now, I need to stay awake. The *Norwegian Bliss*, a cruise ship, is visible in the distance. The AIS says she will pass three miles behind us, and this means we will cross her bow, which makes me nervous, even though we will do so miles ahead of her. It's impossible to tell distance at night, and I carefully watch her green bow light. When the red light on her port side appears, and I can see both red and green, we are directly in her path. Minutes later, the green light disappears and I can relax. We have crossed her bow from a safe distance, and all is well.

The breeze is 9 knots on the nose and we make 4.9. Eleuthera is 511nm away at 199 degrees. We motor on, still crossing the Gulf Stream and lucky to be doing so in benign conditions.

I lay down after the cruise ship is well behind us and nap. When I wake, darkness dominates the world. No sign of life shows itself on the ocean, save for me and *Windflower*. Even *Little Flower* seems lifeless and dark all strapped to the deck and upside down. I lay down for a second nap.

I wake, and all is the same, so I sleep again. I take six naps in a row and decide that is plenty for now, although it only amounts to 2 hours of much-interrupted sleep, I feel refreshed and wide awake as I sit at the helm.

Another boat has been following for a long time. The AIS does not know its name, and I wonder if they are pirates, coming to rob me. Perhaps there will be a gunfight. I have a rifle, a lever-action 30-30, and a handgun, a 357-magnum revolver, as well as plenty of ammunition. I imagine what this would look like, me firing on them with old cowboy-style weapons. I'd have to be a really good shot to win if they had modern arms. Let's hope they are just happy cruisers like me.

Maybe they think I know where I'm going and are following my lead. Really, I'm just guessing. I'm depending on the difference between my magnetic bearing and the GPS course over ground to indicate when we are across the Gulf Stream. I want to be all the way across before turning south. Otherwise we will be sailing against a strong current, and subject to the whimsical weather-conditions of the stream.

I go below to check the bilge, hoping for a dry view of the diesel tank beneath the propeller shaft, but when I lift the floorboards I see the opposite. Water covers the bottom. I taste it, and it is both salty and oily. I spit it back out, and spit a few more times to get the diesel-engine taste out of my mouth, but it doesn't go completely away.

Perhaps the source of the water is in the engine compartment. I pull off the cover and shine a flashlight to see what's going on in there.

What I see baffles me.

It's good to have found the source of the water, but what is it? I see a small copper tube facing up, terminating in a fitting, but with nothing to fit into. In little spurts, it spews water up and bathes the entire engine compartment with warm saltwater. Everything is soaked, including the alternator and various unknown wires and terminals.

What could this be? Why is it here? Is it some component of the engine that needs to be reconnected? Is it part of the cooling system? Is the engine going to overheat? All these questions run through my head as I stare dumbfounded at the engine with its built-in saltwater shower.

I put my thumb over the tube to see how much pressure is behind it, and thus if I might put a stopper of some sort in the tube, and the water is easily stopped. It's warm but not too hot. What could I use as a stopper? The softwood plugs are all way to big. A small piece of rubber would work, perhaps a wad of butyl tape? I release my thumb and the tube continues where it left of, showering the helpless engine with corrosive saltwater, showering the charge controller, the alternator, cables and everything else.

I open the drawer at the base of the steps, break off a piece of butyl tape, and roll it into a ball. I cram this in the copper tube and the water is stopped.

I switch on the bilge pump manually, and nothing happens. I try again, and nothing happens again. Frustration tries to overtake me, but conscious mind pushes it down.

I have to remain calm and logical.

The Whale manual bilge pump is always ready to go, I remember, and I sit in the cockpit and pump out the bilge with the Whale. Afterward, I fetch the hand pump from under the port settee and I pump out the water from the forward bilge into a bucket and dump it overboard. All the while the auto-pilot steers and *Windflower* rocks side-to-side. I'm lucky not to be prone to seasickness, or else this would really be uncomfortable work.

At 4:00am, I check the bilge. There is more water than there was after I pumped it out, but not dramatically more. I pull the cover off the engine compartment and see that the butyl-tape plug has failed. What else could I use? I could just bend the tube over 180-degrees and permanently seal it that way. But what if I later discover that I need to reconnect it to something? I need a very small wooden plug, like a golf tee, or a pencil. Pencils, I have plenty pencils, leftover from my carpentry work.

I quickly find a pencil and sharpen it with a pocket knife. The pencil almost fits, so I sharpen it some more, steepening the angle on the point so it is long and thin. I cram it in the copper tube and the water is stopped. There we go. That ought to do it. I close the engine compartment and hope the problem is fixed.

I make an early-morning salad, since I have no refrigeration and need to eat all the perishables first. The notion of certain foods being appropriate for certain times of day has no meaning here. There is no breakfast, lunch, and dinner; and morning, noon, and night no longer have much relevance. Time of day is meaningless. We are simply "not there yet."

We motor along at 6 knots. Our course over ground is 130 and the magnetic bearing is 150, indicating that we are still in the Gulf Stream. Eleuthera is 513nm away at a bearing of 191 degrees. My destination is two nautical miles further away than it was five hours ago. The wind has been slowly veering, and the true wind angle is now 40 degrees to starboard, so we may be sailing soon. We can make good headway at 50 degrees off the wind. Navionics is working again, so I can take that off the list of things that don't work. Perhaps my luck

is turning around.
8:00am Dec 27, 170nm east of Cape Fear, SC, Day 2

Finally, the wind is in our favor and I cut off the engine. We sail under full main, yankee, and staysail at 5.5 knots. Our course over ground is 110 and the magnetic bearing is 120. The breeze is 11 knots coming from due South, 180 degrees.

Although we sail, and for that I am grateful, I'm not in good spirits. My throat is sore and I worry that I picked up a virus when I went to town, perhaps at the restaurant. Maybe a kitchen worker was ill, or maybe I got it at the bookstore, from touching all the books that other people touched.

The leaks and broken things have me down too. It takes the fun right out of sailing when confidence in the vessel wanes. Sailing is all fun when things are proper, in good weather with good wind and a boat on which everything works. But remove any of these – make the weather cold or rainy, boost the wind or kill it, or make stuff on the boat not work, and sailing loses its fun real fast. It can be blissful and enjoyable, or it can be terrifying and miserable, or anything in between. Today it is somewhere in between. But this is only the beginning of the second day of what I hope will be a five-day passage. I need to cheer up and I know it, but how can one do this? Oh, if I were only in control of my emotions, I would be happy all the time. Maybe if I was more disciplined at meditating then I could more readily achieve control over my emotional state.

The Garmin InReach comes to my emotional rescue and beeps, letting me know it has received a message from someone. This is good news, and I smile at the thought. I like communication with friends and family while I'm out on the ocean. It's my friend Eddie, advising me to tack and head south in order to stay in good wind. Although our course over ground is still ten degrees less than our magnetic bearing, I can't be sure if the two agree when there is no drift, and heading south will take us out of the current eventually anyway, should we still be in the Gulf Stream.

I set the autopilot, then after it's gotten its bearings, I press and hold the starboard button on the remote. The wheel slowly spins to the right and *Windflower* begins a tack. I let out the port jib sheet while pulling in on the starboard sheet, then release it and pull with everything I have on the starboard sheet. The staysail backwinds, and this helps the yankee get across. When the tack is through and the yankee trimmed, I release the staysail, letting it move to the other side of the deck, and trim it tight. I adjust the traveler, pulling the main to center, and we are now on port tack.

9:00am, Dec 27, 33.5593° N, 74.5515° W, 222nm east of Myrtle Beach, SC

Our new course is 210 degrees and we make 4 knots in 8 knots of breeze coming from 260 degrees. I feel better for having some sailing action, and throughout the tack, everything worked as it should. I realize that I have discovered two things that can change my mood for the better: communication with a friend, and tacking.

The wind increases a bit, and we get moving at 6 knots. This is good sailing, out here on the deep ocean, with nothing in sight save for the sky and the water. The sky and the ocean, that's what it's all about. The sky is made of wind, and for that we have sails. The ocean is made of water, and for that we have a hull. Inside the boat is air, and outside is water. As long as this equilibrium is maintained, we float. The sun causes differential heating of the atmosphere, and the air moves. We call this wind, and the sails use this to move us. It's all quite simple, and quiet, and serene. Sailing is all about maintaining equilibrium and slowly moving across the ocean.

sitting at the helm, maintaining equilibrium

It occurs to me that we have burned more than 10 gallons of fuel, and I have ten gallons of diesel in jerry-cans. Conditions are fairly calm, and I recognize an opportunity to put the fuel in the tank, where it belongs. My friend Robin showed me an easy way to get a siphon started, and I use his trick for the first time. I put a short hose in the jerrycan and the other end in the diesel tank. I then wrap my hand around the opening of the jerrycan and the hose, sealing off all but one opening between fingers and thumb. I put my mouth over my hand and blow, increasing the air pressure in the container and thus forcing the fuel up into the hose creating the siphon. Now I just sit back and let gravity do the rest of the work.

Dark clouds line the horizon ahead, and I hope it doesn't start raining while I've got the tank open. I certainly don't want any water in the diesel, and I wonder if have done something stupid. There are so many opportunities for tragic mistakes on a sailboat. Luckily, the clouds stay far away and the operation is over in a few minutes.

Seeing no other ships, I decide it's nap time, and I take two in a row. But when I wake, it's clear that I have a cold. How awful. I never get sick anymore, and to catch a cold right before a long passage is bad luck indeed. I hope it doesn't get any worse. I picture myself with a fever and strep throat, miserable and trying to sail by myself. No, I can't get sick. I simply can't.

At 2:44pm, we make 5 knots at 216 degrees. The wind has backed from 180 to 115, and so we change course to a more favorable 195. Eleuthera is 472nm away at 204 degrees. We point a bit east of Eleuthera because I expect to encounter wind and current from the east as we get further south.

At 5:00pm I decide to take a look in the engine compartment to make sure my plug held. To my great delight, the pencil-plug is still firmly in place, and I feel my confidence grow.

A vague memory of tiny sparks around the cables at the positive terminal post on the alternator, from the last time I looked at it, reminds me to check the cables. This has been an ongoing issue, and it could be that the saltwater bath exacerbated the situation. I check the big positive cable, and it wiggles easily on the post. I'll just tighten it up a bit, no problem.

I grab a small insulated crescent wrench and give the nut on the post *ever so slightly* a twist clockwise. The post snaps off. *Oh my God*, this can't be. But it is so. The charging cable now hangs free, along with another small cable, and the broken post and its nut fall into the bilge, never to be seen again. The post has broken off flush with the alternator body and a sense of tragedy overcomes me as I kneel on the floor, unable to think of a way out of this one.

Remain calm. I can fix this. Surely I'll think of something. Nothing comes to mind. I brainstorm. Epoxy the post back on, no, epoxy doesn't conduct electricity. Solder it back on, maybe but probably not strong enough. Unscrew the post and screw in a replacement; yes, that might work.

I find a small pair of channel-locks and do my best to unscrew the post, but I can't get a grip on it and certainly can't turn it.

Maybe, I think, I should turn for land and go to Charleston, or Florida, but a look at the chart reveals that Beaufort,

NC, is the closest landfall, considering I would have to cross the Gulf Stream again. The thought of returning to the port I just left is crushing and a non-starter.

I pull out the Explorer Chartbook for Eleuthera, to see if I can find a shop that might be able to fix the alternator. RnB Boatyard in Spanish Wells has a big advertisement inside the front cover.

I send Eddie a message explaining what happened and ask him to send RnB an email to find out if they can fix my alternator.

I remember meeting Alex, a mechanic at Lamb's Yacht in Jacksonville. I have his number in my phone, so I send him a message on the InReach, explaining the situation. He gets back quickly, saying that I can still run the engine, but the fuel pump on the Westerbeke is electric and will eventually drain the batteries.

Now I am completely relying on the solar panels to charge the batteries. I need to conserve electricity, and this means I will have to hand steer as much as possible. No problem, I can do that. The big question is whether to go to The Bahamas or back to the States. It's dark out, and I can sense the batteries draining. Will the sun be enough to keep them charged every day? I think it should be OK, but what if it isn't. If the batteries die, I can still sail, but with no navigation, no lights, no radio (although I do have two handheld radios), and no AIS. That would be a dangerous situation, but not completely unmanageable.

One moment I feel like tacking and heading west, the next I want to continue south to The Bahamas. The conflict goes on all night while I sit at the helm steering.

What would I do if I had crew aboard, I wonder. I would have to turn for the United States, no doubt. But I am out here by myself, and am probably willing to take the risk. Am I? Yes, take the risk, go to The Bahamas, complete the mission. But is that good seamanship? That, I do not know. The safe and conservative solution is to turn west and go to the nearest port, or make it to Florida and familiar ports.

I could go to Florida, replace the alternator and do all the other work I planned on doing to *Windflower* after The Bahamas, like replacing the standing rigging. Then I could go to The Bahamas in the Spring. That isn't such a bad idea, except that North Florida is cold in the winter, and I don't want to be cold anymore.

I think about the other option, continuing on to The Bahamas. I'm confident that I can get there without the alternator and surely I can fix it or replace it there. That certainly is more adventurous, and adventure what I am here for.

At 9:42pm, the *SM New York* passes in front of us, 2nm away. Lowly humans cannot perceive distance on the ocean at night, so there appears to be an enormous ship dangerously close, right in front of us. I stare at the ship, thankful to have the information supplied by the AIS. Without it I would be in a state of anxiety every time a ship came into view.

The breeze is down to 10 knots and I hope it comes back, I don't want to have to motor and drain the batteries even more.

It's funny that just yesterday running the engine meant it was no problem to let the autopilot steer the whole time, since the engine was charging the batteries. Now the opposite is true. Running the engine drains the batteries so I don't want to use the autopilot. My, how the tables have turned.

I steer deep into the dark and cloudy night, more than a day's sail from land, while wondering if I should turn towards the States and replace the alternator. Something keeps me heading south, my need for adventure, or my stubborn resolve to complete the passage. Perhaps it is foolhardy to continue, but this is what I do. I can't make myself turn towards civilization and alternators. Instead, I sit at the helm and steer, and my eyes become heavy.

I don't want to give up the helm, since I am now trying to conserve battery power as much as I can. My vision becomes jumpy and my concentration dissolves as a dream tries to take hold of my mind. If I was driving a car right now I would pull over immediately.

Windflower swings to the right and the sails snap across with a bang. The headsails are backwinded and the main has tacked across. *Unbelievable*, I've accidentally tacked, which means I must have fallen asleep for a moment, but I'm wide awake now. I turn the wheel to the right and we go all the way around in a big circle, gybing along the way and getting back on starboard tack. We press on into the darkness. With no stars in sight, I have to steer by the compass or the heading on the chartplotter.

Staring at the instruments and steering by the numbers is anything but fun. Rather it is mind-numbing and I constantly lose focus and have to remind myself to stay alert and awake. My eyes flutter and vision becomes jumpy as a dream-state threatens to overtake reality.

Later in the evening I accidentally tack a second time. I'm glad there's no one here to see me make these amateur mistakes and I wonder if the track shown by the Garmin InReach or the SPOT will have embarrassing little loops on it from my two accidental tacks.

Dec 28, 32.3605° N, 75.3773° W, 270nm east of Savanah, GA, Day 3

At 3:00am, the wind is dying. I wish I could start the engine, but I don't think that's good idea. We need to conserve all the battery power we can. The wind continues to die, and the sails start slatting, going limp, then banging into position in little mini-gusts. It creates a racket that quickly becomes unbearable.

At 4:00am, I take the sails down and try to take a nap as we lie a-hull. But *Windflower* rocks back and forth, pitches, yaws, and rolls in the short-period swell, trying to rock me out of my bunk. I cannot sleep at all, and forty minutes later, I go ahead and start the engine. The sun will be up in a couple of hours and will surely charge the batteries quickly.

We motor directly for Eleuthera heading 201 degrees at 6 knots. It feels good to be making progress again, but the noise of the engine and the fact that I'm on a sailboat and not sailing, but instead motoring, which is the antithesis of sailing, disappoints me, and the broken alternator, tricolor, Navionics, and bilge pump have me down in the dumps. I try to reconcile myself with the thought that at least it is not cold. The thermometer at the navigation table reads 72.3 and I hang onto this number like a security blanket.

Ah, the bountiful wind is back! At 7:30am I shut the engine off and raise the sails, and the silence is glorious. *Windflower* was made for the wind, and she sails the way a dog just freed from the kennel runs across a green lawn. I stand proud and tall at the helm and steer by the wind, as close to it as *Windflower* will allow, watching on the sails and the heeling angle, making small adjustments for the small waves we cross, focused on keeping her in the slot that moves us through the breeze, and all is well with the world.

Why would one sail, all alone they might say
Furthermore without fail, ask if I'm lonely and grey
Wouldn't it be better, to share with another
The fun and adventure, the beauty to discover
They couldn't imagine, at sea all alone
Scared and saddened, so far from home
Isn't it scary, out there in the dark
They would be wary, of depth, madness, and sharks
No, I do tell, lonesome never feel
For my mind is quite well, and my hands on the wheel
I go where I desire, and do as I will
Without becoming mired, in another's needs to fill
The sea is all tranquil, especially at night
And all day I fulfill, whatever I delight
It's quiet onboard, no chattering in my ear
No other's accord, to worry and fear
I risk only me, and my beloved Windflower
No other's safety, is under my power
Rest easy your minds, don't worry about me
I will always find, a fine place to be
The sea is serene, my boat is uncrewed
Better alone it would seem, to seek solitude

I steer for an hour before I remember that since we are sailing upwind, I can try locking off the wheel. Once I feel like we are exactly on course, I hold the wheel steady, then twist the little black knurled wheel on the side of the binnacle to lock off the helm. *Windflower* holds course, then heads up just a little. We make 5.5 knots at a course of 210 degrees. I move the traveler down just a few inches. *Windflower* holds course, and I stand at the helm watching the course over ground, seeing that it stays put. This is a simple method of self-steering that requires no electricity, and a significant development for this journey. I now have a much better chance of making it to The Bahamas.

Locking the wheel is a wonderful way to make the boat steer herself. It is silent, uses no power, and the boat follows the wind, instead of following a compass heading, as the boat does when using an electronic autopilot. This way, as the wind shifts, *Windflower* follows. When following a compass heading, if the wind shifts, the sails suddenly become improperly trimmed.

Riding high on my success at the helm, my thoughts turn to the next problem. I have an idea about fixing the alternator, and, even though it is unlikely to work, I have to try it.

I go below and fish the Makita cordless 4" grinder out from below the aft starboard bunk. I find the vise and a bolt with a nut, then take these things to the cockpit. I clamp the bolt in the vise and cut off its head with the grinder. I then thread a nut to the good end of the threads.

Down below, I search until I find the soldering kit and I get the torch from the electrical toolbox. I attempt to solder the bolt to the broken post on the alternator, but the effort is fruitless. The solder doesn't want to stick to anything. I need a new idea.

4:30pm, 31.3886 ° N, 75.9783 ° W, 283nm East of Brunswick, Georgia

With the wheel still locked off, I notice our boat speed, that is, the speed across the water as measured by a little paddle-wheel under the boat, is 4.5. Our speed over ground, as measured by the GPS, is 5.5. We must be in an eddy of the Gulf Stream, as I had hoped, and we make an extra knot.

The sun lowers to the horizon and the sky becomes brilliantly lit in warm hues. Every cloud blushes with life in colors from magenta through the reds and oranges to bright and almost white yellow and they move like strange, slow, amorphous animals, gods perhaps. The ocean reflects these colors on the tops of the waves, and the motion of the water makes the colors dance in an infinite and random pattern that dazzles the senses. The scene is hypnotic and I can do nothing but stare in wonder as it fills my consciousness and drives away the trivial banter in my head.

I am awed by nature's incredible capacity to create extraordinary beauty. I stand before it as a child before a master, a devout practitioner before the grand altar, a weary traveler before his home. The rest of the world ceases to exist and there is nothing but me and *Windflower* on the ocean facing the colored sky and the all-powerful sun, which bids us good evening.

Is it all real? I wonder, and I feel part of the setting, like a figure in a painting, or a character in a video game. Clearly, I am meant to be here, right here, right now, for this is all that exists and I am one with the world around me.

I hold the steering wheel in my hands as the ocean passes by the rudder. I breathe in the air and the oxygen that has come from the water beneath me. We move across the surface of the ocean, powered by the wind, which was set in motion by the sun. The sun is a star, and we are but stardust, assembled from the atoms sent flying through the universe by the explosion of a star deep in the past. The sun, the air, the ocean, even *Windflower* are all made from such atoms, and we are all one.

The Bahamas are also part of the scene, even if I can't see the islands, still hundreds of miles away. I must remain focused on the objects and numbers around me to stay on a course that will take us there.

By 6:00pm, the wind has backed and our course is 246 degrees, well west of our destination, which is not good, considering the eastern trade winds and current we are sure to encounter further south. But we are now picking up an extra 1.5 knots with the eddy. The wheel is locked off and the sails are trimmed tight on a close reach. There is nothing for me to do.

In reality, the course matches my mind, because I am still unsure whether we are going to The Bahamas or Florida.

I'm waiting to hear back from Eddie about the boatyard in Spanish Wells, if they can fix my alternator. If they say they can, we go to The Bahamas. If not, we go to Florida. Our current course of 246 degrees, which is dictated by the wind into which we sail, aims us between the two destinations, so it makes sense in that regard. It is an undecided course for an undecided captain.

When the sun has disappeared below the horizon, the crescent moon shines bright, and the crescent faces up, like a shallow bowl. Directly above it shines the bright and steady light of one of the planets of our solar system. I do not know which planet it is, but I know it is a planet because its light does not flicker, like that of a star, light-years away.

The effect of the planet over the crescent moon is dramatic and my attention is fixated on the heavenly alignment. It reminds me of a pendulum, yet it does not move, as if time has no meaning out here.

The sky darkens and the moon and planet move their own respective ways, and the perfect alignment is no more. The seas are calm and the wind is fine. I have been hand steering, but now I try to find an equilibrium so I can lock off the wheel. I find the slot in the wind, lock the wheel off there, then watch. I make micro-adjustments to the wheel until *Windflower* holds her course, then I lay down on the bench on the leeward side of the cockpit for a nap.

At 11:30pm, I wake up and see that the wind has backed and *Windflower* steers herself on a course of 190 degrees, directly towards Eleuthera. This is the deciding factor. Logic be damned, we will sail to The Bahamas! Clearly my ship wants to go to the islands. She has spent her entire life in cold New England and now she sees her first chance to visit the tropics and bask in the warm sun *in January*. She will not be deterred, and I will not stand in her way now that she has made her intentions clear.

Ah, but on the other hand, the batteries are low. The

solar panels were leaning away from the sun all day, and the radar cast a shadow over them too. The batteries did not get fully charged today and now we find ourselves facing another long dark night without full battery power.

I am fortunate that *Windflower* can steer herself on a close reach, and I am fortunate that our course is a close reach. If I chose to go to Florida, we would be on a beam or broad reach, and this would require me to take the helm and stay focused. Oh, how I wish I had made installing a windvane self-steering rig a priority. How luxurious it would be to simply not have to steer at all for the entire passage, and for this to use no electricity. The windvane is now officially a top priority. Ironically, I carry an old Aries windvane rig in the v-berth. It only needs mounting hardware, to be mounted, and a wheel boss. I could have done this and had it working right now if I had made it a priority, but I can't do everything right the first time, that would make for dull storytelling.

I nap, and after waking I sit in the cockpit and stare up at the innumerable stars. They are all out tonight. None of them stayed home. It must be a holiday in the heavens, for the streets of the sky are full and the lights shine down from so many points that the individual stars coalesce when taken all in. They are as numerous as grains of sand on the beach and make up not many individual stars, but one big star map, a galaxy visible from the edge of the disc, where sits our solar system, viewed from the blue part of the blue planet.

I sit in the blackness, gliding across the invisible water, and look up at the countless other suns, wondering who might be looking back at our sun from their planet, and what color their planet is.

The alternator is meaningless now, just a toy and a part of a toy. We have sails and solar panels, we don't need the alternator. I have a manual bilge pump and two hand pumps, and buckets. We don't need the bilge pump. The running lights are more than adequate out here where there are no other boats, and I can tell where we are just fine without Navionics on my phone. No. We have all that we need and we are going to The Bahamas, not back to the States. We are going to the tropics, where winter is nonexistent, where the water is clear and the fish are colored like some mad artist painted them with a full palette. We are going to a place where *Windflower* can anchor and rest wherever she pleases. We are going south, to the islands.

Dec 29, 30.3054° N, 76.2156° W, 270nm east of Jacksonville, FL, Day 4

At 6:00am of the fourth day of the passage, the sun rises and chases away the stars and the blackness of the sea. The wheel has been locked off all night, and *Windflower* is happy this way. She has found equilibrium and is well entrenched within.

The sun's rays penetrate the clouds on this fine morning.

The batteries start the day at 12.43 volts, which isn't bad. This number didn't change all night, and for that I am thankful. We make 5 knots in 14 knots of breeze, heading due south at 180 degrees. The temperature is 71 and I wear a light jacket and a hat. Our speed is lower than it would be if I was steering, because *Windflower* is pinching a bit (sailing closer to the wind than is most efficient), but five knots is acceptable and we heel less at this speed. I could probably micro-adjust the helm, but I am remiss to touch the wheel since *Windflower* has been successfully steering herself for so long now. I don't want to risk losing the magic.

I watch the sun color the sky and my mind is free of thought. All it contains at this moment is the field of view before me, a simple scene yet infinite in its complexity, a sight no one else sees. The great ball of flame rises noticeably, yet imperceptibly, and the colors slowly fade and change from warm to cool.

I come back to the ship and check the voltmeter, which reads 12.35, lower than ideal.

I notice *Windflower* has too much weather helm this morning. She tries to steer into the wind and the wheel must be turned to the right to counteract this. I ease the traveler and take the slack out of the reefing lines, tensioning them just a bit to flatten the sail. I furl in some of the jib. I find equilibrium and lock off the wheel. We make 6 knots in 14 knots of breeze. We are less than 300nm from Eleuthera, at least halfway there.

The sky is clear and blue and the ocean is alive but docile. I stare at the water until I desire activity and unlock the steering wheel. I sit at the helm, back in control of my ship, and stare ahead at the horizon.

The wind picks up we accelerate to 7 knots. *Windflower* charges across the ocean and I hand-steer and we are a team. Searching for the perfect slot in the wind and the best course through the waves, I stare ahead and sink into the interaction of the wind and the water and the mechanics of *Windflower*. Steering the boat is meditative and all-encompassing, and reminds me of why I like to sail. I am thinking of nothing, giving over my mind to the wind and the ocean and the ship, so that all may work together to propel us south. It occurs to me that

I'm in charge of a forty-foot, fifteen-ton vessel on the open ocean and we are hundreds of miles from anywhere. This is adventure; this is living large!

Windflower *finds her slot through the wind. The control head for the autopilot is visible under the seahood. The five lighted dots signify that the autopilot is on, as I am taking a photograph.*

Seven knots is fun, but on a long passage, on this passage anyway, I feel like this speed indicates the time for a reef, and I put in the first. It goes in smoothly without me having to leave the cockpit and I congratulate myself for the success. We only lose a half a knot, and 6.5 still feels fast.

The seas are 5-8' and the sailing is lively. *Windflower* cuts through the waves with no resistance and they seem to split apart in anticipation of her arrival. The ride is so smooth that I smile at the thought. My previous boat would have been slamming occasionally. I don't think *Windflower* can slam. She's no punk rocker, rather more of a ballroom dancer.

But something does slam, it's the anchor occasionally being lifted by a wave. It bangs into the new headstay riser, then slams back into the bow roller. I've been hearing it occasionally for long enough now, and I must go do something about it.

I put on the orange bibs and clip my long tether to the jackline. I creep forward as *Windflower* rises and falls. Spray comes over the bow and douses me as I move. I pretend not to notice. The water isn't cold.

At the bow, I clip my short tether to the inner forestay and kneel. I am doubly clipped in and thankful of this since the ocean rises to the bow with each wave. *Windflower* cuts through another wave and the ocean leaps. The bibs save me from really getting wet this time, although my shirt is now soaked. Luckily it is not cotton, but a synthetic long-sleeve left-over from my mountain biking days, and it sheds most of the water.

I take the short piece of rope that I brought with me and tie it to a cleat, loop it through the bow roller, over the Vulcan anchor, and take it back to the cleat. Before I can tie it off, another wave rises as *Windflower* dives, and the ocean greets me again in her wet and heavy embrace. I pretend not to notice. I'm trying to be tough here, and also to keep my focus. I tie off the line, unclip my short tether, creep back to the cockpit, and take off the orange bibs. So dry and safe, the cockpit feels. I like it here; I think I'll stay.

A message from Eddie makes the InReach chirp, and I am gladdened by the thought of his words bouncing off a satellite and finding my little device out here on the ocean, so far from anywhere. He tells me that the boatyard in Spanish Wells has not gotten back to him yet, but also that he looked at the manual for my alternator and describes the mechanism that attaches the post to the alternator. It sounds like I might be able to unscrew the post and bolt on a new one. Even though I already tried that, I might have to try again.

The device chirps again, and Eddie tells me that the wind is going to turn more south tomorrow evening, then southwest on Monday ahead of the next front.

All morning *Windflower* heels away from the sun as if she is shading her eyes, and the solar panels are not able to charge the batteries. The solar panels need a certain minimum angle to the sun in order to charge, and we do not have the angle. I put the second reef in the mainsail in an attempt to get us to heel less and present the solar panels more directly to the sun. As I crank in the second reef, I hear a snap and something falls to the deck and bounces. The sail flogs and lines flap madly in the melee. The blue second reef line hangs limp below the boom, weighted by the block that held the clew. Its shackle is gone. I hoist the main back to the first reef position.

I want to check the rigging with the binoculars, to see if anything else broke. I'm not certain that what I heard hit the deck was the second reef shackle.

Where are the binoculars? I can't find them, and it's making me angry. I've been so good at keeping them in one place, in the cockpit right by the leeward bulkhead, where I could quickly get to them at any time. They've been there for at least a day. Well, the time is now and they are not there. I look all over. I bought them in St Petersburg when I was fitting out *Sobrius*. They were expensive, and I intended to keep them forever. Good binoculars can last a long time if they are not dropped, or lost. But I cannot find them anywhere. I stop looking, hoping they will turn up somewhere.

Eddie recommends going to the Abacos and anchoring near Spanish Cay to wait for the front to pass and catch the northwest winds behind it. I look at the charts and see that this is a possibility. But the Abacos were hit hard by Hurricane Dorian last summer and I worry that sandbars have shifted, debris has created hazards, and navigation may be unpredictable.

I put my phone in its case mounted on the post by the navigation table and think to myself that I should look in the navigation table for the binoculars. Yes, that is their official spot, isn't it? I open the table and there they are, right where they are supposed to be. Perhaps my luck is turning around, or perhaps I'm becoming delirious.

At 12:21pm, the batteries have charged up to 12.63, and my confidence builds. I found the binoculars and the solar panels are charging the batteries. That's two successes in one morning.

I take a turn at the wheel and feel too much weather helm. I should let some more jib out, I think to myself. It's all experimental, but this must be the right thing to do. I hold the furling line in one hand, pop the rope clutch with the other, and the line runs out so fast and hard that it almost sucks the skin of my left hand into the steel device. I should have wrapped the line around a winch before opening the clutch. I've learned another lesson, I hope.

The chartplotter informs me that two ships are coming up behind us and I turn around to look, but all I see is grey ocean and sky. The AIS tells me that *Navig8 Amethyst* is 18.5nm back, of course I can't see it. Perhaps if the Earth was flat I could see a ship that far away. The other ship disappears from the chartplotter before I can get its information.

We make 6.6 knots at 204 degrees in 14 knots of breeze. I'm hand-steering, enjoying the ride, and the temperature is pleasant. I am constantly reminded that I am not cold, and that this is why I am heading south. I utter a vaguely maniacal little laugh with both hands on the big steering wheel, standing with legs spread to keep my balance, the wind tugging at my goatee. I am alone on the ocean, hundreds of miles from anywhere, on my own private patch of Earth, the Blue Planet, master of my own world, happily delirious and immersed in a long adventure.

Time passes and I still stand at the helm with calm mind, steering through the swell. I'm trying to find the slot in the wind, and once finding it, trying to stay in it.

One of the two ships behind me is visible to port, but it should pass without either of us having to change course. I remain alert.

Movement ahead on the water catches my attention.

Something huge rises from the ocean, like a ship sinking in reverse, then falls back in with a great splash. I grab my phone, which, conveniently, is sitting right next to me, and turn on the video camera.

A dark school-bus with a long face leaps from the ocean and for a brief moment becomes horizontal, hovering over the surface like a UFO, and then hits the water in haphazard fashion, slapping its massive body against the ocean sending hundreds of gallons of water skyward.

It's a whale! I yell with delight. It leaps again and again I yell. The whale's head appears, mouth open, coming vertically out of the water, then leans back and splashes again. A fourth time the whale breaks the surface, its head coming out vertically, "spy-hopping" as the behavior is called. The whale might be looking around, perhaps hearing *Windflower* approaching, or perhaps the leviathan is in the process of devouring a giant squid, just caught from 3000 feet below after a heroic battle, and rising vertically to force the slimy and still-fighting beast down its cetacean esophagus.

The whale is sleek and grey with a dorsal fin, a distinct mouth, and a square forehead. I'm no whale expert, but I'd say it might be a pilot whale or a pygmy sperm whale. As we sail by, I think about what kind of damage such a creature could inflict on my boat should it leap out of the water, like I just saw it do, and land on us. We would be crushed instantly. Hopefully it is feeding or playing and not trying to warn me to go away, because we sail right through where I saw it first jump.

As we pass I am conscious of what a wonderful experience this was, an incredible wildlife encounter, and the highlight of the passage thus far. It was almost as good as the hot shower in Beaufort, yet it makes for an even better tale.

A whale leaps from the water off the port bow, providing the day's entertainment.

At 2:30pm, we only make 4 knots over ground, but the speed through the water is 4.6. We are now in a current moving against us, but only a half-knot current. The wind is down to 10 knots and we fly full sails. *Navig8 Amethyst* passes us to port. She is a tanker and 184 meters long. *Century Melody* is coming up on starboard and is a cargo ship 137 meters long. I might have to tack to get out of her way. Even though I have right-of-way since I am under sail, I do not give any credence to this little bit of maritime law.

Ten minutes later, as soon as *Navig8 Amethyst* is completely past my position, I tack. We now head due east. At 3:00pm we tack again and resume our southbound course. As I adjust the lines on the traveler, my knee is braced on the bulkhead, and something beneath my knee snaps. I look down, and see that I have broken my newest pair of sunglasses, which I bought at the Surf Station in St Augustine right before I left town, so they hold sentimental value. I add them to the growing list of casualties.

At 6:00pm, I enjoy a beautiful sunset. Rays of orange light penetrate the stratum and shine down on the horizon through a blue-grey layer of clouds. I like to catch every one, every sunset and every sunrise. The beauty of nature is there for us to enjoy every day, free and spectacular and truly good.

As we close reach in light winds, the sun sets in the background, less dramatic in black and white, but still a sight to behold.

I have another idea about fixing the alternator, and I feel like I have to try it. Without it, the batteries may go completely dead. If I can't fix the alternator tonight, then tomorrow we will have to lie a-hull, towing a drogue so we face downwind, and let the sun shine on the solar panels. Sailing upwind, with the wind coming from the south, we are always heeled away from the sun, and the panels do not charge the batteries on either tack. I have to try to fix the alternator, and now is the time, since the wind is light and the seas are small.

I go below, take out the Makita cordless drill in its big blue case, and fetch the new set of drill bits and a flashlight. Inside the engine compartment I shine the light on the alternator, then put the smallest bit in the drill and sit down. As carefully and as slowly as I can, I begin drilling a tiny hole in the end of the broken post. My hand is braced against the engine so it moves with the boat, and the drill bit slowly digs away at the steel post. It's working! I'm going to win! I can feel victory already. Getting the hole started was the hard part, the part of the job which was most unlikely to succeed, and that the rest of the job relied on. But the hole has been started and now I can't be stopped.

I drill in about a half inch, then switch to the next larger bit, repeat the process, and switch up again. When I have a hole 1/8" wide and 1/2" deep, I put down the drill and get out the three boxes of screws and bolts. I find three likely candidates and take them to the alternator. One seems like it might fit. It's a stainless-steel wood screw with a trim head for a square-drive bit, a leftover from my carpentry job. I fetch the Makita impact driver and a square bit. I'm not certain about this part of the repair, but I'm hopeful as I attempt to drive the wood screw into the steel alternator post.

It works! The screw drives right in and holds fast.

Out comes the electrical toolbox. I strip a length of 16g wire and use it to wrap and tie on the charging cable and the other small cable that were connected to the post before it broke off. I twist it all together as tight as I can, then top it off with an alligator clip. I scoot back to observe my work. The charging cable is reattached to the alternator, albeit in a shoddy manner, but it should work. I stare a bit longer. Have I missed anything? No. All looks good. A bit ridiculous, but good.

I get up and start the engine in the cockpit, then go below to look at it all. I see no sparks or smoke or any other red flags. I check the voltmeter. It reads the same as before, but that's alright, the engine is just idling. I rev the engine, check the voltmeter, and bingo! It reads 13 volts. The alternator is back in action! What a great day this is! I saw a whale and fixed the alternator. Now I just need to fix the masthead tricolor, the bilge pump, the second reef, and the sunglasses.

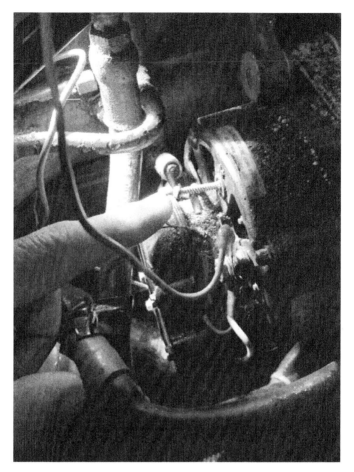

I'm pointing at the wood-screw that I drove into the broken positive post on the alternator.

Monday, Dec 30, 28.8673° N, 76.8479° W, 215nm east of New Smyrna Beach, FL, Day 5

It's midnight and I lay in the gently rolling bunk listening to something rattling around outside. It's a distinct metal-on-metal sound and it's like an anchor that keeps my conscious firmly attached to the awake world. The body of the boat is like a drum or an acoustic guitar and amplifies any noise on the outside, making a sound that is imperceptible on deck into a loud annoyance inside. I assume that I'll get used to all of *Windflower's* sounds, but for now the noise is quite bothersome.

I don't know what it is I hear, but I've tried to sleep through it for two naps, and I've had enough. I get up, strap on a headlamp, and emerge from the cabin into the dark and dynamic world outside. I look to my right and see the problem, it's a running backstay that I left attached. It's loose, but on the leeward rail, and I should have moved it forward before tacking.

The leeward rail is a dangerous place to be when heeling as much as we are, so I clip my long tether to the windward jackline (on the high side of the boat) and creep forward. When I am across from the verbose backstay, I slide on my butt to the leeward rail and clip my short tether to the jackline on that side. I'm like a rock climber maneuvering along a cliff ledge, attached to the rock in two places. The only difference is that to fall off the boat is to die a *slow* death.

I move the running backstay forward. It was also chafing the jib sheet, so I've caught two fish with one hook. I'll have to remember to move them before I tack from now on. It's exciting out on the leeward rail, and I pause to watch the black water and white foam rush past. The darkness of the night magnifies its motion and for a moment the adventure-level is high and the scene nearly hypnotic.

I return to the safety of the cockpit and check our course, the AIS, and the horizon before descending into the cabin, where I lay down inside for another nap. The noise of the running backstay is gone, but another annoys me. Something is banging up front, perhaps in the V berth, a locker door I assume. It bangs, pauses, bangs again, pauses just long enough that I hope it won't bang again, then it does, and I am annoyed. This goes on until I fall asleep, but the sound is there to greet me when I wake.

At 1:30am, I reef the main, move the running backstay forward and set the other one, then tack. The wind is 15 and our course goes from 250 to 140. Eleuthera is 199nm away at 190 degrees. It's impossible to go straight for Eleuthera without dropping the sails and motoring, but motoring 199nm is not on my to-do list. Instead, I find equilibrium at the helm, lock the wheel, monitor, make micro-adjustments, then relax as *Windflower* steers herself.

We sail into both the wind and a current, and the speed over ground is only 3 knots, while the boat speed is 4. Every hour we only move three nautical miles, 3.3 miles, about as far as one would casually walk in an hour, and we are not even going in the right direction. This is more like being in a holding pattern, like an airplane circling the airport waiting its turn to land. Out here we are waiting for the wind to change in our favor.

Slightly saddened by the slowness and poor direction of our travel, I console myself with the thought that this is so much nicer than the sail from Gloucester Point to Beaufort. Locking off the helm and relaxing in the warm night air and looking at the stars is fine indeed, so much better than being cold, even if we are barely moving and travelling in the wrong direction.

Tonight I wear shoes, my waterproof pants, 2 shirts, 1 blanket wrapped around my shoulders, I'm leaning back on a pillow stretched across the curved teak helm-seat, athwartships, and as relaxed as a solo sailor on a moving boat can be.

Napping at the helm, I catch rest 20 minutes at a time.

Two ships pass late in the night: *Northern Jambouree*, a cargo ship; and *Golar Frost*, a tanker. I feel like we are friends now, me and these two ships, since I know their names. Should I see them again, I will wave and say hello, addressing them by name.

I can't see *Golar Frost*, but surely it is a medieval Viking ship, sailed and rowed by enormous men with blond or red beards, wearing helmets with the horns and antlers of terrestrial beasts, skins and furs for their foul-weather gear, and leaning on battle axes and other various weaponry.

On *Northern Jambouree*, a festive crew of jolly men and women dances to old-time music played by a live band complete with an accordion, a lute, and a mandolin while drinking Canadian whiskey and chasing it with beer.

The crew of *Golar Frost* considers sacking *Northern Jambouree*, but after much consideration and a near brawl that only the captain can subdue, they continue on their journey to Vinland, while the revelers on *Northern Jambouree* party on, oblivious to how close they just came to losing their ship and their lives to the Viking marauders.

At 5:00am, we only make 3.8 knots. The boat speed is similar, so we are no longer bucking a current. But the wind speed is 14. Why are we going so slow? I micro-adjust the wheel, check the sails, trim each a bit, and we slowly creep up to 5 knots. *Windflower* is so sensitive, but she's happier now.

I lay down for another nap and try to ignore the banging sound coming from the V berth.

At 6:30am, we are 212nm east of Cape Canaveral, and Eleuthera is 192nm away. We have only gotten 7nm closer in five and a half hours. Its bearing is 195, but we head 130. It's progress, but barely; at this rate, we'll be there is just over eleven more days, and by that time, I'll have completely lost my mind.

At 7:30am, I move the running backstays, ready the sheets, employ the auto-tack on the Pelagic Autopilot, and *Windflower* turns 90 degrees to starboard. I release sheets and pull in the opposite sheets, move the traveler, and shut off the autopilot. At the helm, I put us on course, then lock off the wheel.

A message comes through on the Garmin. It's Eddie, warning of a low-pressure system that will move across the Abacos tonight. He says it will bring squalls that might have powerful winds. I should be ready for gusts in the 30's, but there is some possibility of gusts up to 50 knots, he says.

The news is distressing. I haven't experienced gusts that strong before. *Windflower* should be able to take it, but surely something else will break. Should I leave the bimini up in squalls? Its main purpose is to shield me from the rain (and sun). But I don't know how strong of wind it can resist before tearing apart, or before the screws pull out of the gunwale and the whole thing becomes a missile.

At 8:45am, I start the engine and we motor-sail so the

batteries will charge. The thought of the alternator sending electrons through the little wood screw and into the batteries makes me smile. My confidence runs high this morning.

At noon, we are still motor-sailing at 6 knots, heading 145. The wind is coming from 190, almost directly from Eleuthera, at 14 knots.

The second reef needs to be fixed, as I might need it tonight when the low passes over us. Its clew block is still on the line, it is just no longer attached to the sail. This is the same thing that happened to the first-reef clew block. Both blocks are Schaffer, and probably not sized properly for the job. When I get back to Florida I will replace both with Garhauer 50-13 UB blocks, or perhaps I'll find that they are chafing the sail and I will have to remove them and just run the reefing lines through the clews like everyone else. [They did chafe the sails and I eliminated them at the next refit.]

The main has to be lowered for this operation, so I can access the second reef clew. I put in the third reef. I cut a piece of ¼" Dynema line and tie the block to a carabiner that I used to use for a tether. I use a zeppelin bend, which I learned from the classic book "The Riggers Apprentice" by Brion Toss. I pull the clew of the second reef down into the cockpit and clip the carabiner to the clew. It's done. The main is raised to the second reef, and I leave it in for a while to test the fix, then raise the main the rest of the way.

Ah the feeling of success. I love to fix things. It is so depressing when something breaks, but the good feeling of a successful fix quickly converts the depression to joy. It makes me feel self-reliant, and self-reliance is a necessity out here, hundreds of miles from anywhere, suspended over a mile of water from the dark and cold floor of the unforgiving sea where lurk the giant squid and various other monsters. Without looking after, *Windflower* would drift aimlessly and eventually sink, and there is no one here but me to do the looking after.

Something else needs fixed. *Little Flower* has worked her way off the fenders that cushion her from the deck, and she grinds into the fiberglass like a pebble in a shoe. Red streaks from her paint scar the deck and look like bleeding wounds from the cockpit, and it is up to me to alleviate the situation.

Before we left Beaufort, I felt like she was very firmly and adequately tied down. But perhaps the line stretched, for now she sags toward the leeward rail and needs my attention. I'm already clipped in to the jackline. I try to always have my long tether clipped to a jackline, it doesn't restrict my movement in the cockpit and is the right thing to do, helping me avoid a long slow death bobbing in the sea watching helplessly while my boat sails away from me. I move forward, pulling my long tether behind, then clip the short tether to the mast. I struggle to lift *Little Flower* and cram the fender back underneath, but I get it done.

I look around to check the anchors and everything else. Something catches my eye at the roller furler, something bad. The furling line is tight up against the lid of the drum and the sheath of the line is chafed all the way through. The core is still good, but this is a bad sign. The worst thing that can happen with a roller-furled headsail is that it comes all the way out during a storm. This is exactly what would happen if the line breaks, and squalls are coming tonight. I must fix this now.

I return to the cockpit, go below for tools, then emerge and clip my long tether to the jackline. I creep across the pitching deck to the bow with a flathead screwdriver and a small crescent wrench. I clip the short tether to the inner forestay and kneel at the bow pulpit, ready to move the block that directs the roller-furler line to the drum. I need to move the block down so the line is less apt to chafe against the lid of the furler drum.

As I stare at the boat, it seems to sit still while the ocean rises to the bow, then recedes, over and over again. The ocean leaps over the deck and covers my legs for a moment, adequately splashing the rest of me. I clamp the wrench to the nut on the back and try to get the flathead screwdriver into the slot of the moving target that is the screw that clamps the block to the bow pulpit. Water douses me again. The world moves in all three dimensions and I am reminded how lucky I am that I don't get seasick, for this is the situation that would otherwise bring on the nausea. I'm also lucky that the water is warm.

I play this game for a long while, stabbing the screwdriver at the moving bolt while the ocean throws lumps of water at me. After much effort, the block is lowered a few inches and I return to the relative safety and comfort of the cockpit. Time on the deck in lively conditions reminds me just how nice and safe it is in the cockpit. I *love* it here.

Now I need to move the furling line to try and get it off the drum, so it doesn't chafe the rest of the way through. I uncleat the jib sheet, leaving it wrapped around the winch, and hang on tight, then pull in some furling line while letting out on the sheet. After furling the sail about half way, I let it back out, then go forward again and see that the line is no longer tight up against the drum. Success is mine!

So many things to fix. The old worn-out line goes like this: "Cruising is the art of fixing things in exotic locations." I would modify that to "…fixing things underway while getting splashed." To not fix something like the furling line is to invite disaster. It simply must be done. When I get to The Bahamas I will have to replace the line. If it gets any worse, I'll have to remove my staysail downhaul line and use it to replace the furling line.

I go below and look for more ways to prepare for squalls. I organize and put things away, making sure nothing is able to fall or roll around. I clean up the navigation table and the galley, then check the straps on the water jerrycans.

I need a nap. But inside, the infernal banging continues. *Good grief*, I can't take this anymore. In the V-berth I shove a few things to the side, the shopvac, lifejackets, scrap wood. Thank goodness I have all this stuff. The boat moves up and down, rolls left and right, and I crawl in the tiny space between my pile of essential junk and the ceiling with a short bit of line in my hands. I reach for the swinging door, scurry like a lizard a foot further forward, wait for the door to swing back, and grab it. I've got you now! I run the line through the handle of the culprit, then through the handle of its partner, and tie them together. The doors will bang no more, and I shall sleep peacefully because of it. I scurry backwards and go lay down for a blissful 20 minutes of quiet rest.

At 2:50pm, we sail heading 190 degrees at 4.5 knots. The mainsail has one reef in and the wind is 15 knots. We could certainly go faster, but there is no need since we aren't heading toward our destination anyway. We are in a holding pattern, sailing just for the sake of movement and stability. I make a pot of chili, fill my belly, and take a nap.

At 4:30, the wind has decreased, and I take the reef out. We now make 5 knots at 145 degrees. I lay down and take three 20-minute naps in a row.

At 5:50, I sit watching a beautiful sunset that lights up the entire sky. I love sunsets, and this is a good one, all orange and red with clouds lined in fiery magenta and a yellow ring around the burning sun as it slowly hides beneath the horizon like an animal slipping into its den for the night. I, however, will stay up most of the night. Night is dark and day is light, but I sleep no more in one than the other. I am no longer diurnal, nor am I nocturnal; I am somewhere in between.

I still wear the orange bibs, as well as rubber boots, and a sweater, but inside it is too warm for the sweater and I take it off. I feel the tropics coming on slowly. I smile at the thought that no one is taking their sweaters off in Virginia or Massachusetts right now, on the evening of Dec 30.

Eddie sends me a message saying the low-pressure system is small and that I should be fine, but I might experience some intense cloudbursts. "Point into the wind," he says.

I send Alex a message congratulating myself for fixing the alternator. He responds and tells me that I should tape it up in case it breaks off again so it won't short out on the engine block.

I open the engine compartment and peer at the absurd connection, a wood screw sticking at an odd angle out of the alternator, with the huge charging cable crudely tied on with wire, all with an alligator clip biting into it. I wrap the tape around this mess as carefully as I can, hoping not to spoil the delicate "fix."

I order a weather forecast on the Garmin InReach, and it calls for the wind to start veering at 4:00am, and west winds by noon tomorrow. With a west wind, we could sail to Eleuthera and be there within a day and a half. The island is now 165nm away at 209 degrees.

I put the bimini up in anticipation of rain, but I will miss seeing the stars tonight.

Tuesday, Dec 31, 27.7684° N, 75.4771° W, 265nm east of Sebastian Inlet, FL, Day 6

It's 12:30am and I wish I could see the stars, but instead all I see when I look up is the canvass of the bimini, even though there is no rain for it to deflect. The wind has increased and gusts up to 17, howling slightly in the rigging as it does. I consider reefing; I'm in no hurry and I want to keep my original plan to sail conservatively. I certainly don't want anything else to break. I get up and pull on lines, while my hands protest the abuse, until a reef is secure in the main. I wonder why I have not been wearing gloves while handling lines. I always wore gloves on *Sobrius*, and *Windflower's* lines are under much more tension.

We make only 4 knots at 140 degrees. The wind comes from 200, so the veering has begun. The temperature is a very pleasant 76 and the number on the screen makes me laugh, for it reminds me that I have surely left the cold north behind.

With the journey coming to an end, I reflect on things I could improve, and I write down a short list:
1) Don't store oil and coolant in the lockers under the water jerrycans where you can't get to them.

2) Improve anchor tie-down method
3) Sail with the cockpit cushions below

I occasionally check the oil, but should I need to add any, I'll have to go through a long and difficult process of moving four 7-gallon jerrycans of water, which each weigh 56 pounds, and are all tied in place. It was a mistake to store the motor oil in a locker beneath them.

At 6:00am, we are 278nm east of Port St. Lucie, FL. It still hasn't rained, and I am deliriously tired. I've been dozing off at the helm, laying athwartships with the red pillow behind my head, somewhere in between this world and a dream. My hands move as if to act out the dreams, reaching for things that are not there. I am aware each time I do this, and wonder why my hand grasps at empty space. I wake when this happens, confused, but am asleep in the next moment. I go back and forth so much that I scarcely know which state is the real one. I'm glad I'm tethered to the boat.

At 7:00am, Eleuthera is 149nm away at 229 degrees. If we keep going east, the coming west wind will be of no use. If we were to motor at 6 knots directly towards Eleuthera, we could be there in 24 hours. This would take 24 gallons of fuel and we have much more than that. The decision is obvious, and squalls are coming anyway, and motoring through squalls is easier than sailing through them. This shall be the final leg of the journey. Tomorrow at this time we will be entering the shallow and bright blue waters of The Bahamas and I will fly the yellow flag of the new arrival.

I take the sails down, then check the oil while we drift, so that we won't be heeling which would make the oil check inaccurate. Luckily the level is good and I don't have to spend a half hour digging out the motor oil.

I start the engine and set us on a course of 229 degrees.

I check Navionics to see if it knows where we are. So far it has not known this vital piece of information, but this time it is different and the little icon representing *Windflower* is in the right place. Like the return of an old friend, Navionics is back!

An hour later, Navionics in once again ignorant of our position, and I am saddened at the loss.

We motor across the grey sea under a grey sky. *Windflower* rolls uncomfortably with only the staysail up, sheeted tight to center, to help stabilize us. But we are heading towards our destination for the first time in over a day and this feels like winning.

Rain comes with wind and it blows right under the bimini. I turn on the radar to play with it and experiment. I adjust the rain clutter and the gain until I can see the rainclouds around us. Some pass to our right, others to the left. I look up into the real world and see the dark clouds that the radar identifies as rainclouds. The sea roughens and the rain comes and goes, but we are battered by no heavy gusts. Luck is with me today, and we easily motor through the front.

The chartplotter shows our position and course on the left, and the radar shows clouds on the right.

At 11:11am, we are 130nm away from our destination. The wind is coming back, veering, and is almost at an angle and strength that will facilitate sailing.

An emptiness in my stomach reminds me that I have not eaten in a long while, so I go below to satisfy its demands.

I want to make chili, so I open a can, dump it into a pot, and put it on the stove. I flip the breaker on at the panel, then turn on the propane solenoid with the switch by the stove, and finally turn on the gas and light the stove.

I hear a click moments later and the fire is out. The red light on the solenoid switch is out too, and the switch on the breaker panel has moved to "off." I turn everything back on and light the stove again. The process repeats itself, and I go through the motions over and over again until the chili is hot enough to eat. Now I have another thing to add to the list of broken stuff: the stove.

This really hits me where it hurts. I love my propane stove, and I *need* it. However, if it comes to it, I have a backup camping stove and two cylinders of fuel tucked away in the propane locker. I think back to the Tractor Supply store that I visited in Virginia, where I bought the Muck boots. They had cheap four-packs of Coleman propane fuel that my backup stove uses. I almost bought one. Now I wish I did.

The chili is warm and delicious and my stomach thanks me for the meal. I sit in the cockpit and eat while watching the dark clouds move across the sky and above the sea that mimics their color. The rain occasionally hits me in the face and hands, but it's not cold and I wear appropriate rain gear, so I don't mind the water. Nothing can dampen my spirits now, because tomorrow *Windflower* and I will be in the islands, basking in the warm sun and surrounded by clear blue water.

With the meal finished, I go below to clean the dishes, which consist of a pot and a spoon. I clean the two dishes with saltwater, then turn on the faucet for a freshwater rinse, yet no water comes from the faucet. The tank held 40 gallons when we left Beaufort, and surely I have used only a gallon or two. I suppose some of the water in the bilge was the rest of my precious freshwater from the tank. My list grows yet again and another piece of my happiness is removed. However, all is not lost, I have 66 gallons of water in jerrycans, but my fancy house-style kitchen faucet is useless.

The disappearance of the water is but another of the many mysteries of *Windflower*. But someday, all shall be revealed to me, for I will not stop seeking the answers; however, for now, I am stumped.

By 2:00pm, the wind is up to ten knots and looks good enough to set sail. Eleuthera is now 112nm away at 228 degrees. I point us into the wind to raise the main, then press the buttons on the autopilot remote control to turn it on. Nothing happens. I press them again. It doesn't work. No matter, I have a spare remote control that came with the autopilot, and I go below to find it.

Back in the cockpit, backup remote in hand, I press the button, *Windflower* tacks, and I raise the main while motoring directly into the wind.

With the main up, I shut off the engine, put us on course, and unfurl the yankee. But as I do so, I notice that the staysail is ripped along about 4 feet of its leech. I don't know when this started, but I obviously wasn't paying close enough attention to catch it early. Now it's another thing on the list, along with the remote, the fresh water system, the bilge pump, the tricolor, the alternator, two pair of sunglasses, and the stove solenoid, unless I've forgotten anything.

No torn sail can get me down now, we are too close to the destination, and I can feel success. We are going to make it to The Bahamas, and a dream will come true. There is no other possible outcome.

At 3:30pm, we are only making three knots and this will not get us there before dark tomorrow. I find this unacceptable.

I start the engine. But before an hour is past, the wind comes back and I shut the engine off again. The wind continues to veer and I trim the sails, picking up another knot. I feel more awake now than I have in at least a day. The taste of success has enlivened me. Go ahead, things, continue to break or tear. Whatever happens, *Windflower* and I will limp into The Bahamas with a smile and a joyous yell! Ha! I laugh in the face of broken stuff.

The conditions continue to improve and my good mood remains strong. The wind is veering ever so slowly, and for the first time on this journey, I let the sheets out a bit, then a bit more. Eleuthera, here we come!

At 4:50pm, we make 6.2 knots. The wind has veered all the way around to 345 degrees. The skies are clear and blue and we sail on a broad reach for the first time since approaching Cape Lookout over a week ago, when I was cold. But now the cold is far away and the sailing conditions are beautiful and perfect. The breeze is strong enough to push us along at a good speed, yet the seas are calm, so we move with grace and dignity. There are no offensive waves to bash through, only smooth water that beckons us forward.

My body is tired and my mind is on the verge of delirium, but my good spirits can't be put down. It's simply fantastic to almost be there, a destination that I have longed to be at for months now.

I've learned a few things on this passage, and I jot down another list:

1) You can't skimp on preparation for a long passage.
2) Things move around more than you think they will.
3) Heavy things move even more so.
4) The dinghy and the water jerry-cans need to be secured better.
5) Carry spares for anything you can think of.
6) Sailing a big boat like this is exhausting sometimes.

Raising the main is more difficult than it should be, and I need to figure out why and how I can reduce the friction.

7) Everything needs backups. The Navionics app on my phone has not known my location for the entire trip. If I was relying on it I would be screwed.

8) Steering is a lot of work. I need a windvane autopilot that I can leave on all the time. There is just too much work to do in addition to steering.

9) When I think I should replace something, I should just do it. I almost replaced the alternator in Virginia but I let someone talk me out of it. I should have just done it. The same thing happened with the batteries. I almost replaced them in Massachusetts, and I let someone talk me out of it. I ended up replacing them in Virginia.

10) The solar panels charge only when the sun is above a certain angle. I knew this but didn't realize how important it was. While sailing south, into a south wind, the panels never face the sun. They would be much more useful if I could adjust their angle. I'll have to design something to do this. The panels I had on *Sobrius* could be angled, and I moved them each day as the sun rose or set.

11) I do not like cockpit seat cushions while sailing. I think I will stow them below during passages and pull them out when at anchor. They only get in the way while sailing, are always too wet to sit on, and the windward cushion always slips off when I step on it. Once they get wet, I can't stow them below. This must be done before the passage starts.

The western sky slowly rolls out all the warm colors as the sun sets for the last time on this passage. I switch on the running lights. Since we are sailing, I go below and use the voltmeter to find the wire on the screw terminal on the base of the mast that powers the steaming light. It is the third wire from the bottom and I disconnect it with a Philips screwdriver. We are now recognized as a sailing vessel, with right-of-way over vessels under power.

But when I go back to the cockpit, I do not see the familiar green light illuminating the water on the starboard side of the bow. I go forward to check the light, and just like the last time I approached The Bahamas, the starboard bow light is out. I add it to the list and move on. It doesn't bother me a bit, no, not one bit!

At 9:47pm, we are passed by the *Carnival Pride*, and I speak to the captain, explaining that my tricolor is out and the green starboard running light is out too. I ask if he can see me on the AIS. He takes a moment to reply, and then in a heavy foreign accent, he methodically tells me that he can see me just fine and that he has already altered course to avoid me. I thank him and wish him happy New Year. This seems to brighten his spirits and in a much less-reserved tone of voice he wishes me the same.

After the giant floating miasma of lights has passed by us and is illuminating the horizon to port, I start the engine. The wind has been less than 10 knots for some time now. I hear Tow Boat US from Ft Lauderdale, Florida, on the VHF and wonder how this is possible. Did I really just hear that?

Jan 1, 2020, 26.1767° N, 76.3436° W, 50nm northeast of Spanish Wells, Day 7

At 1:25am, I alter course to avoid the *Zim Rotterdam*, a large container ship.

I study the charts and realize that the approach to the channel into Spanish Wells is too shallow for me to safely pass. This changes my plans. I'll have to anchor out to clear customs there, and I have guns aboard. The Bahamas allows guns, but the customs officials must look at them and record their serial numbers and count the ammunition, at least this is what happened last time I cleared customs.

This adds a wrinkle to my already wrinkled plan. I still do not have documentation from the US Coast Guard proving that *Windflower* is mine. I've been considering getting rid of the guns, and this makes me think I need to just go ahead and do it. They will surely cause many more problems with customs in many more countries if I keep them. I know Canada does not allow handguns, and long guns are allowed only if you are going hunting. I intend to go to Newfoundland in the summer, and I'm not going hunting. I also worry that when clearing customs, criminals may get word that I carry guns, and then I become a target for theft of the guns. And finally, in the end, I am not trained to use them in self-defense.

At 7:00am, we are 11nm north of Eleuthera, the sun has risen and illuminated a cloudy grey sky, and on the horizon appear dark masses of land, the first I've seen in a week.

Land Ho!

Eleuthera is in sight, as well as St George's Cay, Russel Island, Royal Island, and Egg Island.

I go below to make a snack and check the voltmeter. The alternator is not charging. This can't be. It's *fixed*.

I look away and then look back at the voltmeter. Nothing has changed.

The alternator is still not charging. My fix has apparently failed and I must find out why. I open the engine compartment and my heart sinks when I see the charging cable hanging limp. The screw is broken. I check the connection and find that both the electrical tape and the plastic handle of the alligator clip are partially melted. The wire I wrapped around the cable is all frizzy-looking as if it has been abused somehow. I suppose the connection was not tight enough and sparks and heat were produced until the screw broke from the heat. The alternator goes back on the long list of casualties.

Now I'm in even more of a quandary. If the Bahamas refuses me entrance, I'll have to try to sail back to Florida without the alternator, and this is not a risk I want to take. Whether real or imagined, the guns add risk and complication to the situation. They would seem to decrease my chances of gaining entry. I would so much rather simply answer "no" to the question of "do you have firearms aboard."

I'm afraid they have to go.

I can't seem to bring myself to throw the guns overboard. But I feel compelled to do it. They are a weight on my shoulders and I wish to be freed of it. I tell myself, hypothetically speaking, if I were to throw them overboard, what would the first step be? I would bring them and the ammunition to the cockpit. Well then, I'll just do that and have a look at the guns in the light of day.

This I can do, and the Marlin 30-30 and its box of ammunition come to the cockpit, soon followed by the little plastic case that contains the beautiful stainless-steel Ruger 357-magnum. I unwrap the rifle from its colorful Mexican blanket. I take the pistol from its case and I can see the backs of bullets in the chamber indicating that it is loaded. I hold the rifle in my hands, look it over one last time, and say goodbye as I toss it overboard.

It is swallowed by the ocean without resistance, like a piece of spaghetti being sucked into someone's mouth, beginning its long journey to the bottom, over a mile straight down. It was quick and easier than I expected, and I am surprised that I actually did it. The 357 follows closely behind, as well as all the ammunition.

You fool! What have you done?

Remorse sets in instantly. Did I really just do that? Now what am I going to do if pirates attack?

I am reminded of a line in a Lynard Skynard song, "Saturday Night Special," where he asks, referring to handguns, "why don't we dump 'em, people, to the bottom of the sea?" That is just what I did, but I feel foolish anyway.

After the shock of throwing away good and useful tools of self-preservation has faded and been replaced by rational thought, I feel like it was the right thing to do. I no longer worry about customs. I can check in to customs via dinghy without problem, and I will never have to declare guns at any country I arrive at aboard *Windflower*. However, if intruders enter my boat in the night, I will be relegated to hand-to-hand combat, which is a scary thought.

[Throwing away the guns teaches me an important lesson. Before I threw them away, my mind would occasionally imagine a scene in which pirates try to board my ship and I shot them. This happened often, maybe once or twice a day, and I would think to myself "dang, I just killed someone in my mind." After throwing the guns away, this ceases. Although I am not anti-gun, I now feel certain that owning guns poisoned my mind and caused me to imagine killing people.]

At 9:00am, the sun is shining on a peaceful but defenseless ship and the water around us is a deep sapphire blue. Closer to land, where the water is shallow, I can see the bright blue water that I associate with the islands. My eyes fixate on the bright blue as it grows. We sail around Egg Reef, where I surfed and had to dive to free the anchor last time I was here.

I aim for Egg Island Cut, a narrow pass between Egg Island and Little Egg Island. It looks narrow on the chart, but as we get closer, I see its width is not an issue. The water around *Windflower* lightens and the bright sand beneath is interspersed with dark patches denoting the presence of coral.

A small fishing boat crosses Egg Island Cut and we pass through moments later. We have made it to The Bahamas, and a dream has been fulfilled. The destination was unknown for much of the trip, as I almost turned back to replace the alternator. But we are here, alternator or no alternator. We are in the islands now, in a new world that is warm and beautiful, slow and peaceful, majestic yet relaxed.

approaching the islands on the morning of day 7

We sail across water 12' deep, as clear as a swimming pool, bright blue with sand on the bottom. Egg Island and Royal Island rise from the water to port. The contrast between this and the open ocean, which is all I have seen for the past seven days, is dramatic. It's also a stark contrast to Mattapoistett and Gloucester Point. I have travelled from winter to summer in only one week.

I call the customs office, but get no answer. It's New Year's Day, so I assume they are closed. We turn in to Royal Island Harbor and circle around, scouting out the anchorage. A large trawler sits in the south cove, but nobody is in the north cove, where we circle. I select a spot in 11 feet of water with sand on the bottom, ease the throttle to neutral, move to the bow, and with gloved hands, I let the Vulcan, the new Dr. Spock, slowly descend to the bottom. I hold the chain and let it out slowly as we drift backwards. When the little blue indicator strings tell me 75' are out, I set the anti-chafing gear and cleat off the 3/4" nylon rode. We are here, and here is good.

Location: 25.5157º N, 76.8434º W

I strip out of the clothes I've worn for I don't know how many days now and put on my red trunks, which I have not worn since leaving Florida in October. I put on the mask and hang the ladder over the side and leap into the water, which is gloriously cool and I feel clean as soon as I hit it. I swim to the anchor and push Dr. Spock deeper into the sea floor, which consists of sand with a smattering of grass.

The world around me feels like home, a giant swimming pool of water that spans the entire Earth, full of more creatures than any of us can imagine. I am one of those creatures, back in my element, arrived from afar, warm and wet and cold all at once, reunited with my first love, happy in my new home.

Standing on the deck of my vessel that has carried me here all the way from Massachusetts, I rinse with a bottle of fresh water and dry off, then lay down for a long and well-deserved nap, reminding myself that we are at anchor. I sleep without my alarm turned on and without being fully dressed and without my lifejacket on for the first time in seven days.

Hours later I awake, not in a panic, but refreshed and smiling. I take *Little Flower* out for a sunset cruise around the anchorage, thus fulfilling a second dream, to sail in my rowing and sailing dinghy around the islands at which I anchor the big boat.

Windflower, *anchored at Royal Island Harbor, rests after a long voyage.*

    The passage here was both the longest and the most difficult singlehanded passage I have yet made. I was reminded of both why I sail alone, and why it would be nice to have someone else aboard with me. Sailing alone means that I don't have to explain problems or broken things to my crew, or to feel their anxiety and fear. It means that I can make decisions without having to take into account someone else's safety. I also cherish the serenity, the peace and quiet, and the ability to do exactly as I please at all times. Sailing alone builds self-reliance, bravery, and confidence. I also think it would be hard to be a writer with another person around all the time.

    However, as I keep watch and sleep only 20 minutes at a time, I become delirious. Having someone else to share watch duty is certainly easier. Of course, it would also be nice to have someone to talk to and share the experience with, but it's hard to say if this could outweigh the serenity and the attraction of self-reliance that solo-sailing brings. Perhaps the future holds some balance between the two.

Now that I am here, my old life is officially over, and a new beginning is staring me in the face. I've moved through an important transition, from a land-based life to an ocean-based life, from sessile to nomadic, terrestrial to marine. Now I truly live on a boat, and home is wherever my boat is. Right now, home is Royal Island Harbor, tomorrow it will likely be somewhere else. Home is a state of mind. I am home when I like where I am, where I feel comfortable. Mattapoisett was home for a month. The York River Yacht Haven was home for six weeks. Town Creek Marina was home for three days. Cape Lookout was home for two.

The old chapter of my life, carpentry, playing in a band, living in a house, renting out rooms in my house, driving a car, is all over. I've stepped out of society – mainstream society any-way – and into a new life completely.

Instead of a giant Suburban, I've a small rowboat for trips to shore. My little galley takes the place of a large kitchen, a bottle of water poured over my head takes the place of a shower, a small bunk takes the place of my king-size bed. One day I might have a refrigerator, but for now I do without. No longer do I have an overflowing room full of instruments and amplifiers, rather I have one acoustic guitar and one mandolin. I have tools that live in lockers and drawers, but no garage full of shop-tools and scrap wood. My life is simple now.

My home now is wherever my boat is. I move from place to place. I write about my adventures. I live by my own terms and make my own rules. I live very close to nature, the way I was meant to live, like a wild and free animal, not tethered to society and all its ills, rather on society's edge, on its fringes, outside, in nature, in the real world. Society is no place for a wild animal. It crushes the spirit of such. It makes cages and sells them to us. Out here we are uncaged, free to be ourselves, living under the sun and the stars, surrounded by water, na-ture, and other wild animals.

Man was not meant to live in an artificial world. We

evolved in nature and are thus designed to live in the natural world. It is here that we find happiness, fulfillment, satisfaction. Cut off from nature, we experience anxiety, depression, anger, ennui, apathy. We take drugs in vain effort to fix our problems, to alleviate our suffering. We seek excess in the artificial world because excess is the prize that the artificial world offers us. It tells us that success is measured by material possessions, and happiness comes from amassing such.

But real happiness is found in the real world. What is better than riding a wave, or swimming underwater on a coral reef, or hiking through a deep dark forest, standing on top of a mountain looking out over valleys and across ridges, canoeing down a pristine river, sailing on the ocean, staring up at the stars on a clear dark night in the cockpit of a sailboat hundreds of miles from shore? What is better than encounters with wildlife, looking a large wild animal in the eye, seeing a whale leap out of the water, or catching a glimpse of a black bear, the ghost of the woods, before it slips away and disappears?

Nature is the cure for society's ills. It is within her arms that the world gains meaning, where our minds become clear, and where we find peace, tranquility, and happiness. Who can look upon a grand view from the top of a mountain, or a blue seascape, or the scene within a deep dark forest without feeling something wonderful deep inside? Who can dive on a coral reef without recognizing a great creative force at work? Who can ride a wave without smiling?

While some would destroy nature as an inconvenience, it is rather the most important thing for us to save. We are part of it and to save it is to save ourselves. It provides the air we breathe, the water we drink, and the food we eat. The more nature is destroyed, the more dependent we become on artificial systems to keep us alive, and the more artificial we become.

While merging completely with nature is an unrealistic goal for most of us, and an impossibility for all of us, as the carrying capacity for the Earth has been grossly exceeded, we can all benefit from an occasional inundation with the natural world. Immersing oneself deep within nature relaxes, soothes, and renourishes our souls. It reminds us who we are, where we come from, and what is either necessary or unnecessary in life. When faced with the beauty and serenity of the world that surrounds us, we come home, for the natural world is where man evolved, and like any other homecoming, returning to nature creates a deep sense of peace and calm and contentment within ourselves. It is where we are meant to be. It is home.

The sky is but a reflection of our soul, and the sea is the same. What we see when we look upon nature is the barometer of our very existence.

The sail in this chapter is documented in the YouTube video "Chasing the Nomadic Dream, Beaufort, NC to Eleuthera." https://www.youtube.com/watch?v=Ot_7AgItHqE

SPANISH WELLS

Part bird part fish
This manmade thing
Granting my wish
Joy it brings
Suspended high
Above abyss
Magic ally
Gliding bliss
Simple machines
Working as one
Inanimate team
Journey begun
Wheel in my hand
Staring at stars
Heavens shine grand
Venus and mars
Showing the way
Across vast ocean
Sailboat at play
Magic potion
Trip to the moon
Deep space beyond
Destiny soon
Crossing the pond
Blue water here
Shallow and bright
Islands rise near

Sailors delight
Calm harbor now
Anchor does fall
Straight from the bow
Sailor stands tall
Sun on bare skin
Water is fine
Let it begin
Bahamas time

The warmth of the air and the sun, the beauty of the water with the islands floating above, and the friendliness of the people constantly remind me of why I wanted to return to The Bahamas.

I was cold for the three months before arrival, and as I stand on the deck of my ship wearing only a pair of swimming trunks, with the warm sunlight beating down upon my skin, I laugh at my good fortune. All the time I spent in the cold makes me appreciate the warm weather every moment of every day. I am reminded of the warmth when I leave the windows open, when I get dressed in the morning, when I go to sleep under just a thin sheet, when my hair blows in the wind, unencumbered by a warm hat, and when I swim in the water.

The water draws me in like a lover. The coral reefs never get old, the fish and all the other strange creatures still fill me with awe as I look upon them, and being underwater is just as serene as it ever was.

I awake early on the second day of January, and my second day here. The stove is on my mind, since the first thing I want to do is make coffee, so I set out to diagnose the problem. It isn't long before I find the solenoid, near the propane tank in the propane tank locker, and feel that it is hot. I can even see little bubbles coming out of it. This is clearly the problem. I remove it and spend a while trying to bypass it, but the designers of the system had in mind that someone might try this dangerous stunt and in order to prevent bypassing the solenoid, the hoses on either end of it are of slightly different sizes. Perhaps this will save me from blowing up my ship.

I use my portable camping stove to make coffee and oatmeal, and it works just fine.

Still in the mindset of fixing things, and desiring a win, I rewire the two bow lights. Both are heavily corroded, as neither were wired with waterproof connections, rather electrical tape was relied upon to keep the connections dry, which, of course, was woefully inadequate. Bow lights have a tough life, the toughest of any of the ship's lights, right up front, taking seas in the face all day and all night. If any electrical connection absolutely needs to be waterproof, it is the bow lights.

Next up is the mysterious saltwater-spewing copper tube in the engine compartment. I remove the pencil, which did its job well, and fold the copper tube over 180 degrees. I fill the end of it with 5200 and call it permanently sealed.

Since all my freshwater in the built-in tank leaked out, I search around until I find that a hose to the hot-water tank has come undone. Here is a ½" hose clamped to a ¼" copper tube. I found this odd connection to be leaking when I was still in Virginia, and wrapped SOS tape around the tube to increase its diameter so the hose would seal around it. However, the tube still slipped off. More tape is called for, and after wrapping it up, I clamp the hose back on.

I check on the bilge pump and find it functioning properly. Strange, but good. I probably need to rewire it (with waterproof connections).

The shower sump, which I had pumped out a few times during the passage, is again full of water. I have no idea where the water is coming from. I pump it out, study the hoses, and find myself stumped. Nothing is leaking. It has its own through-hull and hose system, so where the water is coming from I cannot tell.

I pull up the floorboards and check the freshwater tank, which, of course, is empty. I add 5 gallons, assuming I found the leak. The other ex-water tank is right next to me and exposed now, so I take off the cover to see how it fared. Water fills the bottom and I pump out about five gallons. It's clean freshwater, so it must have come from the freshwater tank next to it. By what means it moved from one to the other, I have no theories. Luckily all the food and fruit juice I stored in there was impervious to the water.

Keeping the momentum going, I remove the alternator and take it apart. I use a vise and a hammer to knock out the broken post, and then replace it with a bolt. My bolt is a bit larger in diameter than the original post, so I have to modify the alternator housing a bit and I have to use electrical tape to insulate the bolt from the housing. I use two large washers to sandwich the big charging cable terminal and a nut to squeeze it all together.

The engine wants a bit of oil, which I supply, and I also give it a bit of a cleaning to get some of the salt off it. After starting the old engine, and am pleased to see the alternator charging again.

Up until this morning, I felt as though I had to find someone to fix the alternator, and was willing to pay for it, when all I had to do was fix it myself. I just had to take it apart, figure out what was wrong, and fix it, just like I used to do with bicycles. I can fix just about anything if I try. Self-reliance is a necessary trait for the offshore sailor, and it must be cultivated. We do this by attempting things we might fail at, even if failure might be expensive and time-consuming. It is the price we pay for the lessons that make us capable. Out on the ocean, there is no choice.

I almost went to Florida instead of The Bahamas because of the alternator, and I am thankful that I didn't. It was my sense of pride, my foolhardy need for adventure, my love of risk-taking, my inability to refrain from risky activities, and the fact that this book was supposed to take me here, to The Bahamas, that made me press on and stay the course. Why play it safe when you can be reckless and adventurous?

On the third of January, celebrating my 59th month sober, I sail to Meeks Patch, a skinny and uninhabited island 1.5 miles from Spanish Wells. This is as close as I can safely anchor to Spanish Wells, where I need to clear customs. I anchor on the little island's northwest point, sheltered from the wind, and set sail in *Little Flower* on a beam reach to St George's Cay and town.

Location: 25.5230º N, 76.7875º W

This is my first time sailing this little 10' boat across open water, and I am not sure what to expect. I wear a lifejacket and hope for the best, and to my delight, *Little Flower* is a pleasure to sail across the long stretch of open water.

My little sailboat takes me right through the cut and into Spanish Wells Channel where I strap the boom to the mast and start rowing. Both townspeople and tourists alike turn their heads to see the little red sailboat being rowed up the channel. I suppose sailing dinghies are an anachronism, and I feel a bit like a celebrity in my little red boat. It makes me proud to come in under wind and human power while every other boat is burning fuel.

The government dock is concrete and tall, but I find a little stairway and row for it. I am within a few feet of the steps when a water taxi rushes right at me, turns just before hitting me, and backs up to the steps, I row out of the way and find a rusty iron post that I use to climb up to street-level. Two women from *Second Sojourn*, a sailboat I remember seeing at Royal Island Harbor, hold my line and offer a hand as I skin my knee climbing up the dock.

The small yellow customs building is just across the street, and I let myself in. The customs official is very friendly, and I show him my best respect, answering with "yes sir" or "no sir" at every opportunity. I fill out a few pieces of paperwork, and check the "no" box next to the question asking if I carry firearms onboard. He gives no pause to my lack of proper title, and within minutes I am cleared in to The Bahamas with a three-month visa and cruising permit.

The town is bustling with activity as I stroll up the waterfront, past the RnB Boatyard and its workers busy polishing a huge catamaran perched up out of the water. Golf carts driven by tourists and small cars by locals work their way down the pedestrian-filled waterfront street, driving on the wrong side of the road, as we like to say in the States. Colorful houses and small businesses line the street to the right, while docks and seawall make up the left.

Pinders Hardware supplies me with new line for my roller furler, a new bilge pump, a switch for the steaming light, and four bottles of propane for the backup stove. The woman behind the counter recommends OnSite Marine as a possible source for the solenoid.

OnSite Marine is very helpful in trying to find me both a solenoid and an alternator. A few days later, they locate an alternator, but to my surprise, it is more than twice what one costs in the States, due mainly to a 40% duty and a hefty sales tax on top of that. By this time, ironically, I have found an old alternator in *Windflower's* spare parts locker. I suppose I should have looked there first. But I leave it all alone, trusting my repair. The solenoid is never located, but I find that the familiar green Coleman propane bottles are common in The Bahamas.

Pinders Grocery supplies me with a few vegetables, some canned goods, and 10 gallons of diesel.

Rowing and sailing back with the diesel containers full is not the problem I anticipated it might be. They are tied to the center of the little boat and are not even noticed.

With the sails up, we slowly glide down the channel towards the cut. A young boy yells "I like your boat!" and I smile and wave. A horn sounds behind me and I turn to see an enormous ship slowly approaching. I get out of the way and let it pass, and behind it is a huge trawler followed by a line of boats, all of which dwarf *Little Flower*.

The first ship exits the cut, but the big yacht behind runs aground, then revs its engines to power across the shallow spot, turning all the water in the channel brown. I tuck *Little Flower* out of the way as all the ships pass, then tack back and forth out the channel, against the incoming tidal current, as folks watch with amusement from the docks.

We have to tack many times and make less and less ground as we near the narrowest part of the channel. I have to row for a bit, then lose an oar and have to retrieve it, and finally break out of the current under sail *and* oars.

After all that work, the beam reach back to *Windflower*, sitting way off in the distance, is a pleasure, and crossing the expanse of bright blue water is a mini-adventure for sure, almost a full adventure, considering my lack of experience with the little boat.

*propelled by the wind, my little flower, humble though she be
takes me round the bend, with God's power, across the open sea*

Windflower *awaits my return at Meeks Patch.*

I return to Royal Island Harbor, as a front will pass through in the coming days, and this is the best place to sit out the veering winds.

Location: 25.5139º N, 76.8470º W

I'm delighted when a couple in a dinghy pull up to *Windflower* and engage me in conversation. Steve and Sandy, from Massachusetts, recognize *Windflower* and just want to say hello.

I notice that of the dozen boats at Royal Island Harbor, all but one are cutters. The other, *Minis*, is the little sloop of a singlehander from Canada. Lawrence is his name, and he stops by to say hello too.

I invite Lawrence onboard and we have a nice visit, two singlehanders swapping stories and exchanging notes. Lawrence towed his boat on a trailer from Canada to Florida, then sailed to Spanish Wells. He tells of being struck by a gale in the Northwest Providence Chanel and running with the wind under bare poles, getting bruised and battered along the way. It's a fine story and I take note of the good feeling brought on by strangers coming to my boat just to say hello.

I vow to be that guy in the future. I will row to the boats of strangers and just say hello, and see what happens, I tell myself. The Bahamas adventure will be different from the last in that respect. The last time I was here I didn't meet many people at all, but rather avoided others. I still plan to go to empty anchorages on uninhabited islands, but when other boats are around, I will meet people this time.

Indeed, I am already meeting people, settling in to my new life as a cruiser, and enjoying it immensely.

The next day, I move just a bit west to a little cove that looks like it has potential for snorkeling, with a cut leading to the reef on the outside.

Location: 25.5038º N, 76.8730º W

After a long and diligent search for lunch, I am delighted to spear two lobster on the reef, but I am so excited by the second lobster that when I get in the boat, I drop the spear overboard. I don't realize it's missing until I have already started rowing away, and I have to turn around, get back in the water, and search for it. Luckily, I find it. I would have missed out on a lot of fresh seafood had I lost it so early.

The following day I motor out to Egg Reef, the site of a tale I told in "Journey to the Ragged Islands." I surfed the reef two years prior, then found I couldn't raise the anchor and had to dive on it four times, in 65' of water. I lost one of my fins, and finally discovered that the anchor wasn't stuck, I simply was not strong enough to pull it up when all 50' of its chain was hanging vertically.

This time the swell is smaller, and I am able to anchor closer to the reef, in 25' of water, and I put a trip line on the anchor because *Windflower's* anchor is heavier than the one I had for *Sobrius*, and I don't want a repeat of the experience.

Location: 25.5204º N, 76.9021º W

The reef is nearly 2 miles offshore, I am alone, and ready to surf. I toss the 12-0 in the incredibly clear water and climb down the ladder, then paddle across the shoaling reef to the point. A wave that has been travelling across the deep ocean for unknown days finally reaches the reef, stands tall, and I paddle into it.

Gliding across the clear blue water, I watch as yellow, red, and blue coral, black and yellow and purple fish, pass by underneath. I can see them clearly. They slip by as I slide down the face of the waves, come from afar. I too have come from afar, and now I am here, and the fish are here, and the coral, and the waves. We are one.

The waves are my friends and I cruise down the line

looking ahead at a view of water, with far-off islands in the distance. Normally a beach would be in front of me, but out here, water is all around and *Windflower* is my beach.

With deep water just past the take-off zone, the waves are powerful, and since the reef is long, so are the rides. I enjoy the session immensely, but I also know that sharks must frequent this reef, and being alone in such a place brings the fear and anxiety. After six or seven waves, I quit while I'm ahead and return to my boat.

After the surf, I snorkel the reef. The most interesting thing I find is a large fisherman's anchor lying on the bottom and encrusted with sea-life. I imagine a wreck might lie in the area, from some ship many years ago, passing by in the dark of night and not seeing the reef, but though I look, I can't find any treasure or evidence of a wreck. I am always on the lookout for treasure.

When time comes to raise the anchor, after moving the boat directly above it, I pull in on the trip line, thus lifting the anchor, but not the chain. After pulling in about five feet of the trip line, I pull in a bit of the chain, then more of the trip line, and back and forth until I have enough chain in that I can pull the rest of it up without the help of the trip line.

I sail back into the bay and spend an evening anchored off Spanish Wells, where I meet John and Kathi who sail a beautiful Gozzard 44, *Makani*. Little do I know, our paths will cross many times in the next four months.

Location: 25.5385º N, 76.7652º W

In the morning, I pull everything out of the V-berth, which is damp from water leaking in through the hatch during the passage. I lay it all out on deck in the hot sun. The staysail needs to either be repaired or replaced, and I opt for the easier of the two by digging out a sail I brought from *Sobrius*, a small headsail, which I figured might make a good staysail for *Windflower*, and it does.

I climb the mast and repair the masthead tricolor light. Its lightbulb is not securely fit into its seat, and a bit of repositioning is all it takes, although I suspect it might not be the correct bulb.

Any excuse to go up the mast and take in the view is OK with me.

Low tide is coming up in a couple hours, and I intend to sail through Current Cut, to Eleuthera, and anchor near the Glass Window Bridge. I hoist the mainsail about 2/3 of the way, and *Windflower* responds by edging forward while I pull up the anchor.

The sail to Current Cut is a pleasure, broad reaching, jybing once, then racing towards the narrow space between Current Island and Eleuthera.

ELEUTHERA

A new place
To rest my head
And bury the anchor
A daily race
On magic sled
My very savior
Nomadic life
A new world
Daily adventure
Little strife
Within the curl
Deep in nature
Sunrise, sunset
Stars at night
All clean air
New friends met
Or alone I might
Sail without a care
To another place
A beach or a rock
Maybe a town
Smile on my face
No need for a clock
And never a frown

CHASING THE NOMADIC DREAM

The sail to Current Cut does not take as long as I predicted, and the tide is still coming out when we get there. I intended to go through at the bottom of incoming tide. My logic, which I later modified, was that if I ran aground at low tide, the incoming tide would lift me off the bottom and all would be well. Eventually I decided that it is best to cross shallow areas closer to high tide but still rising.

I approach the cut at an aggressive 7 knots under full sail, heeling with the wind just forward of the beam. The cut has a reputation for strong current, and the water on the other side becomes shallow at the end of the channel, but the cut itself is at least 50' deep. We turn to port and I sheet in, putting us on a close reach for the pass through the cut. *Windflower* heels and keeps her speed of 7 knots.

As we get closer, I can see the water moving out like a river, and our speed drops to 6 knots, then five. I figure if I start the engine we will have no problem. But the closer we get, the narrower the cut looks, and the stronger the current. Even with the engine and sails at full power, we slow to 4.5 knots. Rock ledges line both shores, undercut by the running water. According to the chart, the cut is 311 feet wide, but from my perspective, on a sailboat in rough water, the cut looks barely wide enough to pass through safely.

As soon as we enter the cut, an opening to the left catches my eye, and inside the opening is calm, shallow, bright blue water in a rectangular little harbor almost hidden behind the short scrubby trees, a little oasis of calm in an otherwise active environment. The scene distracts me for a moment, but I recover quickly and maintain our course, upstream like a salmon.

On the other side, I am rewarded with a gorgeous view

of bright blue, and obviously very shallow, water on both sides. The depth in the channel steadily decreases and I watch the chart to stay in the deepest part. The tide is almost all the way low, so if we run aground, I won't have to wait long for the tide to lift us free.

The depth keeps decreasing, all the way down to 7', then 6', and I even see a flash of 5.9', which distresses me greatly. Our draft is 6', so I believe, but we are well-heeled and thus not drawing our full draft. The depth slowly increases and I am relieved when it comes back up to 12', where it stays for the rest of the sail.

After reaching the long skinny island of Eleuthera, we tack up to Glass Window Bridge, which is a cut in the narrowest part of the island, in the steep cliff that lines the sound, allowing the water of the Atlantic to spill across and into the sound when the waves are big enough. But the setting is not as scenic as I saw further south, so I turn around and select Muttonfish Point as an anchorage. The point is the largest in the area and I hope it will offer the best protection from the strong southeast winds in the forecast.

Location: 25.4132º N, 76.5916º W

The scenery here is also quite pleasing to my eye, with green trees and grey rocks, two sandy beaches in sight, only one nearby house, partially hidden in the trees, and stately mansions perch on the bluffs overlooking the points to the north. I share my little cove with a catamaran and spend three very quiet nights here while waiting for better weather to continue south.

I snorkel the cove and the rocky shore every day, and enjoy the wildlife, as always. An unending school of little minnows lines the bank, so thick that I can hardly see the rock wall behind them. Grouper hide from me in the many caves, and an occasional stingray cruises along the bottom. Blue tang and queen angelfish swim inside caves painted red and orange and yellow by encrusting organisms, bristling with white antennae-like creatures, and decorated with the occasional cluster of waving tentacles of a sea anemone.

Outside the caves the rocky bank is covered with sponges of various colors, some purple with arms like trees reaching skyward. Orange starfish sit still on the bottom as do the occasional lionfish, beautiful with their long spines and stripes, yet invasive and exotic.

As I poke my flashlight into holes and caves, I am mystified by all the bizarre lifeforms. Sometimes a huge and ugly crab threatens me away with an enormous claw. A brown-spotted moray eel remains calm as I look upon it. Scallops with bright red tentacles cling to rocks, and a strange creature like a millipede, about a foot long, crawls slowly along the rocks. I later identify it as the "highly toxic" green fire worm which can inflict a painful sting. It certainly does not look like anything that should be touched.

The most beautiful of all the fish I see is a juvenile blue angelfish, swimming alongside a spotfin butterflyfish. The juvenile blue angelfish is colored differently than the adult, which is bright yellow with blue accents. The juvenile is mostly brilliant royal blue with curved vertical white stripes, a yellow tail, and a yellow belly. Clearly these fish were designed by some divine artist.

Around the corner and out on the point, a large emergent rock sits in 25 feet of water, surrounded by smaller rocks and covered in purple and red sea fans. Fish swim all about the base, and three large snapper catch my attention. Perhaps these are the "mutton fish" the point is named for.

I take a deep breath and swim down after them, spear at the ready. I briefly get close enough for a shot, but the lack of killer instinct in me makes me pause just long enough for the fish to swim away. I need to be very close for a good shot, since I have but a primitive pole-spear, and any hesitation on a good shot allows the fish to escape. I swim around the rocks and gaze at the fish, all of whom now keep their distance.

I return to the boat without dinner, but with another adventure under my belt, and stored in memory. The underwater world is the main attraction to me of The Bahamas, and every dive is a good one.

Mutton Fish Point has been a nice quiet place to sit out the winds, but after three days of rolling, I am ready to move on. The completely protected harbor of Hatchet Bay is on my mind, and I pull up both anchors and sail away under double reefed main and staysail. I expect strong winds outside the protection of the point, but the wind is not nearly as strong as I anticipated, and I take out the second reef and unfurl a bit of the yankee.

We sail at 5 knots, slowed by the annoying and incessant chop, made up of short-period three-foot waves which are situated just far apart enough to make *Windflower* bounce up and down. We sail south, moving away from shore, for about an hour, then tack and head for Hatchet Bay.

The cliffs of Eleuthera come into view and loom over the windblown water below. We sail close to shore about a quarter mile downwind of the cut into the bay, so I take down the sails and motor up the coast for the last leg of the day's sail.

HATCHET BAY

Short period swell, blown four days wind
Batters us well, the bow it does send
Up and down like a horse, 'til the sails do come down
All a matter of course, taken with no frown

We motor the last bit, to the entrance unseen
By the chart it is lit, and eye though keen
Sees not through rock wall, until it is there
The channel so small, and the rocks so bare
Waves crash all around, it's me they would scare
But I rise to the sound, of water on hull
And see through the cut, where waves they are null

Like Odyseus sailed, through the pillars he dared
We enter Hatchet Bay, only feet to spare
And the water is still, and tranquil inside
And the wheel in my palms, does greatly abide
To the will of my mind, as told by my eyes
To enter the bay, and take the calm prize

A s we motor south along the rock wall that makes up the western edge of the Eleuthera, I look for the entrance to Hatchet Bay. It's very close, according to the chartplotter, yet all I see is a rock wall rising about 25' off the windblown water. Twice I think we are coming to the cut, only to find just a small cove.

We get closer and closer, and still I see no sign of a channel through the cliffs. When the chartplotter says the cut is right in front of us, I marvel that I still see no sign of it.

I notice that two points on the cliff begin to move away from each other. This can't be it, I think, but a red day-marker on one of the cliffs confirms that this is the opening. Not until we are right on it do I see the narrow entrance to Hatchet Bay, and the green marker on the other cliff facing the red. The chart shows the opening to be 100 feet wide, but it looks incredibly narrow from my perspective, especially with emergent rocks on both sides, waves, and visible current that will try to set me on the north cliff.

I turn *Windflower* to port and gave her a bit more throttle. The wind blows directly from starboard, and the current sweeps across the cut, necessitating steering just right of the entrance, but when a wave exposes an emergent rock on the right side of the entrance, I steer for the middle and hope for the best.

One moment we are between the cliffs, and then we are inside. The wind disappears, the water smooths out, and peace settles over *Windflower* and me.

I select a spot on the south side of the harbor, near the dinghy dock at Farrington's Boater's Haven and Convenience Store, and listen to the competing hymns of two churches, as it is a Sunday, while I let the anchor out.

Location: 25.3470º N, 76.4879º W

The main allure of Hatchet Bay is the all-around protection. One can anchor here and stay indefinitely, regardless of the weather, and since sailors typically need to watch the weather every day and move about regularly in order to be anchored somewhere safe from the wind and waves, this is extremely attractive. In places like Hatchet Bay, a sailor can truly relax and go about other business.

The water in the bay is not an attraction, dark green with nothing much to see on the bottom. Up next to town there is a cave, which would ordinarily be something to explore, but this is not the case. The cave acts as part of the town's sewage system, so anchoring near it is not recommended. The side of the bay opposite town is where most people anchor. It's also quieter over there, since loud music often comes from town at night, I will soon learn.

If you anchor in Hatchet Bay, take note that a ferry passes through the harbor and docks at the northeast corner of the bay. The ferry usually came in on Thursday and Sunday evenings while I was there, but other large boats came in on other days. It is very important not to anchor in the way of the ships, which go to the dock in the northeast corner of the bay, next to town. This is another reason why anchoring on the other side of the bay is ideal. The ships don't have a lot of room to pass and anchored boats get passed very close.

I row to the nearby dinghy dock and stroll through town, while most of its residents are in church. The town itself is not exactly picturesque, with the exception of the south-facing beach, and could use a bit of a clean-up. One thing the Bahamians could improve is their trash control. Apparently throwing garbage out of a car window while driving is an acceptable way to get rid of it.

However, the town does have a nice grocery store and at least three restaurants, two of which even have signage declaring them such. The other has to be pointed out by a local, because it is indistinguishable from the surrounding houses.

The town also has public water spigots on a few street corners, and one is within a block of the dinghy dock. I fill up my water containers regularly and find the water to be clean and potable.

I almost leave Hatchet Bay after my first day here, as I am unenchanted with the town. But I meet Emmet at the store next to the dinghy dock, and after meeting him, I decide to stay a bit longer. He tells me of two places I need to explore before leaving. The first is Sweetings Pond, where I might see octopus and sea horses. The other is Surfer's Beach, which is four miles north and requires hitchhiking. I decide to give it a try.

I set out on the main road with a backpack and a surfboard, thinking I will probably have to walk the entire way and resigned to doing so, but I am pleasantly surprised when a small grey sedan pulls over and the local man asks if I want a ride.

"Do you think my surfboard will fit?" I ask. It is 6'8" long.

"No problem mon," he says.

I hesitate for a moment, then decide to go for it. I shove the board in, over the passenger seat and all the way to the back window. The tail is almost touching the windshield and I leave it where my head would normally go, then duck into the passenger seat hunched over and shut the door.

"Thanks! I'm going to Surfer's Beach." I go on to explain where I think it is, repeating Emmet's description.

"Where you from mon?"

"I'm from St Augustine, Florida."

"Well I'm from Eleuthera," which he pronounces "Elootra," "and I know right where Surfer's Beach is."

This is the first of many similar experiences hitchhiking to Surfer's Beach, which quickly becomes my favorite thing about Hatchet Bay and the reason I ultimately stay for three weeks, then return later for two more.

From the main road, the "Queens Highway," where he lets me off, I walk up a quiet paved street to the top of a small hill. I pass a few houses and a little hotel that looks like it wants to cater to surfers, but is empty. As I continue downhill, the pavement ends and the road becomes rocky and washed out. At the bottom of the hill it turns left and short trees form a canopy over the road, which is more of a trail now. The trail ends at a parking area on a sandy road coming from the opposite direction, which turns right and uphill. The trees end and the ocean comes into view.

I'm now on top of a large bluff overlooking a clear left pointbreak. I take a moment to study the setup, but quickly follow the trail down the steep bluff to the beach, where stands a crude structure made by surfers that provides a bit of shade and places to sit and watch the action, but nobody is in the water.

I watch for a while and see that there is a reef to the left and a shallow sandbar just off the beach to the right. The main wave starts way out on the reef and breaks along its edge, providing a fairly long left that works all the way to the beach. The sandbar off to the right is heavy and unruly looking. The waves go from smooth rollers to heaving shore-barrels in a split second, but every now and then I see one that looks makeable. It's windy today, so the waves are far from perfect, but I can see how they work. I decide to try the right first and paddle out to the sandbar.

Right away, a rip-current pulls me out into deeper water and also down the beach, away from the reef and the sandbar I want to surf, so I have to paddle to stay in position. I use a conspicuous century plant on the bluff to line up. I eventually get a couple waves, but they are short and the possibility of getting slammed hard into very shallow water is a constant threat. I ride one in, walk back toward the reef, and paddle out to the main point in the deep water next to the breaking waves.

I'm not sure where the lineup is, so I swim underwater occasionally to check the depth, and I try to position myself so I am in water roughly as deep as the waves are tall.

A wave that looks good comes and I turn and paddle for it. The face is steep and I lean back on the tail of my board as I nearly air-drop into the wave. A hard bottom-turn sends me to the left and out on the face, which quickly loses power, and I cut back into the whitewater. I do this two more times until the wave stands back up and races across the reef closer to the beach. I bottom turn, top turn a few times, then kick out right before the wave slams into the somewhat rocky beach at the end of its journey across the Atlantic Ocean. I paddle back out through deep water without having to duck under any waves, which is a luxury for me, since I am from Florida, where every wave ridden requires many duck-dives to get back out.

Another surfer shows up, a tall guy with a deep tan. We smile and wave hello, and each other's presence helps us gauge where the take-off zone is.

The next day is much bigger and again nobody is out. The forecast calls it 6' at 13 seconds, and the waves are double-overhead (twice the height of a person). Most of the waves close out across the whole area, but whenever I see surf this big, I can't resist paddling out to give it a try and see if I can at least get one or two good rides. Just dropping in on a double-overhead closeout is a thrill, and rare for Florida surfers.

Nobody joins me in the water, but I catch four waves and my board skips across the water at high speed. I should have brought my 7' rounded pintail, which is perfect in waves like this, or bigger. But I expected smaller waves and have my 6' 8" Channel Islands Flyer, which has very little rocker (curvature fore-aft along the bottom) and is made for head-high or smaller waves. The board is skittish and skips across the water at high speed, but this adds to the thrill. However, after four waves I am spent and I paddle in.

Some locals are on the beach and they smile and congratulate me on my rides.

"You make us proud," says George, an octogenarian who I later learn is still a very capable and talented surfer. His comment makes my day.

Surfer's Beach at 6', 13s, onshore breeze

I return almost daily to Surfer's Beach over the next two weeks. The wave is far from world-class, but my standards are low and this wave easily exceeds them. One of the amazing things about surfing in The Bahamas is that the water is clear. I can see the sand on the bottom, or the reef, and sometimes the waves are transparent. The water just looks cleaner and more friendly than what I am used to.

I meet other surfers every time I go to the beach, and we all enjoy the waves together, without any competitiveness or negative vibe. Not only are the surfers friendly, but so are the locals. I get a ride every time I walk on the road, even twice when I'm not even sticking my thumb out.

I suppose one reason the beach isn't crowded or popular with travelling surfers is because the prevailing wind here is onshore. The best times to surf are on the days right after a front passes, when it gets a day or two of offshores while the swell still comes in. While surfers can easily find more consistent and higher-quality waves in Central America, Eleuthera is a good place for the sailing surfer who is already in The Bahamas and doesn't mind hitchhiking.

Surfer's Beach, on a good swell, from the hill overlooking the point. This pointbreak provided either a long sloping left or a faster right into the reef.

This was the inside right beach-break, off the screen to the right in the previous photo. It was very fickle, but when it worked, it broke over very shallow water and provided a fast, hollow, and uncrowded wave. Thanks to Gert Kelu for the photograph.

Down I swim, through clear blue water
propelled by fin, hunting fish and lobster
Bright yellow angelfish, and royal blue tang
sing a song of bliss, turn with soft bang
Inside a cave, a brown spotted eel
I'm not so brave, to make it a meal
Lionfish sublime, in the face of my spear
confident their spines, will keep me from near
Catch me if you can, the grouper do run
they know who I am, not here for fun
Under rocks seek lobster, my belly gets thinner
the creepy little monster, with tail fit for dinner
Through caves swim snapper, the striped schoolmaster,
looks mighty dapper, than me he swims faster
Puffer with big eyes, from afar sees he me
waits to inhale, belly full of sea
I turn from the rocks, fat like the Buddha
watching me mocks, school of barracuda
No fish will I spear, perhaps just a lobster
with barracuda near, like a crafty mobster
They'll steal my catch, off their aim may be
and instead will fetch, a mouthful of me
At the bottom of sea, pick up anchor and go
swim off to safety, with dinghy in tow
When finding a grouper, is out of my power
leap from the water, row back to Windflower

Rocks pile on each other and support a rich variety of life below the surface just outside Hatchet Bay Cut

During my initial three weeks, I find Hatchet Bay to be full of friendly people, and I make many new friends. Emily and Clark Willix, from Emily and Clark's Adventure on YouTube, stop by to say hello because we have a friend in common, Ken Godwin of Captain Ken on YouTube.

They invite me to join them for a hike to the cave just past Sweeting's Pond, and we end up getting a ride in a church van. The cave is big and long and full of stalagmites, stalactites, columns, and flowstone. There's even an old ladder that leads down to a pool of water. A big sign on the main road "Hatchet Bay Cave" clearly marks the dirt road leading to the cave. The cave entrance is in front of the first place one might park a car on the right.

On the way back to the bay, we hike to the pond. Sweetings Pond is accessed by an unmarked dirt road across from a quarry just north of town. The saltwater pond is bigger than the bay at Hatchet Bay, and similar in shape and geology, but it is not directly connected to the water outside, although it must be connected by caves.

According to local lore, the pond was once stocked with fishermen's bycatch by a man who was trying to establish a resort there. While there are many fish and strange creatures to see there, the pond lacks large predators like barracuda and sharks, so one may snorkel completely relaxed.

While swimming around looking for creatures, I notice that Emily and Clark have found something that absorbs their interest. When I swim over, I see they have found an octopus, which I have never seen. The creature is like nothing else on earth; perhaps it is an alien from a different planet. The octopus changes shape and color as we stare at it, dumbfounded. It eventually walks away as if it has more important business than entertaining the earthlings.

I return to the pond a few days later and see two more octopuses, many sea horses, spider crabs, two brittle stars, whelks crawling on the bottom, coral, and a few fish.

The octopuses are amazing creatures to behold. They sit still when they see me and try to blend into the background. But when it becomes clear that I can see them, they brighten up and make themselves as big as they can, trying to either scare me away or convince me that they can't fit in my mouth. They don't try to get away, but hold their ground until it looks like I start swimming away. Then they walk along the bottom using three of their eight tentacles like legs, while the other five are kept ready for defense.

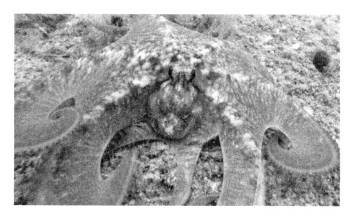

Everywhere they crawl, like creatures from beyond

Strange animals them all, live in Sweetings Pond
Brittle stars like spiders, described by HG Wells
Crawling around inside, sponges and knells
Octopus sit still, until they are seen
Grow bigger they will, and try to act mean
Alien intelligence, eight arms in all
Five for defense, and three to crawl
Seahorse in the weed, has only a tail
No legs do they need, move slow as a snail
Why the horse face, that is unknown
They sit with horse grace, their hiding place shown
Under a rock, look, don't reach in, man
A spider crab's nook, might cost you a hand
Whelks cruise the bottom, as slow as they can
So they don't look like food, to octopus or man
Young coral grows, and little fish swim
In the warm shallows, their life begins
Red scallops on rocks, red tentacles stretch
Like boats tied to docks, with fish-catching nets
Of this alien world, I have grown fond
Surely I will return, to Sweetings Pond

After returning from Sweeting's Pond, and seeing that the breeze is from the east, I row out of Hatchet Bay, turn left, and drop the little grappling anchor from *Little Flower*. I saw grouper in the rocks just to the left outside the cut a few days before, and I am hungry. I swim around underwater, trying to find lunch. I have yet to spear anything except the two lobster near Spanish Wells many days prior, and I want to eat fresh fish.

The water is about twenty feet deep with a flat sand bottom, but near the cliffs that line the shore are piles of enormous boulders and pieces of the cliffs that have fallen into the water, some lying by themselves, and others piled on top of one another. Some even emerge from the water. Orange fire coral grows on the rocks, as well as purple sea fans. I'm careful not to brush up against the coral, as I've been burned by it before. Even though the visibility is only about fifteen feet, I am mesmerized by the underwater scenery.

After chasing a few fish and not getting a shot, I tell myself to swim like a shark, slowly and quietly. A moment later, a hogfish swims right in front of my spear, and he is mine! As soon as I hit the fish, my heartrate spikes and I race to the surface, immediately fearing shark and barracuda that I imagine must be following me just out of view and waiting for me to spear a fish so they can rush in and steal my catch. I am completely a novice at spearfishing and totally unaccustomed to the flooding thrill of spearing a fish underwater, while holding my breath. The moment goes from quiet and serene to death-defying action in a flash. Adrenaline surges when the spear hits the fish, which bleeds and thrashes as I haul it to the surface.

I leave the fish on the spear and drop both into the dinghy, then quickly haul myself over the transom and into the boat. I am sure a shark will soon be on the scene, and I don't want to stick around to meet it with the fish's blood in the water.

Later, I learn to remain calm after spearing a fish, to swim to the dinghy at a normal pace, and to give off an air of confidence to any sharks or barracuda that might be watching. The last thing I want to do is to attract and excite a shark.

Ready to leave, I pull on the anchor line, but it holds fast and does not budge. I try and try again, but to no avail. By now I have convinced myself that a shark lurks just beneath *Little Flower*, and I do not want to get back in, but I have to. Reluctantly, I quietly slip back into the water, swim down, and free the anchor from the rocks, shark or no shark. Luckily there is no shark, and I get back in *Little Flower* with the quickness of the wary and row home.

Far from a skilled fisherman and knowing little about preparing a fish to eat, I get out my little-used fillet knife and I fillet the hogfish as best I can. I leave the skin on and drop the fillets in a pot with a bit of olive oil on the bottom. I prepare a salad, flip the fillets and turn off the heat. As fresh fish always is, the hogfish is delicious.

No sooner do I clean up from the meal than Walter from the Al Morris 65 *Marnie* shows up in his big black RIB, which I think of as "The Suburban of Dinghies," and invites me over for dinner. Having a healthy appetite and, as a singlehander, always ready for human interaction, I graciously accept.

His boat is immaculate, big, and clean. We enjoy much good conversation, as he too is alone until his next crew shows up, and dinner, another salad, this time with shrimp, is excellent.

It is another full day in paradise.

I stay in Hatchet Bay for three weeks, mainly because the surf keeps showing up, and with swell in the forecast, I find no reason to leave. When I am not surfing, I am spearfishing. I explore the coral-covered rocks both to the north and south of the cut leading into the bay. While the wariness of the fish suggests that the area is frequently spearfished, I occasionally am able to get a fish or a lobster.

It's hard to leave, Hatchet Bay
When I believe, west wind's on the way
For the bay will lend, itself to protection
From any wind, from any direction
There's fish outside, lobster and crab
A short dinghy ride, dinner to grab
Surfboard will glide, at Surfers Beach
Hitchhike a ride, the waves to reach
The grocery in town, has plenty of food
And the locals don't frown, 'cause they're in a good mood
There's water too, just up the street
Fill up I do, and people I meet
So it's hard to leave, Hatchet Bay
Another day indeed, I think I'll stay

One fine afternoon, the crew of another boat pulls up in their dinghy. We have friends in common and the owner, an attractive woman approximately my age, knows of me through Facebook. She invites me over for dinner and my interest is piqued.

The sailboat is big, beautiful, modern, and many times

the value of mine, but also much more complicated. Her daughter is aboard with her husband, and a hired captain makes four. I am looking for clues to determine if she and the captain are together, and when she gives me the grand tour of the boat, she shows me her room, and then the captains quarters. I assume she is single and unattached. My interest grows.

We all dine in a salon with shiny varnished woodwork, clean soft cushions, recessed lighting, and quiet music coming from all around. The extravagance of the vessel is astounding, with a washer and drier, refrigerator and freezer, electric coffee maker, air conditioning, and electric heads. However, after dinner, the captain has to start the engine to charge the batteries.

Dinner is divine, and I row home having made new friends.

Two days later, the wind is 20 knots out of the north, and I think it might be a good day to start for the Exumas and sail south to Rock Harbor. But as I ponder leaving, I cannot envision a safe way to pull up the anchor in such wind. My Vulcan is well-buried in the mud under 20 feet of water. It would surely be very difficult to pull up even in calm conditions and the added difficulty of the strong wind makes it seem unsafe.

I think I might bring the anchor line back to the cockpit and pull it in with one of the big winches. This way I could gently throttle forward, steer, and winch the rode in without having to leave the cockpit. But any mistake would send me into the rocks of the jetty behind me. It doesn't seem worth the risk, and at 11:00pm, I call it off.

In the afternoon, my new friend calls on the VHF to say they are leaving for the Exumas right away and invite me to tag along, to "buddy boat." They are going to Staniel Cay. I mention that I want to go to Soldier Cay, north of Staniel Cay, in the Exumas Land and Sea Park, and dive on the Sunken Aircraft and The Aquarium.

I think about it for a second and decide I would be better off leaving in the morning, going through Davis Channel in the daylight, anchoring for the night off Cape Eleuthera, and sailing to the Exumas the following day.

The morning of February 3, 2020, marks five years of sobriety for me. This date, February 3, is something like a birthday to me, only more important. To celebrate, I will spend the day sailing toward the Exumas.

I pull up the anchor at first light, using the winch in the cockpit. The Vulcan is extraordinarily heavy because a huge mass of mud is hauled up with the anchor. I let it hang just below the surface of the water and drive around in a big circle, which cleans it off, before pulling it up into the bow roller. I am certainly thankful for the calm conditions as I go through the process.

With the clean anchor snug in its place, I motor out the narrow cut between the rocky cliffs. The sun rises to my left as I raise the sails and say goodbye to Hatchet Bay, a place to which I am sure to return, and hopefully catch more waves.

A splash and a hiss to my left makes me turn and look and I am delighted to see a dolphin swimming next to *Windflower*. I get up from the helm and carefully walk to the bow, the best place to watch the show. Right away, the dolphin appears and swims back and forth, up and down, riding in the bow wave pushed by my ship. Two more dolphin join, a mother and calf, then two more adults. I stand at the bow for the duration of their visit, until they turn and dart away, off on some other dolphin business. Hours later, in water much clearer, another dolphin, larger than all the others, appears and swims along as if leading *Windflower* to her destination.

I set the autopilot and make my way to the bow so I can get a better look at the dolphin swimming in our wake. The sleek grey mammal rolls and plays in the clear water, barely moving its tail and riding the wave pushed by *Windflower*. It always makes me smile to watch them. However, when I look up, my smile fades. We are off course, something that should not be possible when the autopilot is on.

Back in the cockpit, I realize that the autopilot has power, but is no longer set to "auto," and is instead in "standby" mode. I turn it back to "auto" and watch it. After about fifteen minutes, it loses power, then comes back on, but in "standby" mode. This is troubling, as I rely on the autopilot on long passages and need to be able to trust it in tight quarters.

The protected waters on the west side of Eleuthera are separated from the deep Exuma Sound by very shallow water. To enter or exit in the south, boats have to pass through the Davis Channel, which is about 4nm long. It's about 0.2nm wide and the water on either side of it, which might look like open water, can be as shallow as 2 feet. The channel is unmarked, and I have to rely on the chartplotter to find it.

Luckily, Davis Chanel is easily negotiated. I can see the deeper water of the channel visually, as darker blue, and on the chartplotter, so it is no problem to pass through. I also have a boat ahead of me, as a third means of following the channel.

Cape Eleuthera Marina, at the end of the channel, is an easy place to buy fuel, although I am reminded of the need for fender boards (horizontal boards connecting two fenders) to fend off vertical pilings at Bahamian docks, and I vow to make a pair before docking in The Bahamas again.

I anchor outside the marina in the clear water of Exuma Sound.

Location: 24.8360º N, 76.3470º W

Also anchored is a big beautiful blue sailboat, *Geronimo*, hailing from Newport, Rhode Island. Kids are jumping into the water and swimming around the boat. It is a school ship, I learn after I row over to say hello, and all the kids aboard are taking some sort of class. How lucky for them, I think.

I row over to some dark holes in the water and dive in two strange depressions. I'm not sure if they are natural or man-made. I think they might be excavation pits for the marina and resort, since vertical parallel lines are cut in the rock walls of the holes, however, weeks later, I see the same vertical lines in underwater rocks and determine that it is a natural feature.

In the second hole, the larger of the two, while swimming along a wall about 20 feet down, looking at the little fish that live there, two sharks swim into view to my right. I remind myself to remain calm and continue swimming at the same pace. They look like Caribbean reef sharks, about five feet long, and they just keep on swimming, away from me, minding their own business. I am wary for the rest of the dive, and do not try to spear anything, but I don't see them again.

My new friends call on the VHF and say they are on their way to the Exumas and will go not to Staniel Cay, but rather to Soldier Cay, and meet me there. This makes me happy.

THE EXUMAS

surface of water
flat blue and serene
hides a world beneath
so few have seen
coral heads rise
up from the depths
like external organs
of the ocean itself
fish swim above
through and beneath
invertebrates to you
this scene bequeath
coral build structure
sponges imitate
while anemone wave
tentacles of fate
shrimp hide beneath
rock overhang
patrolling the reef
school of blue tang
lobster will hide
but antennae neglect
moray eel will abide
and lobster protect
big stingray glides
like UFO
escorted by barjack

CHASING THE NOMADIC DREAM

wherever it goes
parrotfish look
like they belong in a book
of fictional creatures
dreamed up by a child
angelfish queen
fallen from Heaven
visits the scene
slips into crevice
barracuda patrol
just out of reach
letting us now
they've a lesson to teach
somewhere outside
my vision I'm certain
shark watches me
like man behind curtain
I drift through this world
an alien visitor
holding my breath
curious inquisitor
I couldn't stay away
even if I desired
the reef calls my name
like the old town crier

I leave at 3:00am to sail across Exuma Sound in order to catch the tide near high and rising at Soldier Cay, since the way in is shallow. I pull the anchor in the dark and motor away from land, being careful to keep Chub rock a safe distance away. Soon the depth drops to over a thousand feet, and we are safe from any hazards on the bottom, and I relax completely.

With the sails up and the engine off and the bimini

down, the night is silent and dark and the stars cover the sky like glistening drops of dew on the morning grass. I sit behind the wheel and stare at the sky while steering by the stars. Nothing could be better. We are on a beam reach in 10-15 knots of breeze, absolutely ideal conditions. This is as good as it gets, enough wind to move at six knots, but not enough to build waves, a pleasant temperature, a comfortable point of sail, stars, ocean, me and my boat. This is certainly what I came for.

As I stare at the stars I begin to steer without conscious thought, and the chattering in my head becomes quiet. My mind clears and simply becomes one with nature, communicating with the creative force through mind only, through silent mind, since words are human inventions and probably meaningless to God. Whoever or whatever God may be, I doubt words are necessary or even useful for communication with God. Allowing the unconscious mind to expand, become silent, and merge with the great unknown vastness that surrounds me, I feel communication is happening on a level deeper and more meaningful than words can portray. Human language would fall short.

The dark and serene night slowly and imperceptibly gives way to the faint light of dawn and the sky turns from black to lavender in the east. The great light is coming. When we are half way across the deep water of Exuma Sound, the massive ball of fire rises above the horizon to port as the sky quickly moves through a display of all the warm colors, finishing its show with the bright blue that a child might paint the sky in a coloring book. The sun is God's face, too brilliant to look at, but looking at us all day, and reflected upon us at night.

The bottom of the ocean here is one mile straight down, and completely invisible from this far above, yet the sun is so bright I can't look directly at it, and it is nearly 93 million miles away. I ponder this as the sun warms me and I put the bimini back up when it begins to feel oppressive.

Six hours after pulling up the anchor, we motor into

Soldier Cay Cut, in the Exumas Land and Sea Park, and anchor near the "Sunken Aircraft" mentioned on the chart, just north of Pasture Cay and West of O'Briens Cay.

Location: 24.3209º N, 76.5581º W

I dive on the anchor and see that it is well set, then climb out of the water just in time to see my new friends pull up in their dinghy. Their boat is anchored way outside to the west, as their draft is too deep to get in to where I am. Like me, they want to dive on the Sunken Aircraft and The Aquarium. These are both well-know and highly-regarded snorkeling spots, and both have dinghy moorings, so we don't need to anchor. Since we are in the Exumas Land and Sea Park, fishing is not allowed, so I expect the reefs to be abundant with life.

The Sunken Aircraft is a little one-seat airplane upside down on the bottom in 15' of water. Around it is a fantastic and healthy reef, teeming with fish.

I swim all around, marveling at the abundance of sea life, taking video as I do. Sea fans wave in the current, sponges, like menorah, rise from the bottom, and corals cluster like scoops of ice cream stacked on top of each other. The corals build structures used by all the fish and various invertebrates on the otherwise flat sandy bottom. The reef is like a city surrounded by desert.

Orange fire coral warns me to keep clear, while soft purple sponges don't care. Flat green coral, finger coral like masses of orange spires, round brain coral, star coral, lettuce coral, and others boggle the mind in their complexity and variety.

Yellow and blue grunt swim in schools under corals, along with pink and white squirrelfish. Brilliant orange and purple royal gramma swim upside down under ledges, black longfin damselfish guard little sections of reef they declare to be their own. Blue tang cruise without a care, while the beautiful yet more reclusive queen angelfish show themselves, then play hide-n-seek in holes and cracks that seem made for their flat bodies. Parrotfish in the gaudiest of colors audibly munch on their favorite food, old and hard coral. They scrape rock and coral with their beak mouths, eating polyps and algae, and excrete fine sand. Curiously, I see no lobster and wonder why. They should be in every crevice on the bottom in a place where they are protected from the human predators.

I follow a yellowtail damselfish, admiring the electric blue spots on its navy-blue body. The hand-sized fish swims away from me as I follow it with the video camera. I am only taking pictures and video today because we are in the Exumas Land and Sea Park and it is a "no take zone." Fishing, spearing, and even shelling are prohibited by Bahamian law. This is a national park where all of nature is protected, so humans can visit and enjoy the sights and so the sea creatures can grow to maturity and reproduce, thus replenishing the stocks of lobster, grouper, and all the other animals that we normally hunt. This is a "take only pictures, leave only footprints" area, and because so, the reefs are abundant. It takes all the creatures to maintain healthy reefs, and the reef around the Sunken Aircraft is testament to this fact.

My new friend is scuba diving while the captain sits in the dinghy, since he is sharing his snorkeling gear with her daughter's husband. I notice she carries a spear, and when she surfaces, I do as well, thinking about a tactful way to tell her that spearfishing is prohibited here, and spearfishing with scuba gear is prohibited everywhere in The Bahamas.

Before I can speak, she yells to her captain, in the dinghy "You've got to come help me get this lobster, it's *huge!*"

"Aren't we in the Land and Sea Park?" I ask her. Suddenly I find myself uncertain that we are in the park, I have a moment of doubt, and wonder about how stern I should be.

"What do you mean?" she asks "Am I not supposed to spear it?"

"The Land and Sea Park is a no take zone. No spearing, no fishing, you're not even allowed to take shells," I explain.

"But it's *dinner,*" she exclaims like a spoiled child not used to be told she can't do something.

"I'm pretty sure we're in the park; it goes from Compass Cay to Shroud Cay, yeah, we're definitely in it. You're not allowed to spear anything." To me, this place is sacred, a special place where we can all come to see nature in all its glory, undisturbed by man. To kill something here would be like killing an animal in a zoo.

The captain takes the mask from the daughter's husband, puts on a neoprene jacket, and gets in with a long yellow spear. I swim away, not wanting to be associated with them anymore, and climb into *Little Flower*.

Moments later I hear her exclaim "Yes!" and a feeling of disgust flows through me like ice water. How could they so blatantly disregard the law of the park? The captain returns to his dinghy with a dead lobster on the end of his spear. He notices the look on my face and tries to justify the killing.

"We need more food on the boat, we're out of just about everything."

I say nothing in response, take off my fins, and row away.

The Aquarium is a little reef, not far from the Sunken Aircraft, along the edge of a rocky bank next to a cut that winds through rocks and cays and shallow sandbars. I tie off to a dinghy mooring and snorkel with my video camera.

As soon as I get in, I am greeted by a school of sergeant major, little fish the size of a teacup saucer with vertical stripes, the same number as their namesake. Coral, both hard and soft, covers the bottom and the rock wall. The abundance of fish is impressive and the display of life mesmerizing.

My new friends arrive, and before long, I notice the spear in the captain's hands. I wonder how I should respond to this affront to environmental law. In the past, with new friends, I too often overlooked their lapses in moral integrity, blinded my lust, or in the case of men, my desire to have a friend. This always led to regrettable situations. Here, at nearly 50 years old, I recognize more easily such shortcomings in people and no longer overlook them so easily.

I find that I lose respect for my new friend, the woman who I formerly daydreamed about sailing and diving with. I no longer find her desirable. After the snorkel, I say goodbye and make no effort to discuss where we might meet again (although she doesn't either). I row back to *Windflower* to continue my solo existence, feeling the loss but firm in my resolve and glad to have been strong in my conviction.

While snorkeling The Aquarium, the battery in my camera died, so I return two hours later and snorkel the reef a second time. But this time the battery on my flashlight dies. The camera and the flashlight are a team, and both are attached to a two-foot articulating handle. The light not only allows me to take video under rocks and in caves, but it also brings out the colors underwater. Water absorbs light, and the colors disappear with depth. Red is the first to go, followed by orange, yellow, green, and blue. As water gets deeper, all becomes grey, before the light disappears completely.

Regardless of the lack of battery power, The Aquarium, with its abundance of fish and coral, warranted a second visit anyway.

The Sunken Aircraft lies upside down on the bottom. The line extending from its nose is the dinghy mooring.

coral and sponges at the Sunken Aircraft reef

A nurse shark rests on the bottom at the Sunken Aircraft.

A variety of hard and soft corals decorate the reef at the Sunken Aircraft.

sergeant major, a schoolmaster snapper, and a yellow-phase coney at The Aquarium

coral along the rock wall at The Aquarium

The anchorage by the Sunken Aircraft is a beautiful spot, but it is also in an area, like much of the Exumas, where tidal currents reverse four times a day, so *Windflower* moves around a lot and faces different directions throughout the day. Anchoring in such a place is a bit worrisome and requires vigilance.

In the morning, I am ready to go to my next destination, Rocky Dundas, a pair of islands in Conch Cut, on the south edge of the Exumas Land and Sea Park. My charts say the islands have caves accessible from the water, coral reef, and dinghy moorings. My friends Pete and Tracey Goss, whom I met in Virginia, are down in that area somewhere, and I hope to visit with them and snorkel the reefs of Rocky Dundas (*Listen to my interview with Pete Goss on my podcast, Offshore Sailing and Cruising with Paul Trammell*).

Early in the morning, I stand at the bow and pull up the anchor, and since the anchor is in nearly 20 feet of water, it is quite heavy, with the 55-pound anchor and 20 feet of chain to lift. I am just able to raise it, but as it emerges from the water,

I am astounded to see the chain all wrapped in a knot around the anchor. I can't leave it like that, and we are drifting towards the reef of the Sunken Aircraft, so I drop the mass of anchor and chain back to the bottom and think about what to do about it.

The Fortress anchor is sitting on the bow roller ready to go, and this is just the opportunity to use it for the first time. I motor forward, pull the tangled Vulcan just a few feet off the bottom, nudge forward again, and drop the Fortress. After we drift back enough to set the anchor, I cleat off the rode and release the Vulcan.

The water is clear and I always enjoy a swim, even if work is involved. I swim down to the Vulcan and wrestle with the tangled chain. I am only able to take one wrap of the chain off the anchor before returning to the surface to breathe.

Out of breath and breathing heavily, I take a moment to swim over to the Fortress, as this is the first time I have used the anchor. I am curious to see how it set, and upon seeing it I am pleased. Its sharp flukes are buried in the sand.

I dive again, two more times, and finally untangle the chain from the anchor. We have been anchored in a tidal current and we must have swung around the anchor a few times. I should have put out two anchors in a Bahamian moor, with one upstream and one downstream, so we wouldn't drift back and forth causing the anchor to have to reset with every change of the tides.

Ahead of us is a narrow route through passes and across shallows, along the inside of the islands, to the Rocky Dundas, so I leave the sails furled and just motor. We maneuver around Bell Island, with its rocky bluffs, sandy coves, a few stately houses, and something that looks like a small resort tucked away in the trees.

One pass in particular, on the northeast point of Bell Island, is just wide enough to get through, and right next to a rocky shore. Luckily the shallows are visible as bright yellow-blue areas, nearly white where the water is very shallow. We have to weave around a bit, staying in the dark blue water, and I use both the chartplotter and my own vision to navigate. I don't think I will use this pass again, it's nearly too shallow and narrow for *Windflower*, and I typically like to play it safe.

Once around Bell Island, the going is easy, and before long we are pulling around to the south of Rocky Dundas. I anchor behind the southern of the two islands, that is, just west of it, and north of Fowl Cay, over a shallow sand bottom.

Location: 24.2769º N, 76.5422º W

I get on the VHF and call Pete to see where he is and if he'd like to join me for a snorkel at Rocky Dundas. The last time we communicated, he was a few miles further south. Pete answers the call and we switch to channel 17. He asks where I am. When I tell him, he says he watched me on the way in, and I assume he means on the AIS. Pete says he wants to snorkel Rocky Dundas too and we agree to meet in the water. The best time to snorkel there is at slack tide before incoming, which is about an hour away.

Before I can switch the radio back to 16, another sailor calls Pete, and I overhear Pete say that he is anchored at Fowl Cay, which is right next to me. I look up and to my left and there I see his boat, *Pearl of Penzance*, a Garcia Expedition 45. Now I understand that Pete literally watched me come in.

I get my snorkeling gear all ready, toss it in *Little Flower*, and row over to the protected little bay at Fowl Cay. I step aboard their aluminum boat and tie the painter to a cleat that looks as if it simply grew from the deck, and am welcomed by Tracey with a hug and Pete with a smile and a firm handshake.

The novelty of meeting friends on sailboats in foreign places fascinates me. The world is so big, yet here we are, friends who met hundreds of miles away, now at the same island, at the same time, in a foreign country.

Later, Pete, his friend, and I snorkel around the reefs

and into two caves at Rocky Dundas. This is just within the southern edge of the Land and Sea Park, so we are not spearfishing. I am delighted to see a large and healthy Elkhorn coral, and also some smaller representatives of this rare species. Elkhorn used to dominate the reefs of the Caribbean, but disease has decimated the population and as I write the species is critically endangered.

a rare specimen of elkhorn coral, a critically-endangered species

inside a cave at Rocky Dundas

the bizarre and uncommon trumpetfish

branched finger coral, in the foreground, just left of center, above the coral swim two blue chromis, on the right is a French grunt

Every reef is different, and every one has its own flora and fauna. At the Rocky Dundas, I am surprised to see two trumpetfish. These oddballs are long and slender fish that sit still and vertical, camouflaged among the vertical branches of soft corals. They slowly approach small unwary fish and crustaceans which they snap up with their big mouths. I also see a brown moray eel, which quickly recedes backwards into its hole, a stunning queen angelfish, the uncommon yellow and black rock beauty, a nurse shark lying on the bottom under a ledge, a gorgeous yellowtail damselfish, various parrotfish, painted wrasse, ocean surgeon, a school of sergeant major, bluehead wrasse, a school of squirrelfish, blue chromis, and one curious barracuda.

The variety of species is fabulous, and indicative of a healthy reef, which is a fine thing to see in this age of world-wide coral reef die-off.

After snorkeling the reef on the east side of the island, I row around the north side on the way back to *Windflower*. I stop at two conspicuous rocks in the sheltered and calm water, and get back in.

Dotting the sandy bottom around the emergent rocks are brightly colored coral heads. One in particular is guarded by a little longfin damselfish, which runs off a much larger blue tang. The damselfish eat algae and encrusting organisms and tend to their territories like a gardener defending their crop from thieves and pests. They will even attempt to run off a human, yet they are no bigger than the palm of my hand.

Back aboard *Windflower*, I wave to *Pearl of Penzance* as they pass by, on their way to Staniel Cay, to drop off their guest who is flying home the next day. I pull up the anchor and move to the northwest cove of Compass Cay.

Location: 24.2773º N, 76.5259º W

As is my practice, I swim out to check on the anchor, and finding it in shallower water than I am comfortable with, I pick it up and walk along the bottom, anchor in hand, to slightly deeper water, where I re-set it. I move it one more time to keep its chain clear of little corals on the bottom which are about the size of grapefruit. Corals this size are fairly common, and as a good steward of the ocean, I avoid anchoring around them because the chain sweeps across the bottom as the boat swings about at anchor, and any corals in the way get damaged or dislodged from the bottom.

Swimming in the anchorage is like being in an endless swimming pool, and I want more, so I swim to a neighboring boat to say hello, then all the way to shore, take a short walk on the deserted beach, and swim back.

On the VHF, I overhear sailors talking about visiting the Bubble Baths, so I look it up on the chart. The baths are right on the northwest corner of the island and the chart dictates visiting at high tide, which is very soon. I grab my mask and a pair of sandals and row ashore. I hike across a broad yellow mangrove flat with little mangrove roots emerging from the firm but moist ground like little brown eels. On the ocean side is a pool fed by waves that occasionally break over a low point in the rock separating the mangrove flats from Exuma Sound.

The water in the sound is clear, but it also surges into the sharp rocks all around. I long to snorkel, so I find a place I can climb down to shallow water and carefully step in, still wearing my sandals.

I swim out through the surge and snorkel in the dynamic but clear water, looking under the rocks for hiding fish, or whatever else might be there, and occasionally looking over my shoulder for sharks.

I carefully climb out, trade my mask for sunglasses, and join three other cruising couples in the warmer water of the Bubble Baths. I introduce myself and learn that the three couples are buddy-boating through the Exumas. For the next week, I occasionally hear them hailing each other on the VHF.

In the evening, I sit and ponder. This has been a full day of activity, starting with diving on my tangled anchor, motoring through narrow passes, visiting my friends, snorkeling Rocky Dundas, swimming at Compass Cay, and the finally relaxing with other sailors at the baths. It all makes me feel young again, and like an athlete. The cruising life is clearly good for me, and I want for nothing more.

In the morning, I work on *Little Flower's* sailing rig, making two key improvements. I add a cam cleat near the bow for the halyard, so I won't have to struggle to tie it to something after raising the sail while the boom pushes up against me, or to untie it after a sail. Then I replace a broken cleat on the mast used to hold the boom down. I also replace the frayed line on the boom for tying it to the mast. I also tighten and secure the plastic sleeves on the oars so they fit into the oarlocks and protect the oars from grinding against the metal.

I sail her upwind for about an hour, all the way to Compass Cay Marina, which requires many tacks and takes us across bright blue shallows and the dark blue and deeper channel over and over again. We weave through the anchorage at the marina, around the ketch of one of the couples I met the day before (we wave) and then turn downwind.

The breeze is strong, and sailing downwind is more challenging than I expected. *Little Flower's* boom has no vang to hold it down, so the boom rises up high in the gusts and the little dinghy rolls from left to right like a drunk stumbling out of a bar after last call. I have to keep my center of gravity low and my concentration high to keep from capsizing, but then the cleat I installed on the mast pulls loose and the boom rises up the mast and my little boat becomes even harder to control. *Little Flower* rolls much more haphazardly now, and the unrestrained boom leaps and falls in the gusts. I sit all the way down on the bottom of the boat and do my best to steer us towards home.

Luckily the current and wind are with us, so we are back at *Windflower* in no time.

As soon as we return, I take down the sailing rig, don my wetsuit, and row out to Conch Cut to catch slack tide before incoming. The tide is already coming in, but I am able to row through the cut to a little cove near the outside. I slip over the transom and into the clear water, then drift back with *Little*

Flower's painter in hand. I keep an eye out for sharks, which I figure are likely to be in the cut for the same reason I am, as I search all through the rocks and coral, looking for grouper or lobster.

It isn't long before I spot two long spiny antennae protruding from under a rock. With spear at the ready, I swim down, see what looks like a big lobster, and release the spear. It's a direct hit, and I push the spear further into the hole, hoping to push it all the way through the little beast so it can't escape.

The spear is jerking as I hold on and the lobster tries in vain to escape the only way it knows how, by using its powerful tail, the source of the meat I desire. I hold my breath and pull until I get it out from under the rocks, then return to *Little Flower*, whose painter I hold in my left hand.

The lobster is indeed a good-sized specimen. I steam the tail in a pot with just a bit of water and eat it with a can of green beans heated up with a clove of diced garlic. If the tail were any bigger, I realize when the meal is over, I would not have been able to finish it.

Little Flower *on the beach and* Windflower *at anchor, Compass Cay*

lobster for lunch, courtesy of Compass Cut

The northwest cove of Compass Cay, Windflower *is on the right. The narrow deep-water channel where it is possible to anchor can clearly be seen as the dark strip between shallow water.*

With the coming of a frontal passage, I need to move to an anchorage protected from all wind directions, and I have had my eye on a spot by Thomas Cay, in the Pipe Creek area, that looks like it will fit the bill.

Exiting through Conch Cut, on the north end of Compass Cay, is easy, however, entering Thomas Cut against the outgoing tide is challenging. Waves from the southeast wind push us into the outgoing current, which is so strong inside the cut that we move at a slow walking pace, with the engine at full throttle, while the water rushes by. It's a bit disorienting and difficult to keep *Windflower* pointed straight ahead in the turbulent water, but we make slow progress.

Once inside the cut, the waters calm and we turn hard to port and into a narrow area of deep blue water, with the rocky bank of Thomas Cay on the left and a shallow reef visible on the right.

I motor to the end of the deep water and scout about, drawing a curved line on the chartplotter denoting water over 9 feet deep. I drop the Fortress anchor at the south end of the anchorage, drift back about 200 feet, then drop the Vulcan. I pull forward about 80 feet, then haul on both anchor lines until they are tight.

I deploy a kellet weight on both anchors. These are old weights from window sashes that I kept from a construction job years ago. I attach the weight to a snatch block, to which I tie a line. The snatch block goes on the anchor line and is lowered down a length just less than the water depth. This way when the tide changes direction and one anchor line goes limp, the weight pulls the line down vertically, lessening the chance that the keel will catch it and hang up on the anchor line. This might sound unlikely, but it has happened to me twice in the past, on my previous boat, and it creates a serious problem. I had to get right in the water both times and wrestle the rode free of the keel.

Location: 24.2383º N, 76.4908º W

With one anchor forward and one behind I now lie to a Bahamian mooring, which is useful in tidal areas or anywhere that swinging room is limited, and this anchorage fits both criteria.

The Thomas Cay anchorage is the sort of place one might see on postcards, or an advertisement for a tropical paradise. Little islands and emergent rocks form dotted lines between larger islands, all arranged linearly with different shades of blue water in between. A few houses dot the landscape, and a few sailboats in the distance decorate the water. *Windflower* and I are alone in the anchorage until a bit later when a blue trawler, *Rita V*, comes in and anchors far behind us, and we exchange waves of greeting.

At the end of outgoing tide, I snorkel the reef next to the boat, and drift out into the cut and catch slack tide. The water in the cut is deep and this is an exciting place to freedive, since it is a bottleneck in the highway of fish. I dive until the current changes and then drift back to *Windflower*, without dinner, but having had another fabulous time in the water.

In the night, I expect foul weather, and get up a few times to check the anchors, but the night is calm and come morning there is no wind at all and the water is smooth and transparent.

Slight creaking of rope
The only sound made
Holding dinghy to boat
On peaceful Saturday

Clear water below
Next to green island
Visible under the boat
Bottom of grass and sand

Birds greet the sun
Rising over palm trees
New day has begun
With barely a breeze

South I will sail
To another isle
Or maybe I'll stay
In Pipe Creek a while

I'll sit and write
While sipping coffee
And leave with the tide
Or stay and go snorkeling

Perhaps I'll sail
My dinghy bright red
She needs no gale
That magic sled

Just a puff of a breeze
To give her power
She sails with ease
My Little Flower

Coral reef beckons
Deep in the cut
A grouper I do reckon

Would make a fine lunch

To stay or to go
No need to decide
For clearly I know
Can't leave before tide

Pipe Creek, looking southwest from Thomas Cay

Thomas Cay Cut. Water flows through here, changing
direction with the tide,
between Pipe Creek to the left and Exuma Sound to the right.

I pull up both anchors, and take some time to switch sides, putting the heavier Vulcan on the left, because the left anchor roller actually rolls, while the right roller is frozen. With both the Fortress and the Vulcan stowed, we ride the last of the outgoing tide through the cut, leaving behind my tranquil paradise and motor south to Black Point Settlement. I passed by this popular anchorage the last time I was in The Bahamas and vowed to take a look the next time. I also want to do laundry and restock water and food.

There is no wind, so we motor and let the autopilot, which is working again, steer. For much of the two-hour trip I stand at the bow gazing down into the clear blue water. I can easily see the bottom most of the way, even when the water is 60 feet deep, and watch as dark blotches of coral reef pass by. I wonder what it would be like to dive out here, and I probably would if the sun were out. Sometimes all it takes to make water uninviting is a cloud between it and the sun.

Dotham Cut is deep and wide and easy to navigate, and soon we are in the bay at Black Point Settlement.

Location: 24.0997º N, 76.4037º W

In the grey and windy morning, since free water is available in town, I do my laundry in the cockpit. While it soaks, I set up the sailing rig and sail *Little Flower* to shore, where I drop off four small bags of trash and fill three 7-gallon jerry cans of water. As usual, *Little Flower* gets a compliment, this time from a local on shore.

While hanging the laundry to dry, I devise an adventure for the day. I want to sail north, around the point, across the cut at the end of outgoing tide, and snorkel the reefs I remember from two years ago, in front of Gaulin Cay South. Then I want to spearfish in the cut on incoming tide, and drift back into the bay. Two hours before low tide, I load my diving gear in *Little Flower*, along with a VHF radio, the Garmin InReach, a bottle of water, and a cliff bar.

The sail out is a fast broad reach. The wind is blowing nearly 20 knots, the sky is only partly cloudy, and *Little Flower*

moves swiftly across the water. Many new boats have anchored in the harbor since the day before, and I wave to a few
sailors on the way out.

When I get to the point, in the lee of the land, the wind
calms and I see reef below. With nearly two hours to kill before
the tide switches, I don my gear and slip as quietly as I can into
the water.

Leaving the spear in the dinghy and taking instead the
video camera, I snorkel on beautiful patches of reef made up of
lobed star coral, various sponges, bits of fire coral, brain coral,
and small patches of young finger coral. Coral reef thrives all
along the edge of land, on the northwest end of the island
(Great Guana Cay) just before Dotham Cut. A large variety of
fish swim all about, including a small school of blue tang, blue
chromis, a beautiful young queen angelfish, margate snapper, royal gramma, schoolmaster snapper, a stunning stoplight
parrotfish, schools of French grunt, a gorgeous yellow and blue
juvenile Spanish hogfish, dusky damselfish, sergeant major,
schools of squirrelfish, spotfin butterflyfish, a chain moray eel
hiding deep in a small cave, and a harem of bluehead wrasse
corralled by a male with the namesake blue head.

A large dark shape catches my eye; laying on the sand
twenty yards away from the reef is the biggest nurse shark I've
ever seen.

Some of the lobed star coral are decorated with spiral-
gilled tube worms, aka Christmas tree worms, that stick their
gills out of crevices in the coral and look like miniature Christmas trees in a variety of Dr. Seuss colors. A pink-tipped anemone slowly waves tentacles from its lair within a coral head
as if competing for attention. Black sea urchins, like living
pincushions, or aquatic porcupines, hide under the coral. Blue
chromis swim in the water high above the coral, little yellow
wrasses meander in a group just above the coral, and nearly all
the other fish swim closer to the bottom. Squirrelfish, red and
white with big black eyes, hide from the sun in schools under
the coral heads. Tiny purple and yellow royal gramma hover-

ing upside-down under ledges catch my eye and make me hold my breath longer.

The current switches directions early, probably due to the strong breeze, and before I get to the cut, I find myself swimming against it. I get as close to the cut as I can, then turn around and drift downstream with *Little Flower's* small grappling anchor in my left hand and the spear in my right. I am no longer sightseeing, but hunting. I want fresh seafood for lunch.

I swim all around, zig-zagging across a wide area of patchy reefs over clear white sand. Since there are no lobster to be seen, and the fish run from me when I approach, I figure the reef is regularly spearfished. Finally, I get close to a schoolmaster snapper and hit it, but the spear pins it against a rock before the hinged barb goes through the fish, and it wiggles off the spear and swims away. I feel bad for injuring the fish, and now it is bleeding, which will surely attract a shark. I move on.

I later learn that schoolmaster snapper are known to carry ciguatera. This is a debilitating disease some tropical fish carry which is caused by toxins, secreted by an alga, that bioaccumulates in some fish, so I was lucky not to land this one.

While on the surface, I spot a grouper swimming between reefs. He sees me too, and darts under a rock. With the spear ready, I take a deep breath, swim down, and sit still on the bottom with the spear aimed at the hole. I see its head and take a shot, but the fish is too quick, and I return to the surface to breathe and wait. I go down a second, then a third time, waiting patiently for the fish to show itself.

Finally I get a shot and hit the grouper in the head. It dies right away, so it doesn't thrash on the way back to the dinghy, and for that I am thankful. Right next to a cut there are sure to be sharks, probably watching me just outside my range of vision, or so I imagine.

I toss the spear and fish in *Little Flower*, quickly climb in over the transom, and pull up the anchor. I push the boom to the side, turn *Little Flower* beam to the wind, take the tiller in one hand and the sheet in the other, and we silently slip away from the reef.

As soon as we round the point and enter the bay, we come out of the lee of land and the wind picks up. I have to move back and forth, leaning back to almost horizontal in gusts and sitting up in lulls, moving the tiller to steer into and out of the strong breeze, releasing and pulling in on the sheet. I feel like a kid again, working the controls and negotiating the challenging conditions. The sail is fast and fun, and once again I am thankful for spending $150 on a sailing and rowing dinghy instead of $5,000 or more on an inflatable with an outboard motor. I'm able to go wherever I want in my humble dinghy, it's fun to use, and I'm getting stronger from all the rowing. I can even see that my muscles are growing.

Cruising life is a healthy life, I'm finding. Every day requires exercise and offers adventure. This is my kind of living. I feel alive and each day is a validation of everything I have done to get here. This is surely the life I was meant for, living on the water, a wild and free spearfishing, surfing, and sailing nomad, enjoying the fruits of nature, the bliss of solitude, and the freedom of remote self-employment.

I occasionally have the notion that if I should die while sailing or diving, it would not matter because I have already lived enough of this good life to justify risking everything. Life is not meant to be wasted chasing after physical objects, numbers, someone else's ideals, or one's own ego. Life is for chasing our dreams, bettering ourselves at every turn, learning all we can, and experiencing the glory of nature in all her forms.

French grunt bask in the sunlight next to lobed star coral. Beneath them is a small finger coral, and a sponge sits in the right foreground.

A coral head rises like a fist from the bottom of the sea.

Little Flower floats above a lobed star coral with a sponge growing out like a chimney.

A chain moray eel warns the camera not to come any deeper into its cave.

A pink-tipped anemone reaches toward the sun from a lobed star coral.

Living on a boat and confined to a forty-foot space makes one desire long walks on land, and living alone at anchor makes one hungry for communication. I set out in the morning to accomplish both. Although there is a cell tower half a mile away, somehow I do not have service [*I later learned that I have to occasionally switch between Aliv and BTC on my phone settings*], so after rowing to shore across the wind, I walk to Deshamon's restaurant, where a group of locals is sitting on the porch drinking coffee, although one is throwing the norms of society to the wind and enjoying a bottle of Guinness.

In the United States, when entering a restaurant, one is typically greeted at the door and directed to a table, given a menu, and asked what they want to drink. In The Bahamas, sometimes one must first find the proprietor, ask if food is being served, and if it is, ask for a menu.

After looking at everyone on the porch, I decide the owner is either the woman wearing a leather jacket and a fur-lined collar, or the man at the table next to her. Not sure, I walk inside, the man follows me in, and that identifies him as the proprietor.

I ask if he is serving breakfast, and he thinks about it, as if deciding if he wants to cook at the moment, then shakes his head. I ask if he has coffee, and he smiles and says "coffee's right there" and points to a pot on a counter, apparently self-serve. I then ask about wifi, my real reason for being here, and he tells me the name of the network. No password is necessary.

After two cups of coffee and a half-hour of communication with friends and family back in the States, the kind man is gone, so I get up to look for him. I ask a woman who is setting tables how much the coffee is, and she returns a look of confusion, as if no one has ever asked her this question, and suggests I ask "him." In the kitchen, I find him, and give him a dollar for the coffee.

I walk off with a coffee to go in search of the trail on the north end of the island that is labeled "not to be missed" on the Explorer Charts. While the walk along the beach is pleasant and yields me some pieces of sun-bleached coral, the trail is nowhere to be found, and I do not recommend looking for it, for the thorny vegetation where the trail is supposed to be is quite unforgiving.

The dozen boats in the harbor when I arrived has become fifty, and I simply am not able to relax with so many boats around, even though none are particularly close to me. I almost pull anchor and leave, but the wind is still 19 knots and I do not feel comfortable pulling up anchor in these conditions with boats downwind of me. Instead I opt for a repeat of the adventure the day before. I will sail out to the reef, spearfish, and sail back.

The sail out is fast and fun, but I notice that our point of sail is just a little bit more downwind than the day before. I sail out onto the reef and get right in the water, snorkeling with the spear in my right hand and the painter in my left.

The reef is just as mesmerizing as it was the day before; the repetition does not degrade its wonder.

Large coral heads rise up from the bottom like bulbous mounds of living yellow rock, but they are usually hollow underneath, and fish of various species love to live inside, as well as other creatures. I always shine a flashlight in caves and crevices and under coral heads, and there is always something to see. Inside one coral is a spotted trunkfish, one of the true oddballs of the reef. They look like a fish drawn by a child who has heard of fish but never seen one. They tend to sit still and pose for photographs. Since their body is covered with hexagonal armor plates, they have little fear of predators.

A spotted trunkfish sits inside a lobed star coral, with a bit of branched finger coral in the foreground.

Inside another coral is a large chain moray eel. Unfortunately I never see its head, so I only get video of its body. Eels are one reason not to stick your hands up under coral to see what's inside.

I keep a lookout for sharks, always trying to be conscious of what is outside the tunnel-vision the mask creates, and I am happy not to see any. I do see the largest stingray I've ever seen, which must be five feet across, gliding along the bottom like a UFO.

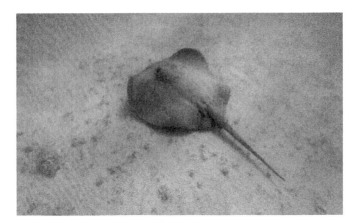

This behemoth cruised across the bottom, paying me no attention, confident in its ability to defend itself from the likes of me, the enormous and uncommon chupare stingray.

    I drift with the tide until we are back in the bay, then leap into *Little Flower*, hoist the sail, and slowly start for the anchorage.

    Something doesn't seem right. *Little Flower* is not able to point at her mother ship, nearly a mile away, but instead we point downwind of her. No problem, I can sail to the other side of the bay and then tack. We trudge along at a sluggish pace, not nearly as fast as the day before, even though the wind is just as strong. I look down and see that *Little Flower* has a few gallons of water sloshing around in the bottom.

    I try to bail as we sail, but all my gear in the bottom is in the way, and the strong wind requires all my strength to hang on to the mainsheet. I don't want to let go because we would then drift downwind, so we sail slowly and awkwardly all the way across the bay. What was yesterday a magic sled is today a tired old barge, chugging across the windy bay, slapping into the onslaught of waves.

    We work our way to a restaurant on the other side the bay, where a man takes pictures as we slowly approach, then we tack back into the mass of anchored sailboats, tack two more times, and finally point at *Windflower.*

As I look at my boat, I wonder why another dinghy is beside her, then I realize the unoccupied dinghy is moving. "Who lost their dinghy?" I yell three times, in hopes the owners will hear, but then again, what can they do? They no longer have a dinghy.

I sail right to the drifting dinghy, grab a hold of the yellow painter, and immediately start drifting downwind. Lucky for me, my neighbor, with a motorized dinghy (all other dinghies here are motorized) comes up behind me and I pass the derelict dinghy off to them, then tack four more times to get back to *Windflower.* The dinghy is reunited with its owner within a few hours.

In the morning, I am ready to leave the crowded and windy anchorage of Black Point Settlement. Just after breakfast, I pull up the Vulcan, which is firmly set. It takes me two tries to pull it free. After motoring out of the bay, sticking to the north side to avoid shallows in the center, I hoist the sails and head south, about 170 degrees, into the 18-knot breeze on a close reach. *Windflower* heels about 20 degrees and cuts through the choppy water at 6 knots. The short-period wind waves make us bounce up and down and send spray flying every minute or so, sometimes over the bow.

The day before, I added a dyneema line to the anchor roller to hold the Vulcan down, and it works perfectly. No longer does it try to jump out of the bow roller when waves hit it from below, and this is a big improvement.

After an hour and a half, we tack, sail towards land, and I start the engine, then take down the sails. The final leg is straight into the wind, and we have to cross through a channel not marked on my chartplotter, but clearly marked on the Explorer Chartbook and on the Navionics app on my phone. The channel leads from the deeper water west of the south end of Big Farmers Cay directly east toward Galliot Cut. The depth never gets less than 11 feet, and we pass through about an hour after high tide. However, looking at the chartplotter is unnerving, because it says we are passing over water 4 feet deep at low water.

Ahead is a trio of uninhabited islands, Big Galliot Cay, Little Galliot Cay, and Tiny Galliot Cay.

My intended destination is Big Galliot Cay, where I anchored two years before. But on this day, the wind is too much from the south and the anchorage is not protected. I motor on to Tiny Galliot Cay, where Navionics claims is a great snorkeling spot, but the island is so small that it does little to block the wind and waves. Finally, we motor over to Little Galliot Cay and find a great sheltered anchorage, all to ourselves, in 9 feet of water, and labeled on the chart as having 7 feet at low tide. The wind is completely blocked, the bottom is clear sand, and the edge of the uninhabited island is lined with cliffs and caves, with big rocks in the water, suggesting habitat for fish and lobster, should I be so lucky. Two goats walk along the top of the bluff overlooking the water, and I occasionally hear them talking to each other.

Location: 23.9222º N, 76.2991º W

This is my first anchorage without any other boats around, nor any houses within sight, so it's time for one of my favorite things: skinny dipping. I climb naked into the water to check the anchor, although I wear my dive knife on my leg. As soon as I get in, a barracuda swims aggressively toward me with its mouth open. I am used to seeing these fish, and they often follow me, but I've yet to be charged by one like this. I pull out the knife and look it in the eye, and even swim towards it, trying to trick it into thinking I am not afraid. The ruse works, the barracuda swims away, and I check the anchor, although in a speedy manner.

With the anchor set, I get my snorkeling gear ready and set out to the edge of the island, this time wearing my wetsuit.

With spear in hand, I swim around little coral heads and big fallen rocks. The area is teeming with life. Schools of margate snapper catch my eye, and a few large schoolmaster snapper. The usual and gorgeous blue tang swim around the rocks, as well as redtail parrotfish and various others. I haven't yet eaten a margate snapper, nor have I speared any snapper for that matter, and I am excited with the prospect of getting one. I saw a Bahamian man catching them in the Ragged Islands, so I assume they do not carry ciguatera.

I find a spot where I can aim my spear into a cave while still floating on the surface and breathing. The margate snapper swim back and forth in the cave, moving as a school and looking at me each time they pass. They all stay out of range at first, but as I sit still, the curious fish move closer and closer until one becomes a target, and I release the spear.

The spear hits the fish and I follow up with a lunge to get the barb all the way through, and the fish is mine! I swim to *Little Flower* toss the spear and fish in, then unscrew the spear tip and pull it out. I hit the fish in the gills and the spear came out of its mouth, so there is no blood and the tip is easy to remove. Still, I row away to another rock just in case a shark is attracted to the area. The fish is eating-size but not a full meal.

The next rock is also adorned with fish, and when I shine the flashlight and look under, I am surprised to see three lobster. I select the one I think is the biggest, spear it, and now I have a proper meal.

The tide continues going out as I dine on my fabulous fresh seafood lunch, but about a half hour before low tide I am shocked by an impact on the bottom of the keel, which is soon repeated. We are bumping the bottom with each passing wave like a car without shock absorbers hitting potholes. I turn on the chartplotter to check the depth, and it reads 5.7, not the 7 feet that the chart claims. Unfortunately, I can think of nothing to do but wait it out. After about a half hour of bumping on the bottom as the small waves lift and drop us, we sit firmly on the sand. I swim down to check on things. I am pleased to see that *Windflower's* keel slopes up just a bit forward of the rudder, so the rudder is not in contact with the bottom.

In retrospect, as soon as we started bumping on the bottom, I could have motored forward into shallower water, grounding the boat and avoiding the half hour of bumping. Then, after the tide started coming back in, I could have reversed back to the original, slightly deeper, location.

I want to snorkel again in the afternoon, without the spear, rather traveling as a tourist across the reef. When the spear is in my hand, I look only for prey, not noticing the other creatures as much, or the general beauty of the scene. I miss snorkeling for the sheer joy of being in the water and observing the reef and all its creatures, and I don't need any more seafood today.

I row *Little Flower* around the point to the right. After rowing as far as I can into the wind and current, I get in and begin drifting across little patchy reefs harboring all sorts of fish. I see two grouper, camouflaged and trying to hide against rocks, lucky that I'm not hungry. I also see a graysby, which is a small and spotted member of the grouper family, and a few queen triggerfish, which are among my favorites to see. It's clear that the fish are all less frightened of me without the spear in my hand, but I'm not sure if it's the lack of spear or just the way I move and react to the fish.

Near the end of the snorkel, a big stingray swims directly towards me, escorted by a bar jack, which swims very close as if investigating me for its host. The stingray passes by within arm's reach, paying me no mind, and comes to rest on the bottom next to the big rocks. I am left with the impression that the jack was escorting the stingray like a security guard, and the stingray was simply curious, as well as fearless, and wanted a closer look at me.

Back aboard *Windflower*, still in the mindset of noticing and appreciating natural beauty, I stand on deck and look all around. Little Galliot Cay is quiet and beautiful, with bright blue water leading away from the island, Galliot Cut is just in view to the southeast, Big Farmers Cay to the northeast, and Little Farmers Cay next to it. This is perhaps my favorite anchorage yet, and a stark contrast to the crowded scene at Black Point Settlement.

In the morning, I move into what I hope to be slightly deeper water, but unfortunately, more into the wind. I am very disappointed when we still bump the bottom at low tide.

I row ashore, determined to hike on the island, explore the caves I can see from the water, and search for hidden pirate treasure, as I often do. I have to climb the rocks to get onto the island, and penetrating the vegetation on top is difficult. The rocks that make up the island, as they are in most places in The Bahamas, are so sharp and jagged that I can scarcely imagine even the goats walking around barefoot. The island is full of caves, and must be completely hollow, like Swiss cheese. I don't find any treasure, but I do come across a stone wall, clearly made by man. I follow it to three primitive foundations of stone walls and one that even employs concrete. I imagine that the goats came from the original settlement. Even with goats, this looks like a lonely place to live.

When I get back to *Windflower*, I am hot and hungry, so I get right at spearfishing. Almost as soon as I get in the water, I see an enormous lobster slowly crawling out from under one of the big rocks. I hit it with the spear, but it gets away. I follow it, take another shot, but this time the spear just glances off the old warrior's back. It swims away under the rocks, but all I have to do is swim around to the other side of the rock. This time I shoot it directly in the face, and my spear goes longwise through its entire body, emerging at the end of the tail.

I cook the big lobster with sautéed onion and green tomato, served over lettuce, and it is as delicious as it sounds.

A meal on a stick

The roots of a tree form a spiral in this cave in Little Galliot Cay.

I like it here, at Little Galliot Cay
No other boats near, nor the rough windy sea
The water is smooth, and the brightest of blue
The anchorage I choose, to make dreams come true

After bouncing off the bottom every low tide for two days, I am ready to move on. Cat Island is less than a day away, and I could be there by late tonight. I could visit the Fernandez Cays at Cat Island, then sail to Conception Island when conditions allow. Conception Island is among the most beautiful places I've ever been. It's a magnificent island full of natural beauty, unfished coral reefs, and tropicbirds flying overhead with their long white tails trailing behind.

I begin to prepare to leave. High tide is in three hours and I need to wait until then, as Galliot Cut has a very strong tidal current. I remember when I came in two years ago it was like a river, with eddies on the edges and waves in the middle.

As I ready *Windflower* for the journey, I remember that Pete and Tracey might be passing by this morning and therefore might stop by for a visit. My AIS is already on, and I switch on the chartplotter to see if I can locate their boat. As I step out into the cockpit, I see a sailboat motoring close by, an aluminum boat, flying the OCC burgee. It's them!

They anchor next to me and I row over for a coffee and a chat. We both are interested in sailing to Nova Scotia and Bras D'Or Lake, then Newfoundland, and then the Azores this summer, so we have much to talk about. Pete has been anchored in this area recently and tells me about snorkeling a nearby wreck and a big barracuda that followed him around there.

After listening to his description of snorkeling Galliot Cut, which is on my mind already, I start to think about staying longer. He also tells of an encounter with a bull shark at Rudder Cut Cay. He saw the shark while snorkeling, but it was moving slowly and swam away, so Pete stayed in the water. But moments later, it swam very close beneath him, from behind, almost bumping him, moving in a quick and nervous manner, jerking one way and then the other.

"That's when you get out of the water," I say.

"I came out like a Trident missile!" Pete says. But as he went to pull up the dinghy's anchor, it was stuck. He had to get back in, swim down and retrieve it. Safely back onboard, he started the engine, but it stopped. He started it again, and it stopped again. He looked at the anchor line, and saw it was wrapped up in the propeller, and he was drifting into a rocky wall washed with waves. Pete took up the oars and rowed back under human power.

After they leave, I pull up my two anchors and start off for Cat Island. I will probably arrive at night, but that should not be a problem, as there are virtually no obstacles on the approach. I look forward to sailing for the rest of the day. Cat Island, here we come!

Moments later, as we motor out of the little shallow anchorage, and pass Big Galliot Cay, and see Tiny Galliot Cay ahead, I think about how nice it would be if we were already at our destination.

I could dive in Galliot Cut between tides, and sail to Tiny Galliot Cay to snorkel the reef I read about. The wind is not ideal for anchoring at Big Galliot Cay, but it is supposed to die down tonight and move to a more favorable direction (east) in the coming days.

I do an about-face and pull in to the anchorage, drive around surveying the depth, then drop the Vulcan.

Location: 23.9241º N, 76.2896º W

I let out an extra 50' of anchor line, intending to drop the Fortress downwind and then pull back the 50'. The changing tidal current in this area will pull one way and then the other twice a day. But as I try to position myself for the second anchor, *Windflower* just sits right above the Vulcan. Wind and tide are in opposition and I have to use the engine to move us to a decent spot to drop the Fortress. As I am dealing with the anchors, I notice a long and slender grey shape following us around underwater, sure to be a barracuda.

With the anchors down, I need to swim and check that they are set, barracuda or not. I am almost surrounded by shallow water, and I am going to rely on the two anchors holding properly through the tidal shifts in the coming days.

Sure enough, a four-foot barracuda is waiting for me when I get in, and is directly between me and the Fortress, which I can clearly see is not set. But as I swim toward the anchor, the big fish moves on and keeps his distance. He is a friendly barracuda, thankfully, not at all like the aggressive one at Little Galliot Cay.

I push the Fortress into the somewhat hard bottom, then check on the Vulcan, which is set in the sand already.

I snorkel around the anchorage and see a lot of fish, but return empty-handed. The GoPro video camera is not charging the battery, so I can't get any underwater video or pictures either.

Once again, the following day, I think I will leave for Cat Island and Conception Island, as soon as the tide starts going out, so I have plenty of time to row to the island and hike across on a trail I saw on the electronic chart.

After landing *Little Flower* on a beautiful and tiny beach, I walk up and over a little hill, across grey rocks and through short and dense vegetation, shrubbery with dark green leaves and stiff branches. As I cross over the top of the island, the dark blue water of Exuma Sound comes into view, followed by a massive rock that emerges straight up out of the water to the right. Below it the tide rushes in like a river, with the current quite visible. When I reach the rocky shore, I turn to the right and hike around the island across impossibly jagged and sharp rocks. I wear boots for this, and any other footwear would have had me turning back for the trail.

Along the way I pick up two purple sea fans, washed up on the beach, and a few pieces of bright white sun-bleached coral, about the size of paper weights. I also dig up a bag of soil for my aloe vera plant, which I had with me last time in The Bahamas. I took this plant from my former house in St Augustine and used nearly all of it for sunburns on my Ragged Islands journey. While at anchor off Long Island, the plant fell into the water and remained on the bottom for an hour. I eventually retrieved it, but didn't expect it to live. Yet live it did, and two years later it is ready for more soil.

Back onboard, with the tide changing in an hour, I think, why not go for an adventure right here, instead of sailing all day to another island. There's still more to see here, so what's the point of sailing away?

I rig the sail on *Little Flower* and set off for Tiny Galliot Cay on a close reach. It's about a half mile away across dark blue open water. When we get there, I have to tack a few times to keep from getting sucked around the island by the tidal current. I anchor in front of the island, on the east side, facing the cut, still in the incoming current.

I put on my mask, snorkel, weight belt, long fins, stick the flashlight in my wetsuit, and slip over the transom with spear in hand. The reef is blissful, stretching off into the distance, beyond my sight, silent, awe-inspiring, majestic. Out here, in front of this tiny island, right in front of a cut, and with open water all around, I am immersed in wilderness, and although I am on the lookout for sharks, I welcome Mother Nature's embrace.

Pete's shark story is still fresh in my mind, and I keep *Little Flower's* painter in hand.

Right away, under a patch of lobed star coral, I see a big grouper, so big that I wonder if I could eat it in one sitting (since I don't have a refrigerator). I swim down for a closer look. The fish is calm and looking right at me, making clear eye-contact. We share a moment, me and this fish, and I decide to let it live, for now anyway.

The current is strong, so I carefully pick up the anchor and drift toward a large shallow reef that I avoided while tacking up the current earlier. I find it to be an elkhorn reef, all full of caves and crevices, and teeming with fish. Much of the elkhorn is dead, but I also see healthy young elkhorn, which is encouraging. I swim all around the reef, admiring all the creatures that live here, and excited to see many large stoplight parrotfish. These goofy-looking fish are bright green and get their name from a vibrant yellow patch on their tail (the caudal peduncle, actually).

After swimming and drifting across the reefs in front of Tiny Galliot Cay, I climb aboard my little sailboat, hoist the sail, and set off for Little Galliot Cay, where I know I can find some lobster, snapper, and maybe even a grouper.

We sail downwind across the open water between the islands, and I crouch low as *Little Flower* rolls back and forth. We gybe, then round the island and sail right back to the spot I fished two days prior.

The rocks along the shore are as full of fish as they were before, and it isn't long before I have a small grouper and a lobster in the boat.

I sail back to Big Galliot Cay, having circumnavigated Tiny Galliot Cay and Little Galliot Cay, and find that I now have neighbors. Three more sailboats are in the anchorage. I tack through the boats, waving as I pass, and clumsily run right into *Windflower*, literally.

I fillet the grouper and toss the body into the water, expecting the friendly barracuda to be there, since it has been hanging about in the shadow of my boat. The big fish does not disappoint and cuts the grouper right in half with one bite, swallowing one piece and letting the other drift. I have heard this is how they eat, but have never seen it in action. The barracuda turns around and picks up the other half of the fish and swallows it too. I clean the lobster and throw it overboard and the barracuda investigates, but is not as excited by the lobster head as it was with the grouper, probably because I kept the only part worth eating.

Pete told me of a way to easily remove the digestive tract from the tail. I break off an antenna, then push it up through the anus and all the way through the tail, and the tail is easily cleaned. This is something I have never done, and I do it with every lobster I get from this point on.

I have another big fresh seafood lunch, rice and beans with lobster and grouper, all cooked in one pot, all eaten by one man. Life is good, and adventure was right here; I didn't have to move the big boat. The meal is a fine reward for slowing down and staying put.

The last time I was in The Bahamas, I felt the need to keep moving from island to island almost every day, like a dog peeing on as many bushes as possible, marking and claiming territory. This time I want to dig deeper and get to know places a bit more. It is becoming clear to me that when adventure is close to home, there is no need to go looking for it elsewhere.

My thoughts the next morning are of Hatchet Bay and catching the next swell, which should be arriving in about a week. I think I might sail north to more islands in the Exumas, then cross to Eleuthera on Wednesday and be in Hatchet Bay by Thursday. But for today, I decide there is still more to explore before leaving, and the reef calls to me like a lover. I must snorkel the cut between Big Galliot Cay and Big Farmers Cay before leaving this place, so I load and rig *Little Flower* and sail away to the north.

I sail by a sailboat that has just come in and invite the skipper to join me.

"Hello, would you like to come spearfishing with me?"

"What?" he replies in a foreign accent.

"I'm going spearfishing, wanna come along?"

"What?"

"Do you snorkel?" I ask while showing him my mask.

"No. Nice dinghy!"

I thank him for the compliment and continue my short journey into the next cove. *Little Flower* tacks upwind and up current until we are at the head of the cut, where I toss out the little grappling anchor.

We drift for a moment, then she comes to a halt and spins to face up current. The anchor holds, and I suit up and slip quietly off the transom, keeping one hand on the boat just in case the current is too strong for me. I am stunned by what I see. The water is deep and clear and I feel like I am inside a magical gemstone, a living sapphire. All around me is bright blue and below is the surface of another planet, populated with aliens in all manner of colors and shapes.

I look around for sharks, and seeing none, I move forward and hold the painter/anchor line, staring at the bottom as I get ready for the first dive.

Deep blue water moves swiftly by and the coral all over the bottom captivates me as I lay on the surface like a flag in the wind. It is gorgeous. I take as deep a breath as I can and swim down. I have to fight the current on the way down, but I hold the anchor line to help.

When I reach the bottom, I pick up the little anchor and we start drifting quickly downstream, as the tide is on its last hour of incoming. The water gets deeper, and I see some ledges ahead. I set the anchor and surface, where I rest and breathe, still holding on to the thin black line.

After catching my breath, I breathe in slowly for four

seconds, then slowly exhale for eight. I do this ten times and keep track with my fingers. Then I take as deep a breath as I can, and swim down. Having to fight the current takes a lot of energy, so even at only 25 feet down, I can't stay more than maybe ten or twenty seconds. I see a grouper, surface, and watch it. I dive again, approaching it from directly above hoping it won't see me, and take a shot. I hit it in the upper back, but it gets free and swims away. I pull up the anchor and drift off, criticizing myself for injuring a fish and not getting it.

The reef continues and becomes more dense and interesting as we drift. Patches of lobed star coral cover the bottom, with soft corals that look like little trees and fans in between. Fish are everywhere. I see another grouper, much bigger this time, and watch it while breathing on the surface, but it swims far away and disappears. He knows why I am here.

I spot another one, probably small, but it's hard to tell from fifteen feet above. I swim down and get him, and within moments I am at the dinghy. But as soon as I have him out of the water, I see how small he really is. I figure he is mortally wounded anyway, and has more meat than a can of tuna, so into the boat he goes.

I swim to the end of the cut, then towards the shore where the water is much shallower, and here I find an eddy, which allows me to swim, towing *Little Flower* behind, back up the cut. When I get back to the deeper water, I notice a large barracuda nearby. I don't want to spear anything with this fish in eyesight, because I have heard that barracuda sometimes try to steal a spearfisher's catch, and might bite the person by mistake. They hunt by bolting extremely fast, like a missile, at their prey, which they cut in two on impact with their sharp mouths. I heard one story of a man who had just speared a fish and was putting it in his dinghy when a barracuda hit his leg and tore off the entire calf muscle. He quit spearfishing for good after that. Then Kathi, from *Makani*, told me of spearing a fish, and before she got it to the dinghy, a barracuda hit the fish on the end of her spear so hard that it nearly broke her wrist.

I swim toward the barracuda and it slowly swims away.

Soon after, I see a school of snapper, and some are big. I follow them. Luckily the tidal current is decreasing, as it is near slack tide, and I'm able to get near them without working too hard. When some of the stragglers of the school are below me, I swim down, slowly, and approach one from behind. We are in about 25' of water and maybe 10' off the bottom. The fish turns to look at me, and I release the pole spear, hitting it in the back. The fish jerks and wiggles with everything it has, which is the sort of movement that attracts sharks and barracuda, and it gets off the spear. Confident that the barracuda I saw, and maybe a massive angry bull shark, is coming right away, I start for the surface, accepting the loss of the fish. But the fish swims in a death spiral, and I turn back, take another shot, and the spear passes through its gills.

This area, in between Big Farmers Cay and Big Galliot Cay, is labeled as an anchorage on Navionics charts, but the bottom is covered in coral reef. Anchoring directly on a coral reef is a very bad idea, both because it destroys the coral and risks trapping the anchor forever. Just west of the cut is sand, so if you anchor in this area, make absolutely certain that the bottom is sand and that your rode will neither foul on coral nor sweep across juvenile coral.

Back onboard, I get ready to clean the fish, but the little grouper is still alive and the snapper is big enough for a full meal. The grouper has been in the shade under a seat in the dinghy, and the water in the bottom probably kept him alive, so, I think, why not let this little guy live? "Good luck," I wish the fish, and toss him in the water. But luck is not with the little fish, as the four-foot barracuda emerges from under *Windflower* and swiftly cuts the grouper in two, gobbles up half the fish, then turns around and swallows the other half.

I suddenly feel very foolish.

I identify the snapper as a mutton snapper, with its

reddish fins, a black spot on the back about the size of its eye, pointed anal fin, blue stripe under its mouth, and orange or red eyes. I was worried that it might be a dog snapper, because I remember from college that they might carry ciguatera. The dog snapper has a row of blue dots under the eye, but not the red fins, spot, or red eyes.

I fillet the snapper and toss the carcass to the barracuda, who is getting fatter.

Again, I am glad to have stayed here another day. The message is getting clear: Take it easy on the passage-making and seek adventure close by; there's no need to travel when what I seek is all around me; slow down and look around; experience what the area I am already in has to offer before moving on. There is no rush, none at all. Live in the moment, especially when the moment is this good.

Every moment in The Bahamas is so good that I find myself questioning the reality of my situation, like everything might be a dream and I will wake up back in my old house in St Augustine any minute.

In the late afternoon, I sit reading "The Unlikely Voyage of Jack de Crow" by A J Mackinnon, a fabulous book that relies not on the adventure, but rather the quality of the writing, something I aspire to. A gentle breeze blows off the land and the air is clean and smells of nothing. My sinuses are clearer than they ever are back in the United States, where pollen and dust and various allergens constantly assault my immune system. A few songbirds sing on the island and quiet fans hum below in the cabin. Occasionally water sloshes or gurgles against the island 150 yards away.

I am anchored next to Big Galliot Cay and sit in the cockpit taking it all in. Big Galliot Cay rises vertically from the blue water as jagged grey and brown rock. The tide is low and the lower four feet of the island is undercut by the water, creating an overhang. At low tide, one could not climb out of the water onto the island. A dark grey line depicts the high-water mark. Above the rocks, halfway up, grey-green shrubs eek out a living, and above, short windblown trees with dark green leaves grow close together, like an endless hedge. A small cove boasts the only sandy beach in view, and there one could take a dinghy ashore, while the rest of the island is unwelcoming.

To the south, beyond the narrow Galliot Cut, is Cave Cay, and to the north is Big Farmers Cay. Little Galliot Cay is to the west, and Tiny Galliot Cay sits opposite the cut to the south. This little trio of islands has kept me interested for six days.

I emerge from the salon after dinner to find a charming and small cutter with a long bowsprit and round portlights anchored near me. A modern Beneteau sits to the north, belonging to the man with the foreign accent who did not snorkel but admired *Little Flower*.

The sun sets over Little Galliot Cay and a line of bright yellow sunlight points from me to the sun. The horizon turns pink and the breeze sings faintly as it blows through the aluminum tubes that make up the solar-panel arch. The sun drops onto the island and the few clouds in the pale blue sky turn orange, and as the sun dips below the island, warm colors spread out before fading away.

Windflower *and* Little Flower *at Big Galliot Cay*

mutton snapper speared in the cut between Big Galliot Cay and Big Farmers Cay

Another cold front is coming, and Hatchet Bay is calling me back. I look forward to the safe and peaceful anchorage, and to more surfing. I pull up the two anchors and motor out of Big Galliot Cay, scraping the bottom as I do.

After carefully motoring through the narrow channel to the deeper water to the west, I set sail and put us on a broad reach. *Windflower* jumps at the occasion and accelerates to 7 knots. The sun shines happily, the water glows in a bright shade of sapphire blue, and the wind blows perfectly. This is truly the best of sailing, care-free and fun, with another island anchorage on the way.

Unfortunately, the autopilot, which has been intermittently shutting itself off, turns off for good. I still have the wheel pilot that came with the boat, and am reminded of the principle of having a backup for everything important. I find myself to be very glad I didn't remove the wheel pilot after installing the below-deck autopilot back at the York River Yacht Haven in Virginia.

I sail past Black Point Settlement and Staniel Cay to the west side of Pipe Cay.

Location: 24.2386º N, 76.5209º W

After dropping the hook and the customary inspection of the anchor, I swim under the keel to have a look, since I have not done so since bouncing on the bottom at Little Galliot Cay. I am dismayed to see what looks like a seam has opened up in the center of the keel, running longwise most of its length. This is going to take some thought, and I go ahead and row to a nearby rock for some uneventful and uninspiring spearfishing.

Back at the boat, it is time for some autopilot troubleshooting. After determining that power is being supplied to the black box that powers the autopilot, I open it up. Looking inside, I can see where it looks like a short has burned one of the components, but that is as far as my almost non-existent electrical skills take me. I contact the company, and am led through some troubleshooting, and it is determined that I need a new black box, which will be shipped to a friend in St Augustine, Florida.

I am depressed, and my sailboat simply feels like a collection of things that will all eventually break.

The next morning, I sail out through Conch Cut and aim for Little San Salvador Island. But the wind is not quite right, and I can't point high enough to aim at the island, so I change plan and change course and aim instead for Cape Eleuthera.

Since we are on a close reach, I am able to lock off the wheel and let *Windflower* tend to herself while I enjoy the view of dark and deep blue water.

The sail is fine, and I anchor just south of where I anchored at Cape Eleuthera two weeks before, but this time, I find better sand for the Vulcan.

Location: 24.8319º N, 76.3480º W

RETURN TO HATCHET BAY

I like big waves, and small waves too
choppy or glassy, either will do
Barrels are fun, to get inside
shade from the sun, watery slide
A pair of baggies, when it's warm
a springsuit, a fullsuit, to adorn
Whatever the temp, I'm happy to go
I'll paddle out, if you say so
Reef or sand, point or beach
step off the land, the waves to reach
I've got a gun, for when its large
a groveler too, small waves to charge
Longboards are easy, like ringing a bell
shortboards can duck, under the swell
Girls on the sand, in little bikinis
skin getting tan, I sure hope they see me
getting a tube, or hitting the lip
they're not even looking, at my head dip
I like to carve, I like to cruise
wipeouts are cool, might get a bruise
It's fun to surf, in new places
drawing curves, on glassy faces
I like big waves, medium and small
riding all day, getting the call

now is the time, with a chick or a bro
surfing is fine, even solo

As the tide drops, I pay close attention to the depth, but in the evening, when I turn on the chartplotter to check the depth, all I get is an error message reading "Update procedure failed, please try update again." I wasn't even trying to update it. I need the chartplotter, and seeing it not working is extremely frustrating.

I find that I can get the depth to show on the Triton display, which I normally use for wind information, and I can use my phone to navigate, but not having the chartplotter will be a serious handicap.

I wake the next morning feeling down, because of the technical and mechanical problems with my boat, but probably also for having left the beautiful and bountiful Exumas, and for the disappointing snorkel the day before. It is clear that my mood is dependent on quality snorkeling and nice weather, but I'm only human.

I need to wait for the tide to come in before going through the Davis Channel, so I figure I will go spearfishing. It's bound to be good around here with deep water right next to the reefs along Eleuthera, but of course, this is also excellent shark habitat. Regardless, the water calls to me and I do not resist.

Three Point cove is just south of me, and I explore it to see if it could be a viable anchorage, since it is labeled as such on the charts, and the only protected cove in the area.

The water in the cove is dark and cloudy, and while entering the cove was easy in a small rowboat, it looks impossible in *Windflower*. Perhaps a shoal draft boat could get in at high tide, but even then, many reefs would have to be carefully dodged.

Outside the cove and upwind of *Windflower*, I row out until I see a dark line underwater. I get in the clear water between land and Chub Rock, an emergent rock 1000 feet from the shore, to see if I can find lunch. The water is only about six feet deep and the bottom is covered in rock and patchy reef.

I look under overhangs hoping to find lobster. The only sharks I have yet seen were here, two weeks ago, so I am wary and hope for lobster over fish because lobsters don't bleed and thus don't attract sharks quite as much as a fish. Perhaps this is wishful thinking, but it gives me comfort, so I hang on to the thought.

The ledge leads out to water about ten feet deep and the abundance of coral and fish increases. Along with blue tang and various grunts, I spy a beautiful queen triggerfish, edible but too pretty and iconic for me to shoot; a queen trigger adorns the cover of my Peterson field guide to tropical fish, a book I have had since college.

The ledge leads me out towards Chub Rock, and when it ends I cross a lone rocky patch towards another reef to the right. All the while, I tow *Little Flower* along by her painter, which is looped over my wrist. In the area between the reefs swims a school of margate snapper, and I do my best to follow without looking like I'm interested in them, but they keep just out of range while I drift slowly away from land, pulled by *Little Flower* who is being pushed by the breeze. I swim back upstream and drift over the reef again, and a third time I drift through the area between the reefs, stalking the snapper.

One fish strays from the pack and I move between the fish and its school. I get close and take a shot. The spear hits but does not penetrate past the barb and the fish gets away.

I'm keeping a vigilant lookout for sharks and now there is an injured fish in the water, which worries me, but I am determined to eat fresh fish for lunch and continue.

I let the dinghy pull me further downwind and move to

the other reef. The abundance of life is impressive. Hard and soft corals cover the bottom, fish of all sorts swim everywhere I look. I follow another school of snapper, then see two larger ones on the edge of the school, and I swim between them and the rest of the fish, separating them from their brethren. I get closer and closer, and the fish tries to rejoin the school, swimming past me, exposing its flank. I take a shot, and the spear hits, but the fish flails and gets away, then quickly swims under a rock. My first instinct is to leave the area. Surely, I think, a shark has been watching me the whole time and will soon be on the scene, agitated and excited by the presence of a wounded fish. But I both want the fish for lunch and feel a responsibility to take the fish, since I shot it, so I swim down to the rock and spear it again, then grab it by the tail and extract it from under the rock.

Quickly, I swim to *Little Flower*, toss the spear and fish in the boat, and climb aboard. It is done!

The snapper makes a delicious lunch cooked in one pot with a can of turnip greens.

I still have time to kill before the tide starts coming in, so I decide to make an effort to fix the chartplotter. I try various combinations of turning it on and off, once while holding the power button down with a boat hook. Finally, I post a question about it on the Bluewater Sailors Facebook group. The advice to simply call B&G comes back and I feel foolish for not having done this first.

I order one day of high-speed internet on my phone, find the contact number for B&G, and finally make the call. It isn't long before the technician on the other end emails me the latest update for the chartplotter, which I download onto a micro SD card. I put this card in the chartplotter, turn it on, the device updates itself without any prompt from me. Astounding! How it is that the information to fix my broken chartplotter could travel by some invisible means onto a card in my computer and be transferred onto my chartplotter is beyond me. Sometimes modern technology is simply magical.

As I motor away from the anchorage, I get a call from the only other boat anchored nearby. The skipper of *Bow Tied* asks about the channel and how deep my draft is. They draw a bit more than me and I say I don't think they will have a problem. Little do I know, I have just made two new friends. That's about all it takes in the cruising community, just a bit of communication, and we feel like we know each other.

I watch the depth carefully, and most of the channel is 15 feet deep, but I see a moment of 9 feet near the end.

I sail on a beam reach at 6.5 to 7.5 knots for two more hours, using the Raymarine wheel pilot when I need it, and anchor in Ten Bay.

Location: 25.1196º N, 76.1553º W

When I dive on the anchor, I see that it's chain is resting against a small coral head, so I pick the anchor up and walk it across the bottom about twenty feet and dig it back in.

In the morning, I set out early and sail on a broad reach at 4.5 knots in 10 knots of gentle breeze. I stop at Lionfish Rock, just north of Alabaster Point for a bit of spearfishing, but the visibility is very poor. The bottom in this area is a fine silt and this makes the water cloudy. I see some lionfish, but after hearing of how painful the stings are, I opt not to shoot any.

My friend who poached the lobster at the Sunken Aircraft told me that she was once stung by a lionfish. She said "I've had two children by natural childbirth, and the lionfish sting was more painful." That was all I needed to hear.

I sail on to Hatchet Bay and anchor in the same place I was two weeks prior, then load my spearfishing gear in *Little Flower*. I row out into the cut and search for lunch while towing the dinghy around by the painter. When I am diving only yards north of the cut, the big ferry comes through on the way out, surprising me, and I am thankful not to have been in the way. I need to pay closer attention.

Fish are all over the area, and I shoot at a big margate snapper in the cut that would have made a fine meal, but I miss. Two black grouper show themselves, but they are both quite wary of my intentions and dart away. French angelfish are not scared of me at all and swim out to get a close look at the human intruder. Quite a few times, I follow a fish that I want to spear under a ledge or into a cave and a French angelfish pops out and blocks my progress, as if protecting the fish I was after, running interference. Porcupine pufferfish do this too, blocking little cave entrances with their long bodies.

A hogfish too small to kill swims within range and I let it live. Beautiful stoplight parrotfish swim about, and I could spear them too, but I don't kill parrotfish, because they help the coral survive, and coral needs all the help it can get these days. They are also another species that is too pretty for me to kill. A school of spadefish swim in the cut, but I don't know if they carry ciguatera or not. I later find out that they are fine to eat, but I never get one. I also see a queen parrotfish, a pair of porkfish, and a few yellow jack.

In the morning, a dinghy motors over with two young guys and they introduce themselves as Will and Grey.

"We're from *Bow Tied*, the other boat at Cape Eleuthera. We called and asked you about Davis Channel."

"Oh yeah, right. I called back to report the depth but didn't get answer."

"Yeah, sorry about that, we went spearfishing after we talked."

I go on to tell them about the snapper I got, and they tell me about the spot they fished. I tell them about spearfishing outside Hatchet Bay, and they say they will come pick me up tomorrow to go spearfishing from their dinghy, which is a nice rigid inflatable with an aluminum bottom and a powerful engine.

I'm learning that making friends while sailing is this easy. Although we only spoke once on the VHF, seeing each other in the same anchorage afterwards is worthy of stopping by to say hello, and stopping by to say hello is all it takes to cement a friendship out here.

I set out for Surfer's Beach and while rowing to the boat ramp, I notice a boat from St Augustine (my hometown), a beautiful Downeaster 38, *Windsong*. A young man with a red beard is reclining on deck reading a book. I meet Erick, who is also a surfer and a freediver, and I tell him I'll bring back a surf report when I return.

The surf is shoulder high and the wind is onshore, so the conditions are far from good, but I satisfy a craving to surf. I get a ride back with a rough looking black Bahamian with dreadlocks who never says a word, but just nods whenever I say anything. He has the radio cranked up, which is playing a recording of a DJ playing to a live crowd who cuts the music and barks something in a loud gravely voice every 3-6 seconds. I am counting. Most of what the DJ says is indecipherable, but I do catch "Throw your hands in the air if you love reggae music!" and, perhaps not getting the desired response from the crowd, "Throw your hands in the air if you're STD free!"

I row by and tell Erick about the surf, then I go spearfishing in the cut again. I see the same two black grouper, and again they avoid me. Big snapper also keep their distance, but some small mackerel swim with me. At one point, I turn around and three barracuda are following me, but they swim away when I look at them.

Back at the boat, since I am already in dive gear, I scrape the bottom of the keel and apply underwater epoxy to the damaged areas, just in case water is getting in.

The next two days are days with neither waves to surf nor good conditions for spearfishing, although I try the latter. But days like these are good days to write, and this is how I spend most of my time, trying to earn the only living that will keep the dream alive. I also finish the book "Three Years Among the Comanches" by Nelson Lee, which is a fantastic nonfiction story about a cowboy who was captured by Indians. He lived with them for three years before making a daring escape through the deserts and mountains of the southwest.

February 23rd is my four-year anniversary for quitting smoking marijuana. Without having quit smoking, I would not be in The Bahamas, or anywhere else on a sailboat. I wouldn't have had the money or the time. The sun is out for the first time in two days, and, of course, I want to go spearfishing.

After filling up water jerry cans on shore, I sail *Little Flower* over to *Bow Tied* and rouse Grey and Will. They come by *Windflower* twenty minutes later and pick me up in their dinghy and we zoom out of Hatchet Bay, turn right, and speed another mile along the cliffs before dropping anchor.

While I love my little sailing and rowing dinghy, this is a real luxury to be able to cover so much distance so fast, and without any effort. However, I have to get used to spearfishing with the dinghy anchored away from the rocks. While I always tow my fiberglass dinghy around and keep it near me, almost everyone else has an inflatable dinghy. These are vulnerable to punctures from the rocks around which we usually spearfish, so the dinghies are always anchored well away. This means that after spearing a fish, one has to swim all the way back to the dinghy while the fish bleeds and thrashes, presumably attracting sharks. However, diving with two other people gives me extra courage, and I get used to spearfishing away from the dinghy.

We dive on six different spots, all chosen by looking for emergent rocks. The water is about twenty feet deep and the large rocks provide plenty of habitat for a wide variety of sea life. Some even have swim-through caves, but at one point my face brushes against something that stings me. There are various creatures on reefs that will sting anyone careless enough to touch them: fire coral, hydras, fire worms, lionfish, scorpionfish, stingrays, sea urchins, and others.

The best course of action is to not touch anything on a reef and to swim in such a way as to not ever brush up against anything; look but don't touch. Another reason not to touch is that coral is very delicate and simply touching coral can kill it. While it looks like a living rock, it is only the surface that is covered with very small animals related to jellyfish and they can easily be crushed. Again, coral should not be touched.

I shoot at a lot of fish, all either grouper or snapper, and end the day with a grouper and a small margate snapper that just swam right in front of my spear.

Grey spears two spider crabs, and gives one to me when we part. I passed by the spider crabs until a local who gave me a ride to the beach tells me the crabs are worth spearing, and I still passed them up until today. They are literally the ugliest creatures in the water, and do not look like something I want to eat, or even handle. These crabs are drab grey and have huge claws on long arms, claws that look like they could snap off a finger. But the truth is, they taste as good as any other crab.

The crabs live under rocks and in caves, and it requires a lot of peering in small dark spaces with a flashlight to find them. While doing this, it is important to watch out for lionfish, because they live in these places too, and they sit still and stick out their poisonous spines when they feel threatened. Should you take a spine to the face, I'm sure it would ruin more than your day.

The crabs also hold on to the rocks with all eight of their legs when they are speared, and it's sometimes hard to pull them out of their hole. Sometimes they hold on so tight that the spear comes out without them. Other times I have to leave the spear in the crab and surface to breathe before returning to the fight.

the mighty Bahamian spider crab

At this point in my trip, I've heard of at least five pointbreaks in the area, but have only surfed one. Erick and his wife Jennifer, from *Windsong*, and I talk about going to James Point to surf. None of us have been there before, but we heard it was a good pointbreak, especially when the wind is south. A day comes with conditions that we think will favor this break, and the decision is made to go. We decide that we might have better luck hitchhiking if we go separately, since three of us together, all with surfboards, might not be able to get a ride.

I set out first, hiking south from Hatchet Bay. I walk a long way, perhaps for 45 minutes. At one point a small car passes with two surfboards sticking out of the windows. The car slows down, but keeps going. Soon after, a pickup truck stops and gives me a ride. We see Erick and Jennifer walking and the driver stops and picks them up. They get in the back and laugh and tell me that they were in the small car that passed me and wanted to stop, but the driver didn't think they had any more room.

The truck takes us out of his way to the beginning of the dirt road leading to James Point, and we walk for the next half hour to the point. On the way there, we pass a house and outside a man is working on his truck.

"Y'all be careful out there," he warns us, "be careful of the waves and the sharks."

"Now, what kind of sharks are we talking about?" Jennifer says.

"Hammer," he says.

"So the point has its resident shark?"

"Yes," the man says as he looks at us and nods his head ominously.

We hike on past a brown salt pond with white foam blowing across the surface, piling up on the edges. A white, broken-down, Jeep Cherokee sits beside the road, long abandoned. Finally, we emerge from the bush and behold a small cove with a rocky beach and a wave breaking over a left point. There is no obvious way in or out of the water, except across the rocks. The sun is obscured by clouds and the water is grey and dark. Nobody else is here. It looks surfable but sketchy to me, and we decide to keep looking.

There is another larger cove to the right, and we stare at this for a while, not sure which cove is the one people surf, but the waves in this cove do not look as good, and we return to the first cove.

Erick and I paddle out and Jennifer stays on the beach and takes photos while we surf. When we first get out, I swim to the bottom and feel it with my hand. It is the same jagged rock often found on land that is hard to walk on while wearing shoes, and impossible to walk on barefoot. This makes me nervous, as does the fact that we are at a new spot, have been warned about sharks, nobody else is out, and we might not even be in the right cove.

Erick catches about four waves before I get my first. I surf very conservatively, but catch a few fun waves before going in and scrambling across the slippery rocks that make up the shore. Returning to dry land is a relief. The place sketches me out.

me (left) and Erick at James Point

We stick around to see if the waves in the other cove improve with the outgoing tide, and I walk to the far end of the point, but the waves over there are even smaller. Looking back, I see a small truck has pulled up to the point.

I walk back and introduce myself to Dennis and his son Riley, from Long Island. I've seen them before at Surfer's Beach. Today is their last day in The Bahamas and we all decide to paddle out at the same spot Erick and I surfed. This session is much more fun. With two more people, it is easier to figure out where the lineup is, although it's shifty, and the sun comes out, which changes the whole feel of the setting.

A family from the Outer Banks, who gave me a ride home from Surfer's Beach weeks ago, shows up, and Jennifer joins us too, and we all have a great session. Dennis gives the three of us a ride all the way back to Hatchet Bay, even though it is miles out of their way, and even though I cut off Dennis on my last wave, which Jennifer tells me about the next day as we walk to Surfer's Beach. I had no idea (sorry Dennis!).

The next day, three of us hitchhike, together this time, and get a ride almost immediately to Surfer's Beach, in a small sedan. The driver is completely unconcerned that all three of us have surfboards. The waves are much better than I expected and I surf two long sessions, catching left after left after left. Erick and I have it to ourselves, but the currents out there are sometimes pulling us out and other times pulling us north. It takes a lot of work to stay in the right place to catch the waves, and the current constantly threatens to pull us onto the reef.

For the third day in a row of surfing, Erick and Jennifer and I walk to the beach at Hatchet Bay, which I walked to on my second day here five weeks prior. Back then it was a cloudy and windy day and the waves were big and unruly. Today, they are shoulder-high and beautiful. The water is clear, the sun is out, and the breeze is offshore. The Outer Banks family is there, but they are getting out of the water when we arrive and then we have it all to ourselves.

I have to go in once to tighten the screws holding my fins in. In the rush to go surfing, I guess I didn't tighten them enough. I get out a second time and put on my mask and snorkel, then swim back out to the reef. I watch from underwater as Erick catches waves. The speed is impressive, especially after the bottom turn, during which the board takes off like a rocket.

It is a feast of waves, and Erick and I both get barrels. He even comes out of one.

Long walk to the beach, surfboard in hand
New friends and I seek, edge of Island
Right point over rock, sculpts waves in water clear
Bright sun is our clock, no other people near
Waves to ourselves, too many to count
Peel over rock shelves, like one endless fount
We feast on the waves, like endless buffet
The barrels we crave, on this perfect day
But to get inside, a hollow tube
Over the shallows slide, daredevil dudes
Rocky seafloor, inches below
Charging backdoor, with leash in tow
Lip throws out, on select few
We duck down, take in the view
Spinning world, all of water
Little round door, do not falter
Come out of the barrel, our only wish
Or eject through the back, like darting fish
The bottom of the wave, may drop out of sight
And throw surfing knave, with fearful might
Over the falls, into the shallows
Wave like a wall, bottom like gallows
But if we should be, lucky and brave
We'll come out of the tube, the watery cave
Emerge from the tunnel, wave spitting spray
Flee spinning funnel, on this perfect day
Throw arms in the air, emit joyous yell
Held in the care, of some magic spell

The next morning, February 27, one of the boats in the harbor is dragging anchor, and *Helacious* alerts them to it on the VHF. I met Brian and Helen of *SV Helacious* the day before. I wanted to say hello because I was attracted to the boat, which looked like a custom aluminum high-latitude boat, complete with integral aluminum dodger. I expected to find a crusty and rough singlehander aboard, but was greeted by a friendly and clean man who looks at me and says "Are you Paul?" Of course, this surprises me and makes me smile. He recognizes me from social media. Brian invites me aboard and I admire his Dix 43, which he built himself. It is a truly magnificent boat, like a hand-crafted work of art. It is no surprise when he tells me he used to be a metal sculptor.

SV Helacious
Listen to my interviews with Brian, episode 12 on my podcast: Offshore Sailing and Cruising with Paul Trammell, which can be found at paultrammell.com

In the morning, the cool air of a passing front and the grey, cloudy sky, lit red and orange by the rising sun, greet me as I emerge from the cabin, coffee in hand. The calm harbor is gently rocking and the wind sings its low tune in the masts and rigging of sailboats at anchor like leashed dogs waiting patiently to run.

Other sailors sit in their cockpits, quietly sipping coffee

and dreaming up the day's adventure, or perhaps sitting in still mind. Mornings are tranquil here. No cars rush to work, no dogs bark. Rather I can hear the crowing of a rooster, a seabird's high voice on the wind, and the sound of moving water. Calm is king.

By 11:00pm, the clouds have dissipated and I sail *Little Flower* over to *Windsong* to see if they want to go spearfishing. Jen comes out and tells me Erick is not feeling well, so I tell her she is welcome to meet me out there if she wants to go. I then sail out the bay, turn left, and sail downwind to the cave, where I drop anchor and get in the still water.

On my first dive, a mass of moving silver surprises me as a school of bar jack swims quickly by. On my next dive, I follow a yellowtail snapper around a big rock, but can't catch up to it. On the third dive, I find a cave with three lobster in it. I shoot one and swim back to the dinghy and drop it in, then go back and spear a second lobster. I could quit right now, I think, but I want to keep diving and hunting. I also want a fish.

I see a big grouper in a cave near where the lobster were, and I return to the cave three or four times, finally getting a shot, but it bolts into the cave just in time to dodge my spear.

I pick up the anchor and move further south and find a great rock pile covered in coral. Massive rocks lay piled on each other, fallen from the cliffs that line the island, and they reach almost to the surface, leaving just enough room for me to swim across the top. Orange coral and purple sea fans cover the rocks, especially on top. Most amazing is the large school of minnows, glistening and moving silver in the sunlight, that make the area look like a mirrored illusion.

I expect grouper to be in the area, feeding on the minnows, and I am not disappointed. I swim across the top, then down into a sunlight-filled hole between rocks. At the bottom is a swim-through and in it is a large cave full of fish. A black grouper darts deep into the cave and out of sight. Another black grouper swims off in a different direction. I also see a large schoolmaster snapper, blue tang, stoplight parrotfish, queen angelfish, French angelfish, and another lobster. I want a fish, so I leave the lobster alone, for now.

While exploring between the big rocks and the cliffs, I see two long ladders underwater, which were probably used by locals to access the reefs in the past. I then swim down into another cave and see a huge green moray eel, the largest I've ever seen. It looks about as thick as my thigh. This makes me think about being very careful when poking my head into caves. Morays are not aggressive, but have poor eyesight and might bite out of fear or ignorance. They are known to be fierce when provoked and their jaws are strong enough to crush bone.

I try a few more times for one of the grouper, by laying still on the bottom in the cave, but I never get a shot. I am finding the black grouper to be much more wary of me than the Nassau grouper. I find the lobster again, spear it, and then call it a day.

I sail *Little Flower* all the way back, which requires many tacks. We sail in the light breeze across still water way out away from the cliffs, then back towards them, out again, and back a few times. I have to short-tack upwind and against the outgoing tide inside the narrow cut to get back into the bay, which is both challenging and fun.

Finally I make it back to *Windflower* and eat, with reckless abandon, all three lobster and a large serving of beans and rice. It has been another full day and a reminder of why I am in The Bahamas. I am reminded of all the freediving I did in Florida, and all the training I did in the swimming pool at the marina at Ortega Landing. It is all paying off, and paying off in lobster and adventure.

Again, the lesson of sitting in one place long enough to discover all it has to offer is making itself clear. In this week, I learned of two new pointbreaks to surf, and multiple spearfishing locations. I also made new friends on a few different boats.

In the morning, I row to town to fill two water containers, and have to walk to the far spigot to fill them, since the spigot near the dock is still broken. Carrying two 7-gallon containers of water is very difficult for me, and I have to stop many times on the way back. It certainly is a lot harder than living in a house, I think to myself, but a small price to pay for living on a sailboat and exploring The Bahamas.

I also stop at the grocery while I am in town. It has become obvious that I should never to pass up a chance to buy groceries. However, my self-control is lacking and I buy a sleeve of cookies, and before the day is over, I eat them all. This is a good example of why I can't drink beer or smoke weed anymore.

Later, I row over to *Windsong* to see if they want to go spearfishing. Erick is still sick, but this time, Jennifer wants to go. Cautious, probably overly cautious, about making sure I don't do anything that would make Erick uncomfortable, I tell her I'm looking forward to sailing my dinghy out there, and that we should take two dinghies.

I sail back to *Windflower* and when I see Jennifer coming in her dinghy, I sail out and we both proceed to the rocks where I fished the day before. I'm impressed with Jennifer's spearfishing and freediving ability, and her gear, which is nicer than mine, but also with her adventurous spirit. She is a woman determined to get all out of life that it has to offer, and will not let her gender be an obstacle.

In my efforts to meet people, especially those on interesting boats, I row over to a small green sailboat and introduce myself to the young captain, Elliot, of *Nortena*, a Pearson Triton. Like myself, Elliot is a singlehander, a surfer, and a spearfisher.

Elliot and I have some fine adventures together. The first is a fruitless effort to spearfish outside on a windy day. It is so rough out that we can barely make headway in his little inflatable dinghy, and we have to go to a cove to the south that is protected. Unfortunately, the cove has virtually no fish.

Later that afternoon, while the sun is about two hours from setting, Elliot comes over and hails me. Worn out from the day's adventures, I am napping. I wake up, somewhat dazed, and go up on deck.

"Have you ever surfed James Point?" he asks.

"I have."

"I think the surf might be good there today. I've looked at it on the map and it looks like it's protected from the south wind. Wanna go?"

"I think you're probably right about it being the place to surf today. But it's going to be dark in a couple hours, and James Point is seven miles away. I don't think it's likely we'd get there before dark. I'm worn out anyway."

"Well, I need to surf, so I'm gonna go for it."

"Rock on brother. Good luck."

I don't think it is a good idea, but I didn't want to discourage him either. I picture Elliot hiking out of the woods in the dark, knocking on someone's door, and sleeping on the floor of a stranger's house. When the sun sets later, his dinghy has not returned to *Nortena*, but when I wake up in the morning, I am relieved to see it there.

Later, he comes by to go spearfishing, and tells me the story.

"I got a ride right away from a preacher. I seem to run into preachers every now and then. Anyway, he picked me up in a church van and when I told him where I was going, and that I wasn't sure where it was, he said he'd take me there. He drove me all the way out a long dirt road, through deep mud holes, over rocks, all the way to the beach."

"Damn, that's a score!"

"Right? The sun was already low on the horizon, and he said he'd come back before dark to give me a ride home."

"What? No way!"

"Yeah, for real. I said he didn't need to do that, I'd be alright. But the preacher said that I wouldn't get a ride hitchhiking at night. Anyway, the surf was small, but I got a few waves. I really had to, since it was my birthday."

"Ah, now it makes a little sense. Happy birthday man!"

"Thanks. So anyway, he came back before dark and drove me all the way back here. Unfortunately, I left my water bottle in the van."

On the morning of March 4, while applying a coat of teak oil to all *Windflower's* exterior wood, *Pearl of Penzance* comes into the bay and anchors behind me. I row over to say hi to Pete and Tracey, but Pete is ill. He picked something up on his flight to Finland. I keep my distance. The Corona virus, aka Covid-19, is just starting to circulate in the news as a potential pandemic. I visit with Pete and Tracey from the safety of my dinghy without tying up to their boat. Little do I know, this will become the way we all visit within a month.

Later in the day, Erick and Jen and I hike to the nearby beach for a surf. Elliot is already there, and the three of us enjoy small clean and fun rights.

After the surf, the four of us go spearfishing in the rocks to the right outside the cut. I swim all around, looking under every rock and inside every cave, and remaining wary of lionfish and moray eels.

Under one rock, I spot a huge crab. His claws look big enough to make a sandwich out of each, or to relieve me of a finger. I send my spear right through him. But the crab holds on to the rocks with all of its eight legs, and I cannot pull it out of the rocks before my lungs demand air, so I leave the spear with it and surface to breathe. I go back down and pull on the spear, but, much to my dismay, it comes out without the crab, and I return to the surface again.

I am determined not to kill the crab and lose it, so I go back down a third time. It is no longer under the same rock, so I look all around for an injured crab on the run. It isn't long before I see a big claw sticking out from between two rocks.

That must be it, I think. I can't get to the rest of the

crab, so I grab a hold of the claw, which is a handful, and pull. Out comes the crab and it reaches its other claw for my hand. I have my spear in my other hand, and I am able to use the spear to defend my right hand before the claw gets me. I surface holding both claws in my right hand, my left hand holds the spear, which is between the claws, but the snorkel's mouthpiece separates from the snorkel and I have to swim to the dinghy sticking my head up out of the water to occasionally breathe with both hands full and a big crab that wants to pinch me just once with its huge claws before it dies. It is a struggle, but the crab is worth it. It makes a meal with leftover beans and rice and a can of Rotel.

On March 5th, Erick, Elliot, Jen, and I walk to the beach at Hatchet Bay, hoping for surf, but prepared to snorkel if the surf is flat. The day is hot and we walk down the long road past the power plant, the dump, and through the scrub to the beach. The ocean is calm and the water glassy. Small waves roll in and break in the shallow water. It doesn't look big enough to me, but Erick likes it. I think there is no lower limit to the quality of wave that he is willing to surf. Mike and Annie from *Precocious* are there and Mike says he is going spearfishing on the beach to the south. I met them a few days before at a jam session.

A few days earlier, I hiked along the beach from Hatchet Bay all the way to Surfer's Beach, looking for places to surf. I didn't find any, but I did find an interesting little "beach" within a circular hole in the rocks. Water rushed in and out with the surge through what looked like a cave. I thought it would be fun to swim through the cave into the ocean and snorkel.

I suggest that we hike down the rocky soreline to this little hidden beach and try to swim through. Elliot and Jen are game, so we hike across the jagged rocks around the corner and out of sight.

Closer inspection shows the "cave" to be nothing we can swim through, rather I declare it looks like a good way to get killed, and we move on, looking for a place we might be able to enter the water.

Finally, we find a little patch of sand we can climb down to. The miniature beach is only about twelve feet wide and between rocks where the waves wash in, but it looks possible to access the water somewhat safely. Jen wants to go, so, we put on our masks and carefully walk into the water, timing the waves and entering between sets.

The water is perfectly clear, but the bottom is somewhat uninteresting, just lines of rock with sand in the valleys between. But Jen keeps swimming further out and I follow, clearly more timid but not willing to let her swim off by herself. I keep thinking she will stop and we'll return to the beach, but she just keeps on swimming further out. The water is incredibly clear, but I am convinced we'll see a big shark any minute, after all, we are in the Atlantic Ocean here, not the protected and shallow waters of the other side of the island.

We eventually find some wide holes in the rocks and come across a large school of mutton snapper. Among them are many other fish, including a very large queen triggerfish, the biggest Nassau grouper I have yet seen, and a huge dog snapper. At one point, I sit down on a rock on the bottom and hold on with my hands, sitting still as if on land while the fish swim all around me. It is the highlight of the dive.

Jen keeps on venturing further away, but I am far out of my comfort zone now. I'm used to having the dinghy close by and I am still worried we'll see a shark and have to swim all the way back to shore, which is at least 100 yards away now, with a big shark following us.

I keep edging us in the direction of going back, but Jen keeps pushing further out. At some point, she feels my fear and I think I spook her.

"Did you see something?" she asks me when we get to shallow water.

"No, I was just getting spooked," I say, a little embarrassed at my lack of bravery.

Getting spooked in the water is a strange thing. It's happened to me while surfing a few times. Once it starts, there is no stopping it, everything starts to look like a shark, every water current feels like a shark swimming up on you, and the fear builds on itself. It's also contagious, passed from one to another through nonverbal communication.

No surf today, at Hatchet Bay
Let's snorkel, I say, if we may
Find a spot, among the rocks
With a bit of sand, where we can
The water get in, and go for a swim
And see some fish, that's my wish
Hike north we do, three hiking fools
Looking for pools, finding a nook
A risk we took, to enter the ocean
Like magic potion, feeling its motion
Like two manatees, mammals of the seas
We've one big eye, turned away from the sky
Looking instead down, at rocks all brown
Sand in between, no sharks on the scene
Mutton snapper in school, over grouper I drool
Pretty queen trigger, dog snapper is bigger

Sit on a rook, fish come for a look
Holding my breath, fending off death
Living the best, life I can guess
An adventure a day, no one can say
That I've not lived large, and followed my charge
Seeking quality of life, and minimal strife
Nomadic and marine, living the dream

I like getting out of my comfort zone, and I'm glad Jennifer pushed me out of it. We saw all the fish out beyond where I would otherwise have gone. Without stepping outside our comfort zones, we never progress. Sometimes it takes someone else to take us there. I later tell Erick that his wife proved herself a badass.

While in Hatchet Bay, I occasionally sail *Little Flower* to the dinghy dock to go grocery shopping, or to fill water containers at the town spigots. Sometimes I sail her outside to go spearfishing. But whenever I sail her, I typically also sail around and wave to the other boats. I am on a mission to meet other people, and my bright red sailing and rowing dinghy is a gimmick that helps. People recognize me because of *Little Flower*, and sailing and rowing her around, as opposed to using an outboard motor like everyone else, differentiates me.

Whenever I meet someone onshore, or later at a different anchorage, they will usually remember me as the guy in the red sailing dinghy.

Rowing *Little Flower* also provides me with daily exercise, and my upper body is developing new muscles as a result.

It seems natural to me for a sailor to have a sailing dinghy. We travel slowly for days at a time to get to our destinations, using our engines as little as possible. So why not continue this practice at our destinations? A sailing and rowing dinghy is much less expensive than an inflatable with a motor. It's quiet and peaceful, provides exercise, and it means we don't have to carry gasoline onboard.

Another advantage of my dinghy is that being fiberglass, it can withstand occasional grinding up against rocks without the risk of holing and deflating. This means I can tow it around with me while spearfishing near emergent rocks, rocky banks, or piers.

Although there are times when I see just how nice it would be to have a fast dinghy that can plane and really cover distance, overall, I appreciate my humble and slow human or wind-powered dinghy. I have yet to suffer from not having a fast one like everyone else.

I met a few other interesting people at Hatchet Bay. Chris told me an amazing story of running into some sort of anomaly while crossing the Gulf Stream in his catamaran. The skies went completely dark, in the daytime, while the wind was calm. The motors and all electronics shut off. But, most bizarre, the compass spun around. For two hours this went on, before the sky cleared, the electronics came back to life, and he was able to continue. He wrote about it in his log and showed it to me as proof.

The captain of a big beautiful ketch told me a great story about a woman he took on as crew. She turned out to be a pathological liar, but he kept her around for most of a circumnavigation because of her "oral fixation."

I met a French Canadian on a little Albin Vega who scoffed at sailors with YouTube channels.

"I don't understand why they want so much publicity," he said in his thick French-Canadian accent. "I'm sailing just for the f--- of it."

I didn't tell him that I had a YouTube channel.

"I'll mention you in my book, if I may," I said.

"No, don't mention me, I'm sailing under the radar."

I met a guy who gave his sailboat a long Greek name.

"Don't ever do that," he told me. "Every time you go under a bridge you have to spell it out, and the spelling doesn't make sense, and no one can pronounce it either. It's a real hassle."

That night, the wind blows hard from the north. Hatchet Bay is a great place to be, since it is protected from all angles, however, should the boat drag, there is always a lee shore to run into.

When I get up in the middle of the night to relieve myself over the side, I see a disturbing sight. My neighbor's boat is very close to shore, and obviously aground. I am at a loss for what I should do. I think about trying to wake them by shining my spotlight on the boat, or ringing my bell, but then I figure they must know that they are aground, it is sure to have woken them up. After much consternation, I figure that there is nothing I can do, so I go back to sleep.

I get up again a few hours later and see that they have gotten free and moved somewhere else, and I am relived, but my conscience is still not clear, and in the morning, I feel bad for not having done anything. I should have at least tried to wake them up with the spotlight.

Seeing this happen makes me worry about my anchor. The Vulcan has so far done a great job of holding me in place throughout the changing wind directions, which would have made the anchor have to reset itself many times, but the wind is blowing 25 knots and I want more protection. I decide to set my other anchor, the Fortress FX 23.

Setting the second anchor poses a few obstacles, the first of which is that I have to maneuver it into the dinghy. The anchor itself is light, since it's aluminum, but the 30' of 3/8" chain is heavy. I drag all this across the deck and lower it into the dinghy, tied alongside the boat, which is bucking in the waves like an angry horse. Once I have the anchor and nearly all its rode in the dinghy, I carefully climb down the ladder into the dinghy, which rises and falls madly in the waves produced by the strong wind. Untying the dinghy from the big boat is challenging, and as soon as I do, we start drifting downwind, the opposite direction I want to go. I quickly sit down and row with all my strength into the wind while the rode pays out from the stern. Headway comes slowly, but we make progress upwind as I lean into the oars.

When all the line is out and only chain remains in the boat, I heave the anchor over the side. But as soon as I quit rowing to grab the anchor, we start drifting downwind fast, and I hope the anchor was far enough away from *Windflower* to be able to set well. Within moments I am back at the boat, scrambling aboard and tying up *Little Flower*.

Standing at the bow, after catching my breath, I pull in the Fortress' rode until it is tight and I immediately feel much more secure, now that we lie to two anchors.

Erick and Jennifer stop by in the morning, a few days later, to say goodbye and we have coffee aboard *Windflower*. I am really enjoying meeting other people, spending time on other boats, and having friends over on my boat. This is in contrast to the last time I was in The Bahamas, when I met very few people, had none aboard my boat, and went aboard nobody else's boat.

[*Listen to my interview with Erick and Jennifer on my podcast, "Offshore Sailing and Cruising with Paul Trammell" which can be found at paultrammell.com.*]

Soon after they leave, I pull up both anchors, which is quite a bit of work. Not only have the strong winds buried them deep in the mud, but they are also in 25' of water, which means I have to pull up all the weight of 25' of chain in addition to that of each anchor and the mud they hold.

I motor through the narrow cut with vertical rock towering over both sides, the cut in which I spearfished so many times, and into the open water on the other side. After motoring a safe distance away from the island, I turn all the way around to face the wind. *Windsong* is just south of me and heading south to Rock Sound. I raise the sails and take off to the north on a beam reach.

The sun is out, the temperature is pleasant, and the wind is just right. For two hours, we sail in these fine conditions, me at the helm, steering and enjoying the ride, all the way to Current Cut. This time, we pass through with the current just after high tide, as opposed to the last time I went through, against the current and at a much lower tide. This time it is easy, and I am more able to enjoy the scenery.

Once through the cut, we sail for another hour in ideal conditions and then pass through Egg Island Cut. I anchor off Egg Island, in a patch of sand next to a boat I remember as one of my neighbors in Hatchet Bay, *Voyageur*.

Location: 25.4953º N, 76.8874º W

I am eager to spearfish on the reef here, which was recommended by Erick and Jennifer, and the clear blue water is more than inviting, rather it pleads with me to get in. I suit up.

In the spirit of friendliness, I row right over to *Voyageur*.

"Ahoy *Voyageur!*"

"Hello."

"I think we were neighbors in Hatchet Bay."

"Oh, yeah, I remember you from there."

"I'm going spearfishing, would you like to join me?"

"I don't spearfish, or have any gear, but my son might like to join you." He then looks down at the water around his boat. "He's snorkeling right now, around here somewhere."

A head pops up and the man gets his son's attention.

Riley looks like a college football player, big and muscular, with the pale white skin of one who lives somewhere cold, and he is game for an adventure. Riley follows me in a kayak out to a reef and along the way he tells me he is curious about spearfishing and just wants to watch and see how it's done. He doesn't have a spear, but later I figure he'll bring one next time he comes to the islands.

We row a good way to a shallow reef marked on the charts and get in the water. As I swim around looking for prey,

I think I might explain to him how to locate lobster so he can point out any he might see, but he beats me to it.

"Hey Paul!" I hear him as I surface. "There's a big lobster over here."

I swim over, hoping he is right, and he points out a lobster big enough for two people to eat. I spear it, but it gets free and the elastic on my spear breaks. Unable to shoot, I try to pull it from the hole by its antennae. Persistence pays off and it's not long before I toss the big lobster in *Little Flower*.

Soon after, he calls me over again and points out a second lobster. With no elastic on my spear, I have to jab at this one cave-man style, and it gets away, but Riley is still looking and calls me over a third time.

"There's a big fish over here!"

This time he points out a big Nassau grouper under the coral, and I jab my spear right through the back of its head. It's the biggest grouper I have yet landed.

"We should probably get out of the water now," I say.

He nods in agreement and we climb into our vessels and make our way back to the anchorage.

I invite the crew of *Voyageur* over for dinner, and Riley and his dad show up. The wife is happy to have some time alone while the men join me on *Windflower* for a lobster-grouper jambalaya. Little do I know, this is the last time I am to have guests aboard for a long time. As much as I enjoy sailing alone, I enjoy having company too. All the alone time makes me appreciate the occasional social interaction more than ever. This time, not only do I end up with company for dinner, I also had a spotter who pointed out everything I speared or even shot at.

The following day, I get in the water to see what is around the boat, and am surprised to see coral. Besides the patch of sand I anchored in, excellent coral reef extends as far as the eye can see, which is a long way in the clear water. Only about 30% of the coral is alive, but fish are abundant.

I land a grouper quickly, and for the rest of the time I swim as a spectator, which is a nice change. I am able to follow and watch two other grouper, and since I don't go after them, they seem unafraid. I see a few barracuda, a spotted drum (for the first time), many parrotfish, wrasses, damselfish, chub, banded butterflyfish, ocean surgeon, a queen angelfish, Spanish hogfish, porgy, French grunt, mutton snapper, a very big unknown snapper, yellowtail snapper, schoolmaster snapper, barjack, yellow goatfish, red hind, graysby, a gag, trumpetfish, squirrelfish, and a few lobster which are too small to spear. The high species-diversity is a sign of a healthy reef, and I smile at the thought.

While swimming around, I notice at least two large coral heads that reach for the surface and are tall enough to threaten *Windflower's* keel. Neither of these navigational hazards are charted, and this is a reminder of how careful we need to be when cruising in the shallow waters of The Bahamas. Just because the chart shows no danger doesn't mean that no dangerous rocks or reef lurk beneath the surface.

I pan-fry the grouper with fresh black pepper and make a big sandwich with sprouts and mustard. This comes to be my favorite way to prepare fresh fish.

In the afternoon, I row ashore and hike on Egg Island, first to the north and around a saltwater pond, then to the south along the rocky shore, collecting purple or yellow sea fans which have washed ashore along the way, as well as some nice pieces of sun-bleached coral. These things are common here, but I assume will be objects of great wonder in far-away places like Canada. I imagine giving them away as gifts to friendly Newfoundlanders when I sail up there in the coming summer.

I wake to my alarm at 2:30 in the morning, eat breakfast, pull up the anchor at 3:30, then very carefully motor out of the anchorage in the dark, using the chartplotter to follow my course from the way in as closely as I can, in order to avoid the coral I saw the day before. When I reach water over 30' deep, I turn into the wind, hoist the sails, and we are off to the Abacos!

As we sail away and the black water gets progressively deeper, I maintain focus on my one obstacle this morning, which is Egg Reef. I keep it well to starboard and *Windflower* in deep water, and when the reef is behind us, the depth drops off quickly to the thousands of feet.

The bimini is down and the moon nearly full and I bask in the unobstructed view of the night sky, which includes at least one shooting star. It is the sort of night when I just want to lean back and look up at the stars, and I do just that. I steer by aligning the mast with the heavens, and my mind is dominated by the specks of light coming from the inconceivable depths of space. Conscious thoughts fade and disappear, and I become one with the universe, I have always been one with the universe, but now I realize this fact, that we are all one, and everything else is one with us, existing only in the mind of the creator, whoever or whatever that may be. But the creation is all around me, and it is me, and I play my role in the game, and my role is here and now. My role is to chase my dreams and realize my destiny, and my destiny is here, on this sailboat, on this ocean, sailing to more islands and looking for more adventure.

The stars eventually fade as the eastern horizon brightens, which begins as a faint greying of the black sky. The grey becomes lavender, and then brightens dramatically as the Earth rotates into the sunshine.

Windflower and I sail on a beam reach at 6.5-7.5 knots in 12-16 knots of breeze through the predawn hours and into the sunny morning, and since I only have the use of the backup autopilot, I hand-steer the whole way and enjoy the time behind the wheel.

The chart shows the deepest part of our passage to be an astounding 13,000 feet, well over two miles deep. I try to conceive of water this deep and picture two and a half miles straight down, but find it hard to do so, and yet I marvel at how easily my boat sits on the surface of water so deep, so high above the bottom.

The swell is about six feet, and I look forward to seeking out rideable waves once we get to the Abacos. But this also means that there are breaking waves on both sides of the shallow cut that we have to find and pass through to enter the protected waters inside the islands. From the ocean, as we approach the cut leading into the Bight of Old Robinson, next to Little Harbor, all I see are breaking waves, though I follow the route marked on the chartplotter with faith in the device, as my eyes see no way in.

The sail from Eleuthera to the Abacos was fabulous!

THE SOUTHERN ABACOS

Lobster in a time of isolation
Takes the blues away
Of the scenes of Armageddon
And the virus that will not stay
In one country or one town
But lobster on the reef
And fish in the sound
Make me smile and see
That food's all around
Lobster in a time of isolation
Takes the blues away
Survival is the new fashion
And nature is the way
To live in all-encompassing peace
Harmony with the mother
On seafood and solitude I feast
There is no greater other
A solo sailor on adventure
Looking for silver lines
Something good will come, I hope
From these pandemic times

The approach to Little Harbor Cut gives me no sense of confidence that we will be able to enter, for all I see are lines of whitewater, the backs of waves breaking across shallow water. I continue towards the cut, following the chart-plotter and hoping it is correct, and I start the engine just for safety.

As we get closer to the cut, a small gap opens in the whitewater, and the pattern I see in the rocky islands beyond starts to make sense. The approach to the cut is from the southeast, diagonal to the land masses, and breaking waves to the northeast and southwest create the illusion of a solid band of whitewater until we are close enough to perceive the gap, which widens to a safe width once in it.

The waves in Little Harbor Cut are not breaking, but they stand tall and threaten to do so. The chart warns that waves break across the cut in large swells, but today's swell is not quite large enough. If it were, I'd have to continue north all the way to Man-O-War. As we pass through, I watch the waves to my right and imagine surfing them. It would be a difficult place to access, and the current might prove an obstacle, but this is the first of many surfable breaks I see in between the islands of the Abacos.

Sailing through the cut is exciting, but I would not want to attempt this cut in a swell larger than six feet. Once inside, the waves subside and the clear blue water welcomes me and *Windflower* to the Abacos. Here is the water one imagines The Bahamas is supposed to have, transparent and reflecting the blue sky, surrounded by low, rocky islands.

I find a quiet and protected place to anchor at the south end of Lynyard Cay, which appears to be mostly uninhabited, although I can see at least one house to the north. A sign on the beach proclaims that this is a private island. I almost anchor in front of a beach, but the sight of a table and chairs and a hammock makes me move a bit further south, thinking this might be someone's backyard beach.

Location: 26.3533º N, 76.9853º W

After I get out of the water from checking the anchor, which is firmly dug into the silty grass bottom, a small power boat with about five people aboard pulls up to the beach and they wade ashore. I spy on them just a bit, with the binoculars, trying to determine if they are the owners of the private island, because if not, this means that the privacy of the island is not enforced. Regardless, I have little reason to go ashore. My interest is held by the water.

Little do I know, a friend of mine from St Augustine is on that boat.

I jury-rig my spear with a piece of shock cord (bungee) and attempt to spearfish in the cut south of Lynyard Cay. Waves break on a shallow reef in the cut, but on the inside, the water is ten feet deep. Although the waves produce a lot of back and forth movement in the water, the snorkeling is interesting and a lot of fish live here. However, I learn that bungee is no substitute for surgical tubing (this is what the "elastic" on a pole spear is made of) and I spear no fish.

Meanwhile, back in the United States, life is changing rapidly. As I sit in my boat sipping on coffee and watching the sunrise, I wonder if I should go back to Florida, or try to extend my stay in The Bahamas. Back in the US, schools are closing, people are told to socially isolate, and grocery stores are being emptied of toilet paper by people who have apparently associated a flu-like virus with overactive bowels.

I think about the possibility of either staying in The Bahamas or working my way south, with the intention of being south of the hurricanes during hurricane season, either in St Lucia, or Trinidad, or Bocas Del Toro, Panama, but I suppose I have plenty of time to decide what to do. It is March 15 and my cruising permit doesn't expire until April 4. My only limitation is my lack of a trusted autopilot.

In the morning, I pull up the anchor, hoist the sails, and sail off without the rumbling of the engine marring the peaceful morning, a feat which always makes me proud. Silently moving across the water, we tack upwind to Pelican Cay, where I sail onto anchor, granting myself another cause for pride. I intend to dive at Sandy Cay, a national park and a no-take zone known for having an extraordinary coral reef.

Location: 26.4038º N, 76.9822º W

I rig *Little Flower* for sailing, gather up my snorkeling gear, and leave the spear behind as I sail off.

Before going to the reef, I sail on a beam reach past the cut to the south to look at the waves and see if they are something I want to surf. Long walls of blue break into churning masses of whitewater in the cut between Pelican Cay and Lynyard Cay, and while the waves are definitely surfable, they don't pique my interest. Something about surfing alone in a cut between two islands in a remote area seems awfully risky to me. I chastise myself for lack of bravery as I sail by, knowing I won't paddle out. I think this area would be a great place to explore the surf if I had some other surfers with me, and maybe a dinghy with a motor.

I gybe and continue on towards Sandy Cay and think about returning, in the future, with more surfers, perhaps on another boat or boats, and we could properly explore this area's surf.

Once at the reef, I tie up to a dinghy mooring, don my gear, and slip into the clear water, feeling a little vulnerable without my spear.

The dinghy mooring is in 25' of clear blue water over flat white sand, but right next to it is a massive coral reef rising, like the mulitcolored crown of a giant king, almost to the surface. Mounds and canyons of coral stretch off into the distance and fish of all colors and shapes swim about. The scene dazzles the eyes. I hold onto *Little Flower's* painter and take in the magnificent sight as a current tries to sweep me away. Only after determining that I can swim against the current do I let go and swim upstream along the edge of the reef.

Twenty feet below, an enormous Nassau grouper comes into view and eyes me lazily, unconcerned about the human in its presence. Since this is a no-take zone, where fishing is not allowed, the grouper has no fear of me and I am able to observe it as the fish slowly swims around the reef. Normally, Nassau grouper immediately hide when I come into sight. I imagine they've all been shot at with a spear and know enough to associate people with grave danger.

I hover above the big grouper for a while, then continue on. The next big fish I see is a huge dog snapper, also unafraid of me. It slowly swims by the opening of a canyon in the reef, and I swim down and through the canyon, looking into caves and cruising slowly, overwhelmed by all the life and movement.

Pink and white squirrelfish hide in the caves and look out at me with big black eyes. A porcupine puffer with even bigger eyes and a square head peers from a dark cave and pokes his head out for a closer look at the human. A yellowtail damselfish darts about a coral-head and tries to run off a school of blue tang. Blue chromis swim above the reef, and bright green parrotfish cruise around audibly munching on the coral. Royal gramma, tiny, yellow and purple, sit motionless upside-down under overhangs, then dart at some unseen morsel. French angelfish and queen angelfish slip in and out of crevices, a school of jack swims by and disappears in the distance, a blue and yellow Spanish Hogfish swims through a cave, a strange filefish hides while mackerel pass by, and a school of sergeant major guard their territory.

As I swim along the edge of the reef, a large dark shape emerges from the edge of visibility over the sand to my right.

Is it a shark? No, it must be a manta ray, I think, and I swim toward it, but it disappears before I can get a positive identification. More dark shapes emerge from the blurry distance and now I see it wasn't a manta. This is a school of enormous spotted eagle rays, the size of dining-room tables, slowly swimming to the reef and along its edge, just off the bottom. They're the biggest I've ever seen, and there must be a dozen of them.

I follow from above, just able to keep up with their slow and graceful pace. These are dark rays with white spots, a long tail, and a conspicuous head that sticks out from the body, unlike most stingrays, which do not have a noticeable head. I swim down for a closer look and I can clearly see the large serrated spine near the base of the tail, which reminds me not to get too close, but the rays take little notice of me, even though I am obviously following them. One has a bite taken out of one of its wings, probably from a shark.

When I get down near the bottom and level with them, off to the side, I can see that the rays have a large body underneath the wings, whereas most rays are flat across the bottom. They have a head and a face, with mouth and eyes, and the face reminds me of dolphin, particularly the mouth. These animals exude confidence, both in the way they glide and the look on their faces. They swim slowly and barely need to move their wings to propel themselves forward. When reef gets in their way, they just clear over the top of it with a minimum of movement.

These are strange creatures, like none I've ever seen, and I follow for as long as I dare, before turning back and drifting with the current towards *Little Flower*. As I drift, I know this has been a lifetime experience, one that I will never forget.

It's been a fantastic dive, and ending it with the spotted eagle rays is called for, so I climb aboard *Little Flower* and take off my mask. But before I get my fins off, I see large dark shadows below, and I know I have to get back in. It's more eagle rays, going in the same direction, and I follow them too.

Before this unforgettable and magnificent wildlife encounter, I had seen many spotted eagle rays, usually when they jumped out of the water, and a few times while underwater, but they were never anywhere near as big as the ones I saw at Sandy Cay. I can't be sure how big the ones I saw were, but they can grow up to 8 feet across and weigh 500 pounds. I'd say the biggest one I saw today might have been that size.

While this was the only time I have ever seen them in a school, these rays are known to gather in schools numbering in the thousands. They eat creatures that live on the bottom, like clams and other mollusks, and they have mouths specialized for crushing shells. They have a large poisonous spine on their tail, but are not dangerous to humans since they don't rest on the bottom and thus can't be stepped on. However, they have been known to wound and even kill fishermen who have caught them.

It's always amazing to see large wildlife, and this was no exception. One of the benefits of being in the ocean is that the animals that live there are not usually scared of humans and let us get near them. Imagine trying to get within ten feet of any 500-pound terrestrial wild animal. I can't think of any that would allow this.

I replay the encounter with the alien-like rays in my head as I sail back to *Windflower*, never wanting to forget the experience and logging it in my long-term memory.

Back onboard, I sail off anchor and move to the south end of Tilloo Cay. Waves are breaking in the cut between Tilloo and Pelican Cays and, riding the high of the morning's dive, I am determined to surf.

Location: 26.4276º N, 76.9874º W

While paddling the 12-0 out to the cut, I begin to feel the current of the outgoing tide. It pulls me into the cut and the breaking waves, and I wonder if I am making a terrible mistake. I turn around and paddle against the current just long enough to satisfy myself that I can out-paddle the current, then turn back around and try to position myself for a wave.

Every few minutes, I have to paddle back against the current, and I monitor landmarks on the shore in order to gauge my position in the cut, since the tide is pulling me out. I am also wary of the fact that sharks like to sit in cuts during the outgoing tide to hunt (or so I imagine).

It takes me a while to figure out the break and get in the right spot. I catch a couple short rides, but I want one of the long waves that I saw from the boat. The wave I saw that convinced me to paddle out started in the cut and broke all the way inside and then broke along the rocky bank of Tilloo Cay.

After waiting patiently and repositioning many times, I see what looks like a good one coming at me. I paddle into the wave, against the current, drop in and turn left, and cruise down the line. The wave reforms and becomes a right, ledges up, and I drop in a second time, then cruise all the way to the inside of the cut and finish the ride near the island.

This is the sort of session where I figure one good wave is a mark of success, and I think I should quit while I am ahead. I paddle back to the boat and smile; this is turning into a day full of adventure.

But I am not finished yet. I have worked up a big appetite and am ready to go spearfishing.

Many years prior, my buddy Joe and I used to call it a triple crown if we could do three sports in one day. Back then it was surfing, skateboarding, and mountain-biking. Today it is going to be snorkeling, surfing, and spearfishing. I also sailed, both the big boat and the dinghy, so I suppose I could make up a new name, but "triple crown" is good enough for me.

I row out to the cut between the two islands and get in, but the water is too cloudy from all the waves breaking, and I don't find any reef, so I move to the shallow water around Tilloo Cay. I find a coral head in shallow water and quickly spear a bluestriped grunt, hardly big enough to justify spearing, but of course it looks bigger underwater.

I move on around the corner, following the bank, and come across what my friend
Dave used to call a "honey hole," a place where the fishing is particularly good. Mangrove snapper school around sunken logs, and I have one in the boat within two minutes. The rest of the school doesn't seem to fathom what I am up to, because I get two more right away. With four fish, I don't think I need any more, and I return to the big boat.

I can't stay where I am because the boat rolls in the swell too much for comfort. Shallow water to the north prevents me from going directly up the cay where the swell won't reach, so I have to go way out through a channel visible only on the charts, then come back to Tilloo Cay further north. When I finally am anchored for the night, I fillet and cook the fish while watching the sunset and have a fine meal fit for the winner of the triple, or quadruple, crown.

Location: 26.4577º N, 76.9912º W

In the morning, I spearfish around Shearpin Cay and Tilloo Pond, where a jetty in shallow water harbors many fish, especially juveniles, and in the pond lives a school of mangrove snapper. I am able to hit a few, but all of them get away. It is times like this that I feel bad about spearfishing. I feel guilty for injuring fish that I don't get. One of the good things about spearfishing is that there is no bycatch, that is, no fish caught that are not meant to be caught. The downside is the inevitability of injuring fish that get away.

In the afternoon, I make contact with my friend Rachael, from St Augustine, who is in the Abacos, and as chance has it, she is planning on moving from Little Harbor to Elbow Cay today. She comes by in a small boat and visits for a bit, and we are able to visit later in the day at the Abaco Inn. It is here that I learn that she was on the boat that went to the beach at Lynyard Cay.

I move north in the afternoon, just before high tide, and am barely able to make the passage across the shallow waters between Tilloo Cay, Lubbers Quarter, and Elbow Cay. The chart shows minimum depths of six feet at low tide, but I am seeing seven feet at high tide, just one foot below my keel.

It is in this area that I begin seeing destruction from Hurricane Dorian. The modest houses on the island are completely destroyed and debris is scattered all along the shore, while the larger houses, obviously those of the wealthy, are apparently better-built and suffered much less. Some houses only have roof damage, while others appear to already have new roofs. Houses close to the water look like waves washed through them and wrecked their foundations. Nearly all the docks are mangled and once-vertical pilings lean at odd angles.

I anchor near White Sound, rowing distance to the Abaco Inn and access to the surf breaks on the other side of the island.

Location: 26.5234º N, 76.9764º W

Excited at the prospect of surfing, I load my red small-wave surfboard in the dinghy and row ashore. I pull *Little Flower* up onto the beach in front of the Abaco Inn and hike across the skinny island, turning left at the road. I climb down a retaining wall that construction workers are building with a backhoe and a pile of boulders, and step into the water at the south end of the   beach next to the rocks. I've been here before, years ago, but the waves are better today.

The surf is about shoulder high, breaking fast across shallow clear water and visible sharp reef. It is a right point-break and the wave stands up just in front of a jagged, sharp rock wall that takes a lot of confidence to line up in front of. But my surfing is honed sharp from all the time spent at Hatchet Bay, and I make all my drops, turning hard at the bottom and propelling myself down the fast but short waves.

After surfing, Rachael drives me around town in a golf cart and we pass debris piles as high as two-story houses, one after another, as well as many large boats, wrecked and sitting on dry land, far from the water, where they will float no more.

After checking the surf at a friend's house, I find a hose and rinse off with a luxurious and seemingly endless supply of fresh water. Even better, when we get back to the Inn, her room is ready and Rachael lets me take a real shower, with hot water, and it is glorious.

Dinner at the Inn is decadent, and since I have not had red meat since before leaving the Chesapeake Bay, I order a hamburger, and it is as fine as Jimmy Buffet's song suggests. The three of us make plans to go after conch the next day, and since I don't know anything about conch, particularly how to clean them, I am excited about this opportunity.

I row home in the dark, and am lucky that there is no boat traffic. I vow to install lights on *Little Flower* when I get back to the States. It occasionally happens that dinghies without lights get hit by other boats at night.

Rachael and Kaitlin pick me up in the morning on a fast powerboat and we zip out to a sunken barge south of Lubbers Quarter where Rachel and I swim around looking for conch and fish. I spear two small mangrove snapper and we both find conch. We then move to a large grass bed off the north end of Elbow Cay, where we find some more conch, and finally go to Johnny's Cay to clean them.

Johnny's Cay is a spectacular place to stop and sit. We anchor in clear shallow water over white sand with a view of the barrier reef where lines of whitewater break over sapphire blue water. The little island boasts a sandy beach, a wrecked house, and palm trees that survived the hurricane.

Kaitlin shows me how to clean the giant marine snails, and the lesson proves useful in the future. First, she uses a hammer to break into the shell at about the third spiral from the point, then she slips a spreading knife in between the shell and the muscle and severs the tendon that holds the muscle to the shell, after which she is able to pull the animal out of its shell. The head and eyestalks are cut off. The gut sack is removed. More internal organs are cut out of the big muscle with a V cut, and finally the grey skin below the foot is stripped away.

We have enough for us and her family to make conch salad, a delicacy I've heard about but never had.

Back onboard *Windflower*, I eat the fish I speared at the sunken barge, then rig *Little Flower* for sailing, and make my way ashore with my red surfboard.

I paddle back out at the same spot, walking past the same construction workers and heavy machinery repairing the seawall. The waves are firing and I count each one. Sometimes I do this, and it makes me stay in the water longer. It also helps me to remember the waves. It's an odd fact that waves I ride don't always register in my memory. It's as if I'm so focused on the act of riding the wave that my mind is too occupied to store the experience. But the waves are steep and fast and I catch 25, and I ride some into water so shallow that I have to make sure I can lay back down on the board without stepping off onto the coral.

The conch salad is incredibly good. The conch was chopped and soaked in lemon juice with diced tomato, onion, and hot pepper. It is basically just like ceviche, and just as good.

I have to make my way back to *Windflower* in the dark again, and the wind is not in my favor. I have to tack in the dark *and* row. One boat comes by and I shine a light on my sail so they can see me. The boat comes near and asks if I am alright and where I am going. I thank them for checking on me and point to *Windflower*, which has its anchor light on.

Before the sun is up, in order to catch the rising tide, I pull anchor and leave for Marsh Harbor, going across shallow water and around Porgy Rock, which is no problem. I anchor outside the Harbor, since the depth on the chart makes the inside look questionable, and row in.

Location: 26.5500º N, 77.0711º W

The destruction from the hurricane is visible everywhere, even from the water, and is extreme. Not one dinghy dock remains intact. Everything on the waterfront is completely destroyed. Only the big commercial port is functioning, and the rest of the waterfront is abandoned and in complete ruins. What was once a bustling harbor, completely lined with restaurants and hotels, docks and houses, is now a scene of total destruction.

My first goal is to try to extend my cruising permit, since the United States is under the threat of the coronavirus pandemic and starting to shut down. My second order of business is grocery shopping, in order to extend the time I might be able to remain self-sufficient.

I walk through town and am awed by the vast destruction. I was here less than one year ago, at the beginning of the delivery of a catamaran from Marsh Harbor to St Lucia. Then, the town was full of activity, cars, people, buildings. Everything is different now. What little structure is left standing is severely damaged, and most buildings are either completely gone or in a state of total ruin. Huge debris piles line the streets. The entire community of Mud is gone. What was once a shantytown comprising about four city blocks is now flat brown dirt, completely barren, and surrounded by a new fence topped with barb-wire. I imagine the fence is there because bodies are under the dirt, which appears to have been graded flat.

One house lays on its side, as if it simply rolled over and died. Boats sit on dry ground well inland as if hopelessly lost. Commercial buildings are ripped apart and twisted steel I-beams poke out of gaping holes where siding and roofing are missing. A sailboat sits on its side leaning against a partially crushed house.

Dust blows about and very few cars pass by. Roofing nails are as common as pebbles on the edge of the streets, daring cars to enter the parking lots of buildings with no roofs. People are scarce. It is a ghost town, post-Armageddon, and a foreshadowing of the pandemic future. Marsh Harbor is depressing. There is no joy in this town.

I make it to the government building, which is completely intact and thus an anomaly, but I am told that I cannot extend my cruising permit until three days before it expires, which is on April 4. Today is March 18.

I leave the government building without having accomplished my goal, but with new information, and head to Maxwell's grocery store, which is big and well-stocked and much like an American grocery. While there, I hear a woman say that "martial law" has been declared and will start at 10:00 tonight. It turns out that this is a bit of an exaggeration.

I stock up with as much food as I think I can reasonably carry in the backpack and duffle bag I have with me, then start the long walk back to the dinghy. The load is heavy and I am exhausted when I return to *Windflower*.

My friends on *Makani*, whom I dined with twice in Hatchet Bay, pull up to say hello before heading out to Matt Lowe's Cay. I stay put, but find the setting to be depressing. I suppose the pandemic had, up to this point, seemed far away, and The Bahamas insulated me from it. But walking through town, seeing the destruction and the lack of people, then hearing about martial law, makes it all real and present, as if the ghost-town status of Marsh Harbor is a glimpse of the post-pandemic future. It all drives home the message that humanity and civilization are fragile and can be wiped out in an instant. Certainly, life as we know it is changing and might never return to what we think of as normal.

I am looking forward to extending my cruising permit and visa and cementing my pandemic escape plan, but now it is up in the air, at least until April 1st.

one of the many boats that will never float again

This appears to be damage from tornado-strength winds.

the house that rolled over and died

In the morning, I pull up anchor and leave the depressing scene of March Harbor and move to Matt Lowe's Cay, where I anchor well behind *Makani*, not able to get as close to the island as them on account of my deeper draft.

Location: 26.5607º N, 77.0213º W

I get in the water and quickly land two lobster near Matt Lowe's Cay, where I also see margate, grunts, and mutton snapper. This is a beautiful setting, with a beach and palm trees, clear water, sunshine, and nothing suggesting the end of civilization. I'm much happier here.

On March 20, the border of the Bahamas is still open, but a curfew is enforced and nobody is allowed outside their place of residence between 10:00pm to 5:00am. The US has issued a travel advisory warning US residents not to leave the country unless they are planning to stay away. Florida has ordered all restaurants and bars that get 50% or more of their revenue from alcohol sales to close and remain closed until further notice. Schools are closing across the country, and some cities are completely shut down. Everyone is being strongly encouraged to just stay home.

I find myself glad to be in The Bahamas and my thoughts are dominated by strategies to extend my ability to stay self-sufficient here. I do not like the idea of being quarantined somewhere in the US. Here, I live surrounded by beauty and an abundance of fish and lobster, although the lobster season will come to an end April 1st.

The propane tank is on my mind and I am disappointed with myself for not having figured out how to bypass the broken solenoid. An idea, a simple and easy fix, pops into my head. I set right to it, drilling a hole through the gate valve in the solenoid. Within minutes, my stove works again, but, in order to maintain the same level of safety that the solenoid provided, I have to remember to shut the gas off at the tank after every time I use the stove. I devise a plan to leave the lid of the propane locker askew while I am cooking, and close it properly only after the tank is turned off. I do this for the next month.

My friends are anchored nearby, but neither of us make any effort to contact each other, besides them driving by and saying hello the day before. I suppose this is the new normal, at least for the time being. I note the irony in that I am on a mission to meet people and make friends while in the islands, but at this point that mission is severely handicapped.

I start thinking about trying to eat seaweed as a way to increase my self-sufficiency. The book "Sailing the Farm" states that almost all species of seaweed are edible, and the only one not edible in the book has a terrible and obvious taste. I munched on a piece of sargassum, raw, while surfing at Elbow Cay, and it was not at all bad.

Caribbean Islands are starting to close their borders, although The Bahamas border is still open. Closed islands include all French Islands, Anguilla, Aruba, Bermuda, the British Virgin Islands, Curacao, Dominican Republic, Saba, St Lucia, Sint Marten, Statia, Trinidad and Tobago.

Open islands include Antigua and Barbuda, The Bahamas, Cayman Islands, Dominica, Jamaica, Puerto Rico, St. Kitts, St. Vincent and The Grenadines, Turks & Caicos, and the US Virgin Islands. Open but with a 14-day quarantine are Bonaire, Grenada, and Montserrat.

Canada has closed its borders and my plans of visiting Newfoundland in the summer come into serious question.

In Central America, Costa Rica is also closed, much to the dismay of my friends Joe and Blakely who run a small hotel, Rancho Cannatella, in Pavones. Also closed is Belize, El Salvador, Guatemala and Honduras. Panama is still open but with a 14-day quarantine.

In the Eastern Atlantic, the Azores are closed, as well as the Canary Islands and Madeira.

The US is still open but is considering closing its borders, and many marinas are closing down. Somehow, boating is being discouraged, as if being on a boat is a danger to anyone.

My brother tells me California is under quarantine and the governor predicts that 56% of Californians will contract the virus. He texts me "Paul, your doomsday predictions have come true... You're as safe as anyone in the world can be right now, and eating lobster. Well done!"

I am indeed eating lobster while the world is shutting down.

More news from the day: Globally 250,000 tested positive for the virus and 10,000 have died. Prisoners in New York and Los Angeles are being released, and arrests in LA County are down from 300 per weekend to 60. Two senators have been accused of insider trading on knowledge of the pandemic, and our president downplays the pandemic, even calling it a hoax. I wonder if the global response to the pandemic is in some way related to stock-market manipulation, because the numbers don't seem to justify the measures, but it's impossible to see the big picture from my boat in The Bahamas.

On the good side, the due-date of federal taxes is pushed back to July 15.

I try to forget all about this news while I go spearfishing, and I come back with a grunt, a grouper, and a lobster. I leave the grouper in a bucket of water and save it for dinner, but in the meantime, I read the news.

In The Bahamas, non-essential businesses are ordered closed. Able to stay open are grocery stores, gas stations, banks, hotels, and many others. People are ordered to work from home if they can. Liquor stores and gaming houses are to remain closed. Gatherings are severely restricted, and inter-island sailing is prohibited. I think this means I won't be able to surf in front of the Abaco Inn anymore.

I figure this is a good time to stock up on more food, since I might not be able to in the future, or I might end up isolating myself at a remote and uninhabited island. I motor back to Marsh Harbor, row, then hike to the grocery store, and then anchor at Mermaid reef.

Location: 26.5554º N, 77.0548º W

Any reef with a name labeled on the chart is a place I want to see, so I row out to the reef and slip into the clear water. Right away I see schools of snapper, live coral, two grouper, lobsters, blue tang, angelfish, squirrelfish... The grouper hide from me and never come back out, and the snapper also seem aware of what I am up to. I return to *Windflower* with one small mutton snapper and two lobster, and I cook them with fresh tomato, onion, jalapeno, and lime juice, and lunch is as good as lunch gets.

While eating, I read a message from Cristina; she's forwarded me a "Level 4 Health Advisory" urging United States citizens to return to the country immediately unless they are prepared to stay out of the country indefinitely. I feel like I am clearly in the "unless" category, and do not feel like the advisory applies to me. I certainly am not ready to go back to the US. Home is wherever my boat is, and today home is next to the bountiful Mermaid Reef.

My friend Mark, who is a nurse in St Augustine, texts

me saying that all his Air B&B guests cancelled their reservations and his guest house is all mine if I need it. I tell him I am planning on staying in The Bahamas and he replies "That's the safest thing to do for sure. It's a strange feeling around here. So many people ignore the news and the obvious data coming from other countries."

At this point, our president is still downplaying the pandemic, saying it will magically just go away, and it is "just the flu" etc. My friend, the nurse, has a newborn baby at home and is nervous about picking up the virus at work and giving it to his child.

The news on March 22 reports that the Florida Keys are on lockdown "closed to all tourists and leisure visitors." Lodgings will no longer accept reservations or extend current reservations, including RV parks, timeshares, and transient marina rentals. Congregations are limited to 10 people or less.

Cristina forwards me a letter from the Coconut Grove Sailing Club stating that sailing is now prohibited. Boats on moorings can still be accessed, but sailing them or having work done to them is prohibited.

I return to Mermaid reef before noon the next day and forget all the bad news as I hunt, but all the lobster I saw the previous day are nowhere to be found. It is as if they all got together and agreed to do a better job of hiding today. However, after an hour of looking under every coral head and into every cave and crevice, I am able to land one.

Later, I want to make my own conch salad, and have all the ingredients save the conch. So in the late afternoon, I go searching. After swimming all across the grass-covered bottom for at least an hour and having found no conch, I return to the reef and bag another lobster.

Back on board, I read a text from my father stating that Louisiana is on lockdown, like California and New York, for at least the next three weeks. Louisiana has the fastest growing number of cases. Luckily, cousin Gary, who lives next door to my parents, is returning soon and will resume cooking (he is an expert chef) and delivering gourmet dishes to their back-door.

In the news, Germany bans groups of more than two. The mayor of NYC warns of more deaths if more medical supplies don't come in, and says April and May will likely be worse.

I am seeing some discussions on social media that the virus is either a hoax, or real but engineered in a laboratory. Some politicians sold stocks right before the market tanked, and I assume they will buy again when the market hits its low point, right before the rebound.

Who will profit from the pandemic, I wonder. Those who had inside information and play the market certainly will, perhaps hospitals, mail-order companies like Amazon, medical equipment manufacturers and suppliers, the makers of masks and gloves, suppliers of internet data, and companies that can secure monopolies during the shutdown. But the big winners will be whoever the government gives money to, like they did after 9/11 in the endless wars, like Haliburton and weapons manufacturers.

When governments breed mistrust, and the people lose faith in the information that they receive from the government and the media, the people are easily misled by conspiracy theorists and charlatans. This appears to be happening in the USA, because social media is full of conspiracy theories and claims that the whole pandemic is either a hoax or a contrived scheme.

Little do I know, the virus will hit home in the future, but the numbers are, at this point, still not very impressive. The US has 26,000 confirmed cases and 340 deaths, worldwide there are 300,000 cases and 13,000 deaths.

After all the musing about conspiracy theories, I feel the need to further stock up on food, so I return to Marsh Harbor and go to Maxwell's two more times. On the first trip, I buy a pressure cooker, so on the second, I buy a lot of rice and dried beans. Also on the shopping list are cans of Rotel, cans of vegetables, spices, olives, granola bars, cans of chili, and cans of soup.

Again, I leave Marsh Harbor and anchor off Matt Lowe's Cay, this time closer to my fishing spot, and quickly bag a bluestriped grunt and a lobster.

Location: 26.5665º N, 77.0173º W

My mother texts me and tells me to be careful, and that I am her safest child at the moment, which I think is ironic, since I am spearfishing alone, one of the most dangerous things I've ever done. She once told me that she was certain that she would outlive me. My, how times have changed.

In the news, Republicans are pushing for a 1.5 trillion-dollar bailout/stimulus package (which reminds me of the bailout/stimulus of the George Bush Jr presidency) and the Democrats are calling it a slushfund, saying it does too much for big businesses and not enough for the workers. Politicians giving away all of our money is something I hoped never to see again, yet here it is, just like after 9/11. They will bring on a recession, or perhaps a depression, while a select few become disgustingly rich. What good is all the money if you lose your soul?

The following day, March 24, the Bahamian airports all close. Costa Rica closes their beaches, and our president insinuates that he will open up our economy in weeks rather than months.

I head to Fowl Cay for some diving.

Fowl Cay is a National Park and a no-fishing zone and it's known as one of the best places to dive and snorkel in The Bahamas. I wanted to see it when I was here in 2016, but was outvoted by the rest of the crew. No longer, now my vote is the only vote.

I anchor inside Fowl Cay, near Scotland Cay, in the clearest water over pure white sand. It is a spectacularly beautiful place. Unfortunately, I can't stay overnight because the swell wraps around both sides of the small island and comes together where I am anchored, creating a chaotic roll. It isn't bad for a day anchorage, but I wouldn't want to sleep here.

Location: 26.6320º N, 77.0539º W

I row around Fowl Cay to the south, then out through a small cut, and further out to the first reef, which isn't too impressive. I hoped it would be, since the next reef is much further out, and I am alone out here, in the ocean, already 0.2nm from shore. The main reef is 0.5nm out, which seems far just because it is out in the ocean, but it's a calm day and I row out and find a deep hole in the reef that reaches all the way to the surface. Waves break on the outside edge of the reef, and they look big enough to ride. But I am not here to surf. I locate a deep patch of water surrounded by shallow reef and I get right in.

I enter a foreign world, clearly an outsider, an alien even, I am in this place. Immediately, I sense my entry back into the food chain. No longer am I a safe human floating above the ocean in the world of air and land, the world that we clearly dominate. Now I hold my breath and hover like a flightless bird, awkward like a duck crossing the street, wide-eyed like a farmboy in Time Square, or a child inside a candy store for the first time. I try to swim gracefully, but I am no fish. I am an imposter in this place, yet it fills me with awe and the glory of the reef makes me feel more alive than ever.

I find myself in a deep circle of the reef, like a corral. Walls of ancient coral rise from the flat sandy bottom. Two enormous snapper swim about, look at me, and continue their fish business undisturbed. Thousands of caves and crevices hold countless fish and small strange creatures, and none mind my presence in their ocean utopia.

A narrow canyon leads out of the pen and I drift above surveying what is below me like a condor flying above, gliding into the open water inside the long barrier reef. I swim out through the canyon, with vertical walls of coral close on both sides of me, pulling *Little Flower* along by the painter. On the other side, I am greeted by a large barracuda, who, thankfully, doesn't follow me around, as they often do.

The silence of the water is like gold in my ears, and the weightlessness a euphoric drug in my veins. The invisible water passes by and stills my soul like a savior. It brings me joy and awe. Surrounded by such power and beauty, I can only exist and observe, for I am an alien here in this other world that hides below our realm.

The water is about 25' deep, and the coral forms a long wall of living rock defending the Sea of Abaco from the mighty Atlantic Ocean beyond. Waves break on the outside of the reef, but inside, the water is still and calm. To my left is only clear water above a flat sandy bottom like an endless swimming pool. To my right is endless reef. I follow the reef, watching all the colorful reef fish go about their business and enjoying the completely clear water, unlike the somewhat cloudy water I have become used to. Here, there is no water to see, and I can't help but imagine that I am flying, not like a bird, but more like a drifting balloon.

Occasional patches of coral rise like little mountains to my left, over the flat white sand inside the barrier reef. One in particular is about 100 yards across and rises from the bottom all the way to the surface. The little mountain of coral is mushroom-shaped and ledges overhang dark caves below.

Unable to resist the attraction, I drop *Little Flower's* anchor to the bottom and swim down to explore some of the caverns below. I swim under a ledge and into a dark cavern that leads deeper into caves than I am willing to go. I swim in and out of the Swiss-cheese rock and coral formations, into darkness and back into light, never pushing my luck, but experiencing the thrill of holding my breath with a rock ceiling overhead.

After getting my fill of swimming in and out of caves,

I take the anchor back in hand and swim slowly all the way around this structure. On one side, a large Nassau grouper and a large hogfish swim casually about. Both are the biggest I have yet seen, too big to spear had we not been in a no-fishing zone, and a real treat to watch swim about, fearless of me. On any other reef, where fishing is allowed, these fish would run and hide from a human, or would have been killed before reaching such a size.

Rounding a corner in the massive reef, I am greeted by a group of big rainbow parrotfish, which I have never seen. The color of their face and tail is astonishing, a deep yet metallic and lustrous brick red. I hold my breath and stare at these gorgeous fish, and am not able to identify them until later, back at the boat, when I look them up in my guide. I chastise myself for not having a working underwater camera. The batteries on the GoPro will no longer take a charge. I had an opportunity to buy a Chinese knock-off of the GoPro from another sailor in Hatchet Bay, but I didn't bite, now I wish I did.

Windflower *anchored at Fowl Cay, Scotland Cay is in the background*

The water calls to me, I have to get in
For beneath the sea, all the fish swim
Yellow angels, green parrot
Blue damsels, butter hamlet
Blue chromis, above yellow coral
Patterned reef, little colors floral
Purple sea fans, wave in the flow
The doctorfish can, cut on the go
Barracuda follow, wherever I roam
The grouper will swallow, fish near his home
Lobster betray hole, antennae protruding
Scorpionfish's goal: sit still brooding
Little purple and yellow, fish upside down
Under a ledge this fellow, the royal gramma is found
Damselfish protect, algae patch if they can
Fend off the attack, from the blue tang clan
Anemone wave, one hundred soft hands
Trying to say hello, to this lost man
Who swims like a seal, and breathes from the sky
His face like a wheel, sees through one big eye

After this extraordinary dive, I climb aboard *Little*

Flower and row across the channel to the north, out of the park, to a rock off Scotland Cay. I begin to put together my spear, which I had in the boat but kept disassembled just to show that I was not using it in the park, in case I was questioned by authorities. But while screwing it together, the endcap that holds the elastic falls into the water. I quickly toss out the anchor, put on my mask and fins, grab the spear, and slip into the water, but since the elastic is no longer attached, the spear slips from my hands and falls to the bottom, 20' below.

Feeling foolish, I swim down and retrieve the spear, then follow the anchor line to the endcap. I screw it back onto the spear, then dive again. On the way down, I spot a large pair of antennae sprouting from a little crevice in the rock bottom, and when I reach it, I am delighted to find a big lobster. I spear it right under the face, which I have found is the best place to spear them, and return to the dinghy with dinner. The row back to *Windflower* is long and difficult, but the adventure was well worth the effort.

I hate to leave this beautiful place, but I can't stay on account of the rolling produced by the waves coming from both forward and aft, wrapping around the island, so I pull anchor and sail to Great Abaco near Water Cay, because a breeze from the west is in the forecast.

Location: 26.5925º N, 77.1553º W

Here the rocky shore is covered by the trees lacking most of their foliage, still unrecovered from the destruction of Hurricane Dorian. But unlike the buildings of man, which are in complete ruin, the trees have shed leaves and branches, but retained their trunks and roots, and life is now emerging again, slowly, in new leaves that show in small clusters of green, not high in the branches, but lower. It is an odd landscape, not with the usual green roof, but rather topped by leafless branches with bits of green poking through beneath.

On March 25, the Bahamian border is closed and a 24-

hour curfew is law; The Bahamas is on lockdown. However, the order is set to expire on the 31st. Airports, docks, ports, and beaches are closed. This means no more surfing for me, and I feel very fortunate to have stocked up on food, but I wish I had topped off fuel and water already.

Every person in The Bahamas is confined to their place of residence, which includes their yardspace, and are ordered to avoid contact with persons outside the family. Essential workers are still allowed to travel to work, and residents are still allowed to travel to the grocery store, banks, pharmacies, doctors' offices, and gas stations.

Each person, alone or with family members, is allowed 1.5 hours of daily outdoor exercise from 5:00am to 9:00pm, and everyone is required to keep six feet apart. Schools and churches are to remain closed, as well as all non-essential businesses. Businesses who can remain open are ordered to limit the number of customers to one per every thirty square feet of space in the store, and everyone has to keep six feet apart.

Airports are closed to incoming international flights, seaports are closed to international boats, and inter-island travel is prohibited.

Even the Olympics are cancelled, as well as most sporting events worldwide. The feeling is weird and apocalyptic, but so far, the numbers of cases and deaths are unimpressive and I remain skeptical.

At the Water Cay anchorage, which is not at all like the other Water Cay, in the Jumentos Cays, I use the morning to make fender boards from 2x6 I scavenged from debris at Marsh Harbor. I also start cutting wood to make a short tiller that I can use for sheet-to-tiller self-steering, to get us back to Florida, since neither autopilot is working. With the pieces cut from the ¾" wood, I laminate three pieces together with epoxy and clamps.

Fishing quickly yields two lobster, but no fish, even though I see a grouper and many snapper. After a big meal, I read Jack London's "Sea Wolf."

I wake to the faint smell of smoke, the kind produced by fires on land from burning debris. I remember seeing smoke over Great Abaco to the north, so I know before I rise that the wind shifted this way, as expected.

After coffee and breakfast, I set out for Treasure Cay, hoping to buy diesel and water. We motor at six knots as *Little Flower* tows behind. I watch her carefully, hoping that she won't fill with water from the dagger-board slot, and I think I see bits of water spraying up, but it is hard to tell. However, it is impossible to miss the oar that slips out and drags behind. I don't think it could get away though, so I leave it be, but *Little Flower* is assuming a new angle, leaning back more, as would be expected if she was taking on water.

I think about how I could address this if it gets bad. I would need to stop *Windflower*, or at least slow way down, pull the dinghy up alongside, and bail her out.

I put the throttle in idle and haul *Little Flower* alongside. She is incredibly heavy and as she gets close, I can see that she is nearly full of water. Only her built-in floatation and the two fenders I tied under the seats keep her afloat. I climb in as we slowly idle forward and spend some time bailing her out while the waves rock us mightily. I imagine how foolish I would feel if at this point she broke free. I would have to decide between rowing for *Windflower* right away, with the dinghy full of water, or continue bailing and then start rowing. Neither are attractive thoughts. Luckily, the job ends in success and without embarrassing disaster.

After calling Treasure Cay Marina and the fuel dock three times each, I almost give up. But one final call to the fuel dock gets a response, and I am delighted to hear the Bahamian woman say that they are open and that my six-foot draft is not a problem.

I put the engine in neutral and drift while I put the new fender boards down, then motor into the narrow channel, which is marked with pilings which may or may not have had red and green labeling before the storm. Ironically, the wind is blowing from the dock, and my fender boards never touch the pilings, but I feel good for having them.

Right as I pull up, a worker on shore wearing a mask greets me with the questions "Are you local?" and "Where are you coming from?"

"I've been in The Bahamas since January, and I've only been to Marsh Harbor since the quarantine started." This seems to be a good enough answer, and they take my lines.

I have to wait while a truck fills their diesel tank, which sits above ground. The fueling station is temporary, as the old one must have been blown away and scattered.

"Do you have water?" I ask.

"No, all we have is city water," she says as she points to a hose bib.

"Is it potable?"

"Yes," she says, with some hesitation.

"Do you drink it?"

"No, I drink bottled water."

"Do other people drink it?"

"Yes, it's city water, just like from your tap in Florida, but we don't have a hose."

"That's alright, I have a hose, and tap water is all I ever drink."

"How long is your boat?"

This catches me by surprise, as I don't see how it is relevant to the water discussion. "Forty feet."

"It's 30 cents a foot."

"Oh, well I need about 60 gallons."

"We don't have a meter on the water, so we just charge by the foot."

"Ah, so it'll be twelve dollars. That's fine."

I begin filling my jerry-cans and empty fruit juice containers, and then think about laundry. I pull out my dirty-clothes bin, set it in the cockpit, and fill it up, adding detergent too. After topping off the fuel tank, I pay and tell her I'll be a few more minutes with the water. I then empty the laundry bin and fill it again for the rinse cycle.

I have to turn around in the Treasure Cay mooring field, which is empty because the marina and resort are closed, due to hurricane damage, and I wave to the fuel-station workers as we pass by.

While motoring out of Treasure Cay and wondering where to anchor next, I spot the iron apparatus of a barge protruding from the water off to my right. I get out the binoculars and confirm that it must be a sunken barge. I anchor as close to it as I can get, which is about a quarter mile away.

Location: 26.6598° N, 77.2895° W

After rowing to the wreck and anchoring *Little Flower*, I slowly swim through the shallow and slightly cloudy and green water to the rusty old barge with spear in hand. Three big spadefish sit still in one corner outside the barge. I could spear one, but I am not sure if they carry ciguatera or not (I later learn that they do not). A large mutton snapper swims away when I approach it, and a nurse shark sits still under the bow as I swim around another corner. Inside the barge is a school of mangrove snapper and a school of juvenile bluestriped grunt, but I am not able to get close enough to the snapper for a good shot.

The barge is certainly an interesting dive, and it is full of fish, but, mainly due to the compromised state of the elastic on my spear, I am not able to get dinner.

I sail off anchor to the nearby Fish Cays. Surely, I think, I can get fish at a place with such a name, and the cays should provide protection from the coming northeast wind.

Location: 26.6361° N, 77.1631° 9.51' W

One other sailboat is anchored nearby, and when I row to the island I see a dinghy in which a woman follows around a man in the water while he spearfishes. When I swim over to say hello, she recognizes me, and I laugh at the coincidence. It's Annie, from *SV Precocious*, whom I met at Hatchet Bay, and her husband Mike is in the water.

On the windward side of one of the small islands, I find a school of snapper swimming around rocks. Mike is also hunting there and we say hello in the water. The water on this side of the island is moving back and forth with the surge and getting close to the rocks and fish is tricky.

I follow a snapper to a rock and spear the fish underneath, but it gets away. I look all around for it and give up, but later I find it, wounded and swimming blind, and I easily get it this time. I return to the big boat with four fish and have a fabulous meal, which I need after all the rowing. Since I was not able to anchor very close to the islands on account of shallow water, I had to row a long way. All the rowing and swimming I have been doing really work up an appetite and is burning fat and building muscle, and at 49 years old, this is a nice surprise. I feel like I'm in better shape than I can remember.

In the morning, I work on the tiller. I suppose I might really need sheet-to-tiller self-steering to get back to Florida, or wherever else I go after The Bahamas. The Raymarine wheel pilot, which is my backup autopilot and the only one working, has been making odd noises, like the squeaking of excess friction building up inside it.

Although I don't know where I will be sailing next, I will need an autopilot regardless. I can only day-sail without one, and any passage will require either autopilot, sailing on a close reach so I can lock the wheel, heaving-to while I sleep, or the addition of crew (which is highly unlikely).

I occasionally wonder if I would enjoy having another person onboard, particularly a woman, but I am suspicious of my motive since these thoughts generally occur at night. Going to bed alone every night is in no way ideal. Overall, I really do enjoy my solitude, making my own decisions, and the extra range that my solo status affords me. One extra crew would mean that my provisions would last half as long, or probably even shorter than that, since I am accustomed to "bathing" only in the saltwater.

After putting a few layers of fiberglass cloth soaked in epoxy on the short tiller, I row to the southern Fish Cays to join Mike in some more spearfishing. I find a pile of tree branches on the bottom with a school of snapper and many other fish swimming around. I am learning that mangrove snapper, aka grey snapper, like piles of tree branches. But while I look at the snapper, two pair of large eyes emerge from the sand and look at me.

Southern stingrays, defensive but dangerous creatures, are reminders to pay close attention when near the bottom. While sharks are a scarier thought, these are a more real and present danger. A wound from a stingray is painful enough to make a strong man cry. Their poisonous barbs not only cut and poison, but also break off under the skin and leave nasty, infected wounds. Even though stingrays do not attack, they make me cautious because I often swim along the bottom while looking sideways at a reef.

I wait patiently, laying still on the bottom with my spear aimed and ready, but don't get anything. I move on, then return later for another try. But this time, a large barracuda, its bright silver scales reflecting the sun, swims slowly through the area with its mouth wide open. They usually swim with their mouths slightly open, but this one is positively gaping, and I interpret it as a sign of aggression. When it swims through like this a second time, I move on, ceding the hunting grounds to the resident predator.

I try my luck in the channel between the southernmost islands, which is full of soft corals that look like little trees between which occasionally swim large mutton snapper. One of these would provide a true feast for me, but I can't get near them. Luckily for me, the conch can't get away, and I take three, then put one back, thinking two will surely make a big conch salad.

I swim to the next island and find a lobster deep in a small cave, shoot at it, but miss. I keep returning to the cave, hoping it will show itself again, but instead I see two mangrove snapper swim in, and one ends up on my spear.

The fish make a fine sandwich with mustard and fresh sprouts, and the conch fill a bowl with chopped meat, much more than I expected. It is difficult to chop so much conch, and my right arm is tired afterwards. Into the bowl I add one and a half diced mild jalapeños, 2 slices of chopped red onion, one chopped tomato, and the juice of three limes.

I let the conch salad sit for an hour before eating it with crackers in the cockpit while reading Jack London's "Sea Wolf" which is turning into a great book. While the conch salad is good, it is not as good as the conch salad I had at Hopetown. I think the red onions were a bit too strong, the conch should have been chopped finer, and I should have let it soak in the lime juice longer.

After dinner, I read the news, which seems like it comes from another world. On March 27, the USA overtakes China as the nation with the most cases of the virus, with 86,000. Deaths in the USA are at 1,300, China has 3,296, and Italy 8,215.

Congress passes a two-trillion-dollar stimulus bill.

Later in the day the news states we now have 97,000 confirmed cases and Trump invokes the Defense Production Act, forcing private industries to produce items required for national defense. He has been using the word "war" at every opportunity, as if he wants to define himself as a "war president." It all seems absurd to me.

In the late afternoon, I move to the main anchorage at Great Guana Cay, where I was four years prior with friends on *SV Monkey's Uncle*. Back then this was a busy place, a party-scene, and full of boats. Monohulls, catamarans, sportfishers, and trawlers filled the anchorage, and a bar on the beach had a party in full-swing. The houses were full of life and the anchorage was not the forlorn place it is this evening.

Windflower is the only boat here and the scene is quite different from 2016. The docks are all destroyed. What houses are still standing are lifeless. No people are visible, and with the pandemic as a backdrop, the scene is post-apocalyptic. It could easily be imagined that this was a war-zone, or that the pandemic has already destroyed civilization and all that is left is the wreckage of our former world. It is depressing.

Location: 26.6670º N, 77.1188º W

The pandemic is like an ink-blot test, a mirror on our own psyches. Some people, which I see on social media, are all negative, scared, and paranoid, while others remain positive. Some accept the news and the lockdowns, while others decry it all as a scam and call for civil disobedience. I am not sure where I stand, but it doesn't look right. The numbers are still not impressive and the government is about to give away two trillion dollars, and whenever that happens, you can be sure corruption is at work.

The latest conspiracy theory on social media is that China released the virus on purpose, and that they already had a vaccine prior to the release, in order to cripple the economy of the west and buy up all the stocks and companies and bonds while the prices are low.

In the morning, a barge pulls into the anchorage and passes very close, probably over my anchor line, then pulls in to a little boat ramp where earlier I tied up *Little Flower* to unload trash, and I'm glad I am not still there.

The barge unloads one large truck and four shipping containers, as well as a load of poles, like telephone poles or those that might be used for building docks.

Mike calls on the VHF and says they are headed to Red Bay. I pull anchor and leave before the barge has a chance to pass close to me again.

We sail on a broad reach in 14-18 knots of breeze and hit 7.5 knots at one point. Apparently, I have not yet learned the lesson about towing *Little Flower* this fast, and so she fills up again, in order to remind me. This time she gets to the point of being bow-up and draining out the back, worse than last time.

I slow down by reducing sail, and at just under 6 knots she takes on no more water, but she is already almost full. Since we are close to our destination, I choose to let her be, I don't want to take all the sail down to bail her out.

I don't see *Precocious* until we are 0.5nm away. As I slowly motor in a circle to pick a spot to anchor, *Little Flower* turns broadside and I see she is totally full of water. It is only her floatation that keeps her on the surface. At least now I know for certain that she cannot sink.

Location: 26.6030º N, 77.1822º W

Mike and Annie come over and, staying in their dinghy, say hello and tell me where he saw fish and lobster are. I empty the dinghy and row out to the rocks near the shore.

The water here is somewhat cloudy and green, so the visibility is poor, but I quickly spear a large lobster. After a fine dinner, Annie and Mike stop by again, staying in their dinghy and keeping 15 feet away. We tell of our catches and he marvels at how many lobster are here. We agree that it is due to the lack of sailors. I remark that we were the luckiest people in the world to be here, in such a beautiful place all full of lobster and fish, while the rest of the world suffers and has trouble finding groceries and toilet paper.

This is how we buddy-boat now: without boarding each other's vessels and without getting near each other.

I don't feel afraid of the virus, yet I still don't invite them aboard. I suppose my sense of self-preservation is a lot stronger than my need to socialize.

In the news, the South Florida Sentinel reports that the state is "opening I-95 checkpoints to screen New Yorkers…

Drivers fleeing the New York coronavirus hot zone will be pulled over and screened at a new I-95 checkpoint," Governor Ron DeSantis says. Checkpoints are also being set up on I-10 to screen those coming from Louisiana.

At this point, New York has 500 deaths and Florida 54. Residents of Boca Raton, Ft Lauderdale, Palm Beach, and others are being told to shelter in place.

Schools are moving to online classes. The USA has 115,00 confirmed cases and 1,840 deaths. The world has 640,500 confirmed cases in 150 countries and 29,848 deaths. Trump threatens to quarantine New York City, but later backs off this threat.

Meanwhile, out on the water, I am feeling stronger than I have in years, perhaps ever. Sailing, pulling up the anchor by hand, rowing *Little Flower* every day, spearfishing and swimming every day provides constant exercise.

Living closer to nature and putting myself back in the food chain is strengthening my mind too. I am becoming braver, getting over some of my last fears, particularly of sharks, although I have so far only seen the two at Cape Eleuthera many weeks before.

I am living the sort of life that I have always desired and dreamed about. I used to think it would be in the forest or the jungle, but it has turned out to be on the ocean. I am free, living close to nature, moving from place to place, killing my own food, and becoming closer to the fearless man I want to be.

I finish reading "Sea Wolf," and give it 5 stars. It's a fantastic story of endurance and the transformation a man undergoes when living at sea, which to some degree mirrors my current experience.

On the VHF, I listen to the Green Turtle Cay Cruiser's Net, and am dismayed to hear The Bahamas is not renewing visas. I am determined to stay and ride out the coronavirus in the land of fish, lobster, clean clear water, and quiet anchorages.

Mika and Annie call and say they are heading down the bay to anchor and fish and they motor away. I don't want to use any fuel unnecessarily, so I sail off anchor and very slowly sail downwind and onto anchor a bit further out than *Precocious*, a Catalina 36 with less draft than *Windflower*.

Location: 26.6002º N, 76.2005º W

They are just getting in their dinghy as I set up *Little Flower* for sailing. I load my spearfishing gear and tack upwind to just past where Mike is fishing, so as not to get in front and fish all the spots ahead of him, yielding right-of-way, since he was here first.

Waves rock the shallow water as I drift downwind and search for fish, but finding none, I settle for a lobster. I am actually getting tired of lobster, which is odd, especially since before I started succeeding underwater I was so used to eating canned tuna. Fresh lobster is in every way superior to canned tuna, I tell myself.

The wind is not ideal for where we are, and *Precocious* motors off, first further downwind to continue fishing (Mike never seems to stop spearfishing) and then to the same spot we were the night before. I hoist the sails and try to sail off anchor as I used to on *Sobrius*, hoisting the mainsail first, and letting the boat try to tack upwind while I pull in the rode. But *Windflower* protests and remains in irons (facing straight into the wind) as I struggle with the anchor line. The sail just provides resistance as I try to pull in the line, working against my great efforts. I end up using the manual windlass, but I think this is more work than pulling the anchor up without it.

We sail upwind, tack once, and sail back onto anchor in the same place we were in the morning.

I find myself to be depressed most of this day, probably because of the news about the cruising permits not being extended, but the murky water and my fruitless effort at spearing a fish also contribute.

After anchoring, I am still determined to get a fish, so I get back in the water, just as Mike is getting out, even though the sun will set soon. I usually don't spearfish anywhere near sunrise or sunset, for fear of sharks, as I've read that they are more likely encountered at these times. I follow two grouper, see a big mutton snapper, and return home with only a lobster.

On the morning of March 30, I hear on the Green Turtle Cruiser's Net that visas *are* being extended, and this makes my morning and erases any lingering depression.

I motor off anchor and begin heading for the north end of Guana Cay, intending to anchor on the outside and dive the barrier reef out there. But as I debate about the use of fuel, which is now precious, and the possibility of running aground, and the fact that I cannot spend tonight outside Guana Cay, I decide to instead stop at the Fish Cays, which is a peaceful and beautiful setting and a place I can spend the night. I anchor close to shore on the east side of the biggest island and get in the water.

Location: 26.6386º N, 77.1542º W

Two hours later I am eating four fillets, panfried with freshly ground black pepper, on a big overflowing sandwich on artisan bread with brown mustard, green tomato, jalapeños, and sprouts on the side. The big fish sandwich is fast becoming my favorite meal.

I go out again for dinner and am surprised by a big shark that swims very close to me, before turning and laying on the bottom. Lucky for me, it's just a harmless nurse shark. While they are harmless, they are still large and ominous and this one reminds me of the reality of sharks, and I keep *Little Flower* even closer than usual. I spear two more snapper, which I eat with beans and rice. I am beginning to think of the ocean as my refrigerator.

The beauty of the setting cheers me up. With the calm

conditions and the clear water, I can see all the details of the sandy bottom through the bright blue water while standing on the deck of my mobile home. The little islands sit still above the sapphire blue water reflecting the bright sun that warms my skin. I am happy and my mood is certainly affected by the surroundings and the quality of the diving. I need beautiful scenery around me, as well as clear water to dive in, of this I am sure.

The day before, I started the book "Lost" by Thomas Thompson, and I finish it in the evening. It's an inspiring and terrifying true story of three people trying to survive on a capsized trimaran in the Pacific Ocean. I can always look back on stories like this when I am going through hard times, and in comparison, my times don't seem so hard.

In the morning, I pull the anchor by hand, and without the engine pushing us forward, in 14 knots of breeze and declare that I will not attempt this in 15 knots or more. We sail off anchor, and when I let out the genoa, I snub the furling line with my foot, which works well, and only unfurl half the sail. I then point into the wind and raise the main and we take off on a beam reach at 7.4 knots with the wind gusting to 20. I put one reef in the main and we slow to 6.5. Thankfully, *Little Flower* is in her davits and thus not filling with water.

We anchor behind Sugarloaf Cay.

Location: 26.5523º N 77.0187º W

Pendant, I believe a Tayana 37, pulls in from the south and anchors ½ mile behind me. I call on the VHF, introduce myself, and invite the skipper to go spearfishing with me. He says he isn't a spearfisherman, and so I tell him "I'll stop by if I get anything extra."

Today is the last day of lobster season, and I am in the right place. I spear a big one right away, soon followed by 2 more in caves along the walls that line the shore. I let one of these go because it is small and still has a lot of fight in it after

I drop it in the boat, but I soon spear another large one.

I spear a Nassau grouper deep in a hole within a cave, but I can't get it out of the hole. I leave the spear and the fish in the hole and swim out of the cave and to the surface to breathe. I go back and try again, then back to the surface, and back and forth a few more times. I hit my head once on the rock overhang so hard that I pull bits of crumbled rock out of my hair, but somehow, there is no bleeding.

I have to leave the fish, and I feel bad for mortally wounding it and not landing it. I am still thinking about this fish and feeling guilty when I go to bed. Sometimes spearfishing is brutal and cruel and this incident is both a reminder of this fact and a lesson. I need to be more careful about spearing fish that I might not be able to extract from their hiding place.

I cross a gap between Sugarloaf Cay and an unnamed rock, and the water gets deeper, to about 20'. Down on the bottom are some big rocks and lots of fish: mangrove snapper, mutton snapper, Nassau grouper, black grouper, and a big sea turtle resting on the bottom. I also see a complete but empty lobster shell, as if it just molted.

I row out to *Pendant*, across much wind, and hail the skipper, who is very pleased when I hand him a lobster. He invites me aboard, but I decline, citing social distancing, and he remarks that out on the water it's so easy to forget about the news of the day. We chat for a few minutes while I hold position in the dinghy with occasional stroke of the oars.

I then row over to *Silver Girl*, who is buddy-boating with *Pendant*, and hail the skipper, who emerges out from the center scuttle, it is a Pearson 424, and smiles when I say "Hello, I've got a lobster for you."

"How much do I owe you?" he replies. I don't expect this response, but I suppose he doesn't know me at all and I haven't made it clear that the lobster is a gift, so it takes me a moment to respond.

"Nothing. It's the last day of lobster season, and I thought everyone deserves a lobster today. I don't have a refrigerator, so I can only eat one, but I speared three so I could give one to you and one to *Pendant*."

He is nearly bursting with joy as I hand him a good-sized lobster, still wet from the ocean and barely dead. His wife emerges from the scuttle and gives me a jar of peanuts, saying "One good turn deserves another."

She looks at the lobster with admiration and awe. She says something about having only dealt with the tails, so I take it back and remove the tail from the body, clear out the digestive tract from the tail with an antenna, and hand it back to them.

They are so happy, and their happiness makes me happy, and I am glad I went out of my way to spear three lobster and row over to these boats with gifts. This is an easy way to make strangers happy, to make me happy, and to make new friends.

We visit for a while, and when she tells me that she used to be a librarian, I mention that I am an author, and this pleases them even more. She goes below and comes back with a plastic grocery bag with four books in it, as a gift for me. After a long and enjoyable visit, I begin to row away.

Windflower is about a half mile away, upwind, and *Silver Girl* is not close to shore, where the wind is deflected. I lean into the oars, fighting the wind and pulling hard. With a loud crack, my arm retracts as the right oar snaps and we begin drifting downwind fast.

Instinctively, I row once with just the left oar, but this only turns *Little Flower* on her center axis and provides no forward thrust at all. I call myself a fool, and since the oar doesn't break all the way, I turn it around and row a few strokes, but it flexes mightily and is useless. I need a remedy right away, as we are drifting again, and so I pull the oar in and break off the upper portion, then begin rowing with one short oar and one long oar. This works, but is clumsy, slow, and inefficient. I have to row two strokes on the right for every one on the left.

I turn us toward shore, which is quite a few hundred

yards away, just in case I begin to lose ground. I don't have a radio and downwind is two and a half miles of open water, followed by the north end of Elbow Cay and the Atlantic Ocean. After an extraordinary effort, I am able to get back to my ship, where I catch my breath and then eat the third lobster.

It rains in the morning, and the sky is finished, I row with the short backup oars, which are clumsy and inefficient to say the least, but I am glad I have them. I am so used to the long oars that this is like learning to row all over again, and with substandard equipment. The wind, especially where it comes through between the islets, makes the rowing a challenge. But I make it to the area where I fished the day before, hoping to get fish, as lobster season is now over.

There are a few times, after the season ends, that I am tempted to spear lobster, but I am determined not to, especially after getting upset with the woman in The Exumas who ordered her captain to spear the lobster in the Land and Sea Park. But just the urge to do so makes me a little more forgiving and understanding of her crime.

The water is a bit cloudy, on account of the wind stirring it up, and I do not see as many fish as the day before. But I see a big sea turtle lounging on the bottom under the ledge of a rock. Seeing such a massive air-breathing creature, one that looks like it belongs on land in the time of the dinosaurs, lounging under a rock at the bottom of the ocean is almost like hallucinating.

After a few dives, and seeing nothing to spear, I swim along the shore, which is a vertical wall, and peer in all the caves, looking for grouper. I swim across the biggest gap between islets, and inside the current is like a river, but on the other side, the water is calm and clear.

A large Nassau grouper sits on the bottom, looking at me, at the first rock I come to. I swim by as if not interested, watching it out of the corner of my eye, but facing away. But the fish does not fall for my ruse and hides under the rock.

I swim down and look in, and can clearly see the fish, which I very much want for lunch, but I'm not sure I will be able to get it out from under the rock. I surface and breathe and watch the rock, going back down a few times to look in. While on the surface, I see a flash of movement from the rock to the wall on the shore. I swim to the wall and find three holes, and in one is the fish, trying its best to sit still up against the rock in the dead-end cave. It has nowhere to go, and I spear it, but the fish has to come backwards out of the hole and its fins prevent this. I am determined not to lose this one, so I leave the spear in the fish and go to the surface to breathe. After a few tries, I finally get a hold of it with my gloved left hand and am able to pull it out of the hole.

I eat the grouper with a can of beets, which I realize that I really like (the canned beets), and the meal is delicious.

Later, I move to the south side of Marsh Harbor, anticipating north winds. I also want to go to town the next day, and try to extend my cruising permit.

Location: 26.5370º N, 77.0475º W

In the morning, I row to shore, with the short oars, beach *Little Flower*, and begin wandering around a neighborhood, looking for the way to town, but every street I walk down is a dead-end. The first car to come by is a small black sedan and it stops and young black man asks if I am all right. My American instincts have me expecting the guy to ask if I want to buy weed, but I couldn't be more wrong. He asks where I am going and when I say the government building, he says he will drive me there, and he does, and refuses my offer to give him something for the gas.

Wilson is his name, and I ask if he is from March Harbor, which he is, and if he was there for hurricane Dorian, which he was. He says he moved to Nassau after the hurricane, and he points to where his house used to be, which is now an empty lot. I ask what it was like, being in a house while it got destroyed by a hurricane. Wilson pauses and only says "I can't describe that," and I don't press the issue.

Customs and immigrations is closed at the government building, but the woman at the administration desk, who wears a mask, tells me to try at the port, which is not far away.

I have to leave my driver's license at the port gate, and am directed to a white portable building which holds the customs office. The dock is noisy and full of activity, and stacks of building materials sit in neat rows, unloaded from cargo ships and waiting to be transported to construction sites.

I am greeted by two friendly women, not wearing masks, in the office, and they readily extend my cruising permit for one year, and charge me $500, which is what I expected to pay.

I walk to Maxwell's, the grocery store, but turn away when I see the line outside. The store is limiting the number of people allowed in at any one time.

I use the Navionics app on my phone, which has been tracking my movements, to find my way back to the neighborhood and *Little Flower*, who patiently waits for me on the beach.

I sail off anchor to the lee of Sugarloaf Cay.

Location: 26.5448º N, 77.0231º W

I waste no time in getting in the water, and right away I find a conch, and set it in the boat. While swimming along the edge of shore, a school of schoolmaster snapper swims towards me, clearly running from something, and this sets me on alert, expecting a shark to come around the corner. Soon after, I come across the culprit, a goliath grouper that looks like it weighs at least 50 pounds.

I don't get any fish, but on the way back to *Windflower*, I find a coral-head with schools of snapper and grunt swimming around it. I try to spear a snapper, but am unsuccessful. I hit two, and even hoist one out of the water, but both get away.

I cook the conch with a can of Rotel, and it is edible

but tough and not particularly good. The conch waste comes in useful later, as I return to the coral-head at sunset with the fishing rod and use the conch guts to catch four grunts for dinner.

Between April 2 and 3, 1000 people in the US died of the coronavirus. There are 216,000 confirmed cases in the US, which is the most in any country. Personal protective gear is in short supply, and states are competing for masks. New York City is a hotspot for the virus, with 47,500 cases and 1,300 deaths. Bodies in the city are overwhelming the morgues, and are being stored in refrigerated trucks.

Florida, Georgia, and Mississippi are under lockdown with people ordered to stay home. In the UK, Wimbledon is cancelled. In the US, 6.6 million people have claimed unemployment – the most in history.

In the news, Dr. Li Wang in China, in December, tried to warn other doctors of a new virus emerging in Wuhan, and was accused by the police of scaremongering. Dr. Li Wang later died of the virus. China told the World Health Organization of the virus on December 31. By mid-January, people were travelling in China for the New Year, and 200 cases were reported in Beijing, Shanghi, and Shenzen. By January 23, Wuhan was on lockdown, having had 18 deaths. There were 570 cases reported worldwide at this point, in Taiwan, Japan, Thailand, South Korea, and the USA. A week later Iran reported cases.

On February 23, Italy had a surge in cases. On March 23, Britain ordered a three-week lockdown. On March 26, the US overtook China with 86,000 cases. On April 2, yesterday, the US had 217,000 cases.

Also on April 2, the commander of the US aircraft carrier the *Theodore Roosevelt* was fired after saying that the Navy didn't do enough to protect the personnel on his ship from the virus.

As I sit at the navigation table, I tune in to the cruiser's net from Hopetown. During "open mic" I share with the net how I renewed my cruising permit. The host asks if I also renewed my visa, and, in the ensuing conversation, I learn that in order to legally stay, I need to renew my visa, and that the cruising permit only allows my boat to stay in the country. My visa expires the next day, April 4. I need to take action; I am not ready to return to the US.

I motor to the harbor at Marsh Harbor, row ashore (with the long oars, which I have repaired with epoxy and fiberglass cloth), and walk to the customs office at the port, where they tell me I have to go to the immigration office at the government building. I walk there, only to find that it is still closed. I ask at the administration office and they say that immigration will not open until after the lockdown expires, scheduled for April 8.

I leave and walk to Maxwell's and stand in line. Luckily, I have my Kindle and I read while we all wait. Inside are signs stating that we all should stay six feet apart, which isn't a problem, since there are few people inside.

I am tired when I get back to the boat, but I rally after a rest and motor to the lee of Matt Lowe's Cay, on the south side of the island, a new anchorage to me.

Location: 26.5595º N, 77.0134º W

I get in the water and spear a snapper. But the most interesting thing I see is a large spotted eagle ray that swims right up and slowly circles me before swimming away. I can see its big barbed spine, and it seems like a territorial display, like the big ray is saying "Hey, who are you? This is *my* neighborhood."

I hear from Erick and Jen on *Windsong*. They are heading back to Florida via the Berry Islands. They heard about sailors being harassed by the police at Eleuthera if they are moving about and not heading home. They report that Bimini has a blockade and people are having trouble leaving.

I am happy to be in the Abacos, where nobody is bothering me. I suppose they have bigger problems here, and there are very few sailboats around here anyway.

The next morning, I tackle a project that has been on my mind since I bought the boat. Every time we sail, water runs into the shower sump from somewhere, and I have to empty it after sailing. I think it must be coming from the anchor locker. The fiberglass tabbing on the bulkhead in the anchor locker is separating from the plywood, and conceivably letting water pass through, water which comes in through the anchor locker drains. These are underwater every time we move because of the bow wake.

I pull everything out of the locker, clean it of debris, sand the bulkhead and tabbing, and add a layer of fiberglass cloth over the seam. This bulkhead is also where the inner forestay chainplate attaches, so it has to be strong, and if the tabbing is separating, it needs to be fixed anyway. The repair is successful.

Mike from *Precocious* emails me a letter from the police commissioner in Nassau, a Remain in Place order, stating "… all boaters are to remain onboard their vessels." Provisions are to be obtained by delivery only. However, at the bottom of the letter are instructions for emailing a request to extend a visa, which includes sending photos of the passport and visa documents. I am happy to see this, since I've already invested $500 in the cruising permit, which is useless without extending my visa.

My mother, when I ask her how life is different, says every day is "rich with change." She sees many families that she has never seen before out on the walking path in the park across the street, as well as many more bicyclers. However, some of her friends complain of being bored, which I'm sure does not impress my mother. "Read a book," she always used to say if I complained of boredom. She and my father are mostly staying isolated, but still go on occasional hikes with friends, keeping six feet apart when doing so, which is the new normal.

In the news, our president fired the inspector general of the intelligence community, Michael Atkinson, who alerted congress to the whistleblower that led to his impeachment, a clear act of revenge, a petty motive for a common man, and, in my opinion, unacceptable for the president of the United States, but not unexpected behavior from him.

In England, people are burning 5G towers, or "masts" as they called them in England, in response to a conspiracy theory that 5G suppresses the immune system, or that the towers are being used to selectively infect victims with the coronavirus.

States and the federal government are starting to feud over access to N95 masks, particularly over the federal government's stockpile of the masks. Apparently, Jared Kushner, the president's-son-in law, has been put in charge of the medical supply chain that delivers critical items to doctors and nurses – a clear case of nepotism and likely corruption and pandemic-profiteering.

On April 4, there are 300,000 cases in the US, and just over 8,000 deaths. Globally, there are 1.1 million cases and 60,000 deaths. New York City has 63,036 cases and is asking for more doctors and nurses to come to the city to help.

The problems of the pandemic are far away, and while they threaten to make my time in The Bahamas a bit less convenient, and will probably ruin my chances of going to Canada in the summer, my days are as they would be regardless: sailing, spearfishing, and moving about from anchorage to anchorage as the weather and my whims dictate.

Meanwhile, I am trying for the second time to use my pressure cooker to make beans and rice. The first try was a failure, and I had hard beans and mushy rice for dinner. This time I use more water, and have better success, but this thing is not as easy to use as I expected.

I wake up on the fifth of April surprised to be facing

away from land, and I feel lucky to still be in 11 feet of water. This is a reminder to never assume the boat will not swing around the entire anchoring circle. Sometimes I want to drop the anchor as close as possible to land, even though the water past the anchor is too shallow for my boat's draft. I would have been aground on this morning if that was the case.

I also should have paid closer attention to the weather and moved the day before.

While passing Matt Lowe's Cay, an exceptionally beautiful island when viewed from this angle, a depressing thought occurs to me. The scenery is beginning to look normal.

Beauty is often surrounding us, but unless we stop and take a moment to appreciate it, unless we remind ourselves to do so, it will become normal and uninspiring. Beauty relies on a state of mind, and sometimes we need to cultivate this.

I anchor at Man-O-War Cay, a place I have been wanting to visit for a long time, but now that I am here, unfortunately, I am unable to go to shore.

Location: 26.6065º N, 77.0819º W

I find a nice coral reef right in the anchorage, but all the fish there, and there are many that I would love to eat, are quite wary of me and do a good job at staying away. Meanwhile, I meet another singlehander, Holt, on a Caliber 40, who is heading back to Beaufort, North Carolina. He says he doesn't feel welcome in The Bahamas anymore. He fears that crime will eventually increase as the economy dies. The Abacos are already suffering greatly from the fallout of Hurricane Dorian, and there are very few cruising boats here this season.

We talk for a while, with me in my dinghy and he standing at the bow of his boat, discussing singlehanding issues and the situation for cruisers in The Bahamas. It is unclear and vague what the orders are, and whether or not we are being ordered to leave, or to just stay off the islands. Certainly the local economy would be happier if we stayed.

Meanwhile, my mother and father attend virtual church, I'm sure a first for everyone involved. Our president wants to open America back up, "so that the cure won't be worse than the disease," he says. I am inclined to agree with him, which is also a first, but the future will prove otherwise.

The lives of my friends are apparently much different from mine during the quarantine. James Slack, one of my friends, wrote the following:

"Day 12 – We have started stripping wallpaper to use as toilet paper. The only food we could get from the grocery store was 32 boxes of the Kroger version of Hamburger Helper and 61 cans of Turkey Spam. The TV screen is pitted and chinked because the kids keep shooting it with their BB guns whenever Trump makes a statement. My wife is alternating fantasizing about Dr Fauci and Gov Cuomo. I have rediscovered solitaire. The pets now hate us all. We have made DIY hand sanitizer out of Early Times whiskey, Robitussin Nighttime cold medicine, and Crisco, and facemasks out of old underwear. With no barbers or hairstylists available, we look like The Beatles after they overdosed on Rogaine. The good news: Not one Jehova's Witness has knocked on our door since we were ordered into isolation."

On the sixth of April, the US has 337,274 cases and 9,619 deaths, of which 4,159 were in New York. However, at this point, 75% who have been hospitalized have been released. In the UK, Boris Johnson is in the hospital suffering from the virus.

I overhear on the VHF that a sailboat tried to cross around Whale Cay, heading west, but had to turn back because waves were breaking across Two Rocks Cut. The swell is 10', so this is not to be unexpected, as the chart states that waves break across the cut in large swells. The pass around Whale

Cay is the only way to continue sailing northwest through the Abacos, and I plan to pass that way soon.

It is a rainy morning, and I am reading "Don Quixote," which I am enjoying immensely, when I hear a man hailing *Windflower*. A man in a boat holds up a badge and introduces himself as the local Chief of Police.

He is friendly and almost apologetic in informing me that the Prime Minister of The Bahamas has declared that foreign boaters are no longer allowed to go to shore. He also says that the Prime Minister recommends that all foreign boats should leave the country and return to their home ports. The Bahamas is on lockdown and residents are not supposed to leave their homes. The government is afraid of the virus reaching the out-islands where medical facilities are scarce.

When questioned, he doesn't say that I have to leave right away, and I tell him I plan to stay here tonight and will be heading west in the morning. I ask him about the local economy and how it will recover from Hurricane Dorian if all the cruisers leave. He says, with head downturned, that he doesn't think it will ever recover.

In the morning, I pull anchor and set sail and experiment with my new sheet-to-tiller arrangement while sailing wing-on-wing, downwind, in 5-9 knots. It doesn't work at all. [*In retrospect, I had it rigged wrong for downwind, and the breeze was probably too light anyway.*] I also try it on a broad reach, again without luck, and on top of it not working, the line I used to hold the block for the sheet in the cockpit breaks. I also think the tiller might be too short.

I have to study up on this before the passage to St Augustine, and re-read the chapter about it in "Singlehanded Sailing, Thoughts, Tips, and Techniques" by Andrew Evans. When sailing straight downwind, a sheet-to-tiller rig would use a storm jib poled out on the headstay opposite the genoa. I simply had the staysail set as normal and the sheet run to the windward side of the cockpit. On a broad reach through a close reach, the staysail or storm jib is sheeted to the centerline of the boat and the sheet is run directly to the windward rail and from there to the cockpit and tied to the tiller, which is balanced by elastic, preferably surgical tubing, on the other side.

I sail to the Fish Cays, where I sail onto anchor off the northernmost island and go spearfishing, but I return empty-handed and continue on to Red Bay, to take shelter from the coming south-southeast wind.

Location: 26.6018º N, 77.1851º W

I anchor at Red Bay in time to hunt around a rock jetty by the entrance to the commercial marina that sits tucked in the rocks. The sun is low on the horizon and the water is a bit cloudy and dark, but the jetty houses hundreds of fish. But sometimes, even when surrounded by fish, I still can't get one, and this is the case here. My spear is still powered only by a bungee cord, and is nearly useless against fish, and lobster season is over. I return empty-handed, again, but having experienced another unique underwater world.

Back at the navigation table, I check noonsite.com and see that foreign boats in The Bahamas are not permitted to move unless they are on their way home. I begin contemplating going back to the United States.

There might still be a chance of going to Canada in the summer, if the border opens back up soon enough. If so, I would need to get back to Florida very soon and get to work replacing *Windflower's* standing rigging and making other repairs. Even if Canada remains closed, I could still go to Maine, which would be a nice adventure. Or if I miss my opportunity to go to Newfoundland, perhaps I could sail to the Azores instead.

But with the economy crashing, I feel like I should be as frugal as possible. Perhaps I should replace the standing rigging myself, or not at all and skip the long ocean passages. Perhaps I need to prioritize survival.

This whole affair with the pandemic, coupled with the

post-Armageddon feel of the Abacos, makes me feel like I should keep *Windflower* stocked with survival gear. I should get proficient at catching rain, and have lots of fishing gear onboard. It would also behoove the survivalist to have the boat in as strong and ready a condition as possible. If the economy totally crashes, money will have no value, while goods, like a well-set up sailboat, will be priceless. This is an argument for repairing and replacing everything *Windflower* needs. This also makes me wish I still had my guns.

The morning is quiet and peaceful, the sun shines bright, and the air moves only slightly. I motor over to Treasure Cay later in the day to get protection from the west winds coming in the night and the next day.

Location: 26.6582º N, 77.2844º W

I look around and see no other sailboats, which is becoming the norm. I begin to feel like I am the only cruising sailboat left. The day before, I saw five boats sail out of the area, heading west. Everyone seems to be going home.

I ask my father, a retired surgeon, if he thinks the risk posed by the virus justifies the worldwide quarantine measures. He writes back saying that is a difficult question. While some epidemiologists think we would have been much better off with only social distancing the high-risk people and let the virus run its course like any other flu. This way we would reach "herd immunity," a phrase becoming popular in the news, much quicker.

I fear the end result of the quarantines will be the loss of many small businesses which will be replaced by bigger companies. Monopolies will be achieved and the gap between rich and poor widened. I also fear that our freedoms of movement and travel might never be fully restored.

In the news, ABC reports that in November, intelligence officials warned of a contagion in Wuhan "changing patterns of life and threatening the population" could be a cataclysmic event. This warning made its way to the president's daily briefing.

Our president has been going back and forth between taking credit for early action and claiming that the virus took everyone by surprise. It was on January 31 that he restricted air travel with China and March 13 that he declared a national emergency. He also fired the entire pandemic response team well prior to the pandemic, and at one point said "it's just the flu" and that it would just go away.

On April 8, the US has 398,000 cases. Globally there are 1.4 million. Wuhan has ended its lockdown.

In the afternoon, I row upwind to the sunken barge for another go at the snapper that live inside. My first strategy is to sneak up to the window before all the fish know I am there and surprise one with my spear. But as soon as I approach, all the little bluestriped grunts that hang around outside the window bolt in and alert the larger snapper, who move deeper into the barge, and they all stay out of range. This appears to be an example of interspecies nonverbal communication.

My next strategy involves crushed up cheese crackers, courtesy of Holt on the Caliber 40 at Man-O-War, which I brought with me in a plastic bag. They are inedible to me, but I think they might attract small fish, who might cause a curious larger fish to come see what's going on. I take the crackers out of a fold in my wetsuit, open the bag, and release the contents, which makes a cloud in the water. Unfortunately, the fish don't like the crackers and the fake cheese any more than I do.

I return empty-handed, but at least having tried a new strategy. It might have worked with a snack that the fish actually liked.

The rest of the day is cloudy and windy and I spend my time writing, but the wind, as it does, makes me feel restless. I feel better in the late afternoon when it calms down. The wind calms even further at dusk, when the sun sets as a red disk over the low island and the only sound is the gentle sloshing of water against the hull. No other boats are in view, and no man-made sounds can be heard. It is a peaceful evening, as most of them are.

Meanwhile, the world's economy is predicted to suffer as never before. The UN states that 81% of the world's work-force is out of work. In the US, 16 million people seek un-employment benefits. It is predicted that half of the world's population could end up in poverty.

Bernie Sanders has dropped out of the presidential race, and our president has been accused of owning stock in the company that made hydroxychloroquine, the drug that he has been pushing, as if he knows anything about medicine.

On the tenth of April, the US has 462,000 cases and 16,500 deaths, while the world has 1.6 million cases and 950,000 deaths. New York has 159,937 cases and 7,000 deaths.

At this point, it is predicted by the WHO that 2,140,000 lives have been saved worldwide by the quarantine methods, yet the world's economy is in ruins. I become curious about how the deaths from the virus compare to other causes of death in the United States, and find the following data on deaths of Americans for the year 2017:

Total deaths: 2,813,503
Cigarettes: 480,000
Heart disease: 647,457
Unintentional injuries: 169,936
Chronic Lower Respiratory Disease: 160,201
Stroke: 146,383
Alzheimer's: 121,404
Influenza and Pneumonia: 55,672
Kidney Disease: 50,633
Suicide: 47,173

I still find the Covid numbers to be unimpressive. It's strange to be so removed from the problem of the disease, and to see such harsh measures, such as the world has never seen. I have trouble making sense out of the situation.

I intend to sail to Great Guana Cay as soon as the wind veers and take shelter there for the night. But I wait all day, and by 5:00, the wind still hasn't moved, so I make peace with the idea of staying where I am for the night.

I study the charts, looking for interesting places to see on the way through the rest of the Abacos. The little islands in the far northwest attract my attention, as they look remote and surrounded by reef and small cays. One in particular, Double Breasted Cay, sticks out as one I should visit, but it also looks difficult to anchor there, unless the wind is north, and the wind has been moving around a lot since I have been in the Abacos. The reviews on Navionics praise the beauty of the island, but also warn of its many dangers.

After dinner, I pop my head out of the companionway and am surprised to see that we are now facing north, and the wind has veered 90 degrees in the last hour. We need to leave this anchorage, and we need to leave immediately if we are to get to Guana before dark. Luckily, *Windflower* is ready to go and I start the engine and pull up the anchor.

As we motor away, I unfurl the headsail, then put on my harness and take the mainsail cover off, something I always do before leaving, but this time there is no time.

We hit nearly 7 knots, so I shut the engine off, but we still make 6.5, which is too fast for towing *Little Flower* without her filling with water, so I furl a bit of the genoa. The breeze eventually decreases, and I unfurl the genoa in response as we pass the Fish Cays.

The breeze further decreases, and I start the engine.

While we sail, the sun sets, and the sky to windward blackens. Dark clouds are approaching and I can hear the distant rumble of thunder and see faint flashes of light coming from behind.

We reach Great Guana Cay and the main anchorage at

Delia's Cay just after sunset, but before total darkness. I anchor as close to the same spot as we were before, as told by the few mooring buoys in the water, and just as I do it starts to rain.

The rain falls heavily, the sky becomes completely dark, and lightning flashes all around. I work quickly to get the sails put away, and while doing so I step through an open portlight (an opening window), right through the screen, and skin my shin. I make a mental note to keep these closed while sailing.

In the news, deaths from the virus are starting to level off and are predicted to decline. The US has 475,000 cases and 18,000 deaths.

Conspiracy theories are flying around on social media, and one of the most outlandish states that there is no virus and that the sick people are getting sick from 5G, and that the stay-at-home measures are in place so 5G can be installed in schools.

Dr. Fauci is discussing issuing immunity certificates to those with proven antibodies, and that such tests are said to be available the following week.

THE NORTHWESTERN ABACOS

Its lonely here
In the Abacos
The trees are bare
The houses bulldozed
Precious few
Are cruising boats
Where once were many
Now there are none
Green shores now brown
Leaves blown off the trees
Tourists have all gone home
Borders closed for the disease

At 8:30am, I leave Great Guana Cay under full sails and with the bimini down, taking in all the beauty of the sky, the islands, and the blue water. Windflower is on a broad reach in 12-14 knots and making 6.5 heading west, out and around Whale Cay.

As we sail through the channels and cuts, little cays and emergent rocks pass on either side, in water either bright or dark blue, depending on the depth and composition of the bottom. We pass Whale Cay, a jagged rocky little island that takes the full force of ocean waves every day of its existence, and through Two Rocks Cut, a narrow but simple entrance to the protected waters on the inside.

As we pass Manjack Cay, I overhear a boat being hailed by an official on land. The boat is heading from Manjack to a cove on the west end of Green Turtle Cay, without plans to go ashore and for the purpose of anchoring in more sheltered water, the captain explains. The official on land has all sorts of questions regarding where they have been and if they have permission to be moving. This conversation ends any thoughts I have about anchoring at Manjack, and we continue on towards the other destination I have in mind, which seems better for the coming winds anyway.

Crab Cay is a long skinny island that shelters a large bay, which is protected from wind from the south, east, and north. I've never been there, and am looking forward to exploring a new place. As I get closer, I can see two sailboats in the bay, and one of them is *Makani*, my friends John and Kathi whom I met at Spanish Wells, again at Hatchet Bay, and again at Marsh Harbor.

After I get my anchor set, a man motors over in a dinghy. I hope it is not some official coming to interrogate me about my plans.

Location: 26.9181º N, 77.5923º W

It is not this at all, but rather a man from a small trawler tucked way up close to shore. He introduces himself, then offers me "crawfish." "Crawfish?" I say. "Lobster," he says. I know he means lobster, but I'm surprised because lobster season is over. I can see someone poaching and eating them, but to brazenly offer a poached lobster to someone else, I think, is bizarre.

"They're out of season," I say.

"Not if they jump on your spear," he says.

"No, thanks, I don't want out of season lobster."

"You won't eat them tonight?"

"I don't even want them on my boat."

He looks dejected and like he is about to leave, but I want to continue talking, so I ask about the area. He tells me of a blue hole behind the small cays, and a sunken barge nearby, neither of which I find.

I get my gear ready and row over to *Makani.* John tells me they left Manjack when things started getting strict. I relay to John how distressed I was to hear the words "kudos to whoever ran off the boat trying to come into White Sound yesterday" on the Green Turtle Cruiser's Net the day before. He nods in agreement when I say "What is the world coming to? We are sailors and should be going out of our way to help each other, not run off a boat trying to enter a harbor. They probably needed water and fuel."

I go spearfishing around Crab Cay and the main island (Little Abaco Cay), and find mangrove snapper in a cave in a cove east of the cut. The cut itself is also full of fish, but the incoming tidal current is strong. I hit one snapper and shoot at two more, but none end up in my boat.

Sadly, my elastic breaks. It was already in a sorry state, with the remaining piece of surgical tubing in a small thumb-loop tied to a long piece of bungee. It provided little power, and with the last bit of surgical tubing broken, I am again relegated to caveman-style spearfishing: no elastic, just a spear to jab at the fish.

On the way out, John loaned me a radio and told me to call if I got into trouble and needed to be towed in. When I return it, he gives me a new elastic band for the spear, a priceless gift, and I thank him profusely. This is just what I need to ensure that my diet of fresh fish will continue indefinitely.

The following day, I catch the last of the incoming tide, just before noon, spearfishing in the channel between Crab Cay and Little Abaco. The tidal current is very strong in the cut, so the only opportunity to spearfish in the cut is near and during slack tide. Otherwise, even if I drift through, I can't swim against the tide in order to effectively hunt.

In the cut are sea fans, sponges, little patches of coral, numerous small holes and larger depressions in the hard bottom, and a wide variety of fish. When the current sweeps me deeper into the bay, the bottom becomes grass and the current eases, and I get back in *Little Flower*, row back to the cut, outside the current on the Little Abaco side, where I sneak around the point in the shallow water and eddies, then drift through again. At slack tide, this is an easy operation, and once the current shows any sign of switching to outgoing, I leave the area. I don't want there to be any chance of me being swept out to sea and not be able to row back in.

While drifting through the cut, I often see a fish I want to pursue, like a grouper that swims into a hole, and I hook the little anchor on the end of the painter to the bottom and hold my position. But in the strong current, it is still hard to maintain position, even with the anchor. I feel like a water-skier, who, after failing to get up on the skis, continues to hold the rope as the boat pulls him through the water.

I don't spear any fish in the cut, but it is such an interesting dive that I let the current pull me through many times.

As the strength of the tide increases and the current becomes too much to deal with, I row out of the cut and along the shore of Little Abaco, past the beach with its coconut palms and around a shallow rocky point, past the little trawler where the man with the out-of-season lobster lives, all the while looking for an interesting place to fish. I find it in a dark channel that appears to be manmade with a rubble jetty next to it. The channel leads out of sight into mangroves and I think for sure there will be mangrove snapper somewhere in there.

This is a strange place to find a jetty and a manmade channel, since there are no houses in sight or any town nearby. Regardless, I row into the channel and tie *Little Flower* to some mangroves in shallow water over hard rock bottom, then slip into the dark water.

The bottom is silt, so I am careful not to stir it up as I swim slowly and quietly up the channel with my spear pointing forward and the new elastic stretched between my hand and the butt of the spear, ready to shoot. It isn't long before two good-sized snapper swim down the channel towards me, then pause, probably wondering what I am and if I am a threat. I spear one, but it gets away and swims back the way it came. I follow, but the channel, which started at only about 12' across and 10' deep, gets narrower and shallower and I know there is a very good chance that a shark will be coming my way and we will have to pass each other, and on top of that there is a wounded fish in the channel now. I picture a bull shark coming down the channel towards me, getting nervous when it sees me, and me pressing up against the side of the channel as it brushes by.

Moments later, a shark does come down the channel, just as I predicted, but it is only a small shark, 4' long at the most. It gets nervous when it sees me and turns around, then comes back and we pass each other on opposite sides of the channel, almost exactly as I predicted. I recognize it as a lemon shark, identified by two dorsal fins of equal size. Nurse sharks also have two dorsal fins of equal size, but they are also distinguished by the tail fin that has no lower lobe, barbels on the mouth (like the whiskers of a catfish but shorter and pointed down), and the first dorsal fin begins well behind the pectoral fins. The lemon shark has a mouth that looks like that of a typical shark, a normal tailfin, and its first dorsal fin begins above the middle of the pectoral fins.

I continue up the channel, which eventually pinches off in a shallow mangrove flat, but I find another nice snapper and land it, thanks to the new elastic on the spear. I have to swim with the fish, holding it out of the water, all the way back to the dinghy.

Wanting more, I tow *Little Flower* with me back up the

channel, then down the channel where it gets deeper and wider. I pass over a spring in the bottom at one point, see grouper, mackerel, barjack, and more snapper.

Out on the point of the jetty, which is made up of a pile of rubble, which fish love, is an entire school of snapper rounding the point going in either direction. I sit still, holding onto the rocks with my left hand and the spear ready to fire in my right. It isn't long before a snapper swims in front of my spear and I let it fly. The spear hits the fish in the side and it thrashes and bleeds while I hoist it out of the water and swim to the dinghy, which is anchored right behind me.

I return to the jetty and see two nice-sized snapper heading into the channel. I follow and stretch the elastic on the spear, ready to shoot, and descended to the bottom where the fish are. They speed away, but then I see a grouper and follow it to a hole where it disappears. I wait to see if it will come out, staring at the hole in the silty bottom, all grey and smooth, but the fish remains hidden and I return to the surface to breathe.

I swim slowly back to the point of the jetty and lay down on the bottom with the spear ready for action. Mangrove snapper swim by in both directions while I hold my breath and remain perfectly still. I let a few small fish swim right by the point of the spear. A bigger one comes around the corner, sees me and speeds up, but it isn't evasive enough and in a flash it is on the tip of my spear. I swim to the dinghy with the fish out of the water and drop it in the boat.

I now have three good fish in the boat, but I am excited to be getting fish and start back toward the jetty when an enormous barracuda, its bright silver scales reflecting the sun, its mouth open as a show of confidence, its great teeth bared, swims right by me and towards the jetty, right where I just speared the last fish. I figure this is a good time to call it a day, so I turn around and get in the boat, pull up the anchor, and start rowing for home. I can see the barracuda following us, and I am glad to be out of the water. I wonder, as I row and look at the dark shadow in the water, if the barracuda was watching me all along.

April 13, report from Culebra, (between Puerto Rico and the Virgin Islands, a popular anchorage for cruisers): "DNRA are not letting any new boats into the bay, even if they are US flagged…boats are being turned away."

Noonsite is recommending that sailors should stay where they are if possible, as most countries on cruising routes have closed their borders.

Countries with borders still open, although most require 2-week quarantines upon entering, include Barbados, Montserrat, St Vincent and the Grenadines, US Virgin Islands, USA, Mexico, Nicaragua, Panama, Argentina, French Guiana, Turkey, Eritria, Tanzania, Japan, Myanmar, Papua New Guinea, Singapore, Tasmania, and Guam.

French Polynesia is turning people away.

I speak to my father and ask him about the situation, as I am still not impressed by the numbers of cases and deaths, and he explains that the quarantines and lockdowns are necessary in order to prevent hospitals from becoming overwhelmed.

He tells me the walking path outside their house looks like a daily parade. Gas is $1.50 a gallon. Everyone who can work from home is doing so, and everyone is learning how to use the internet to have meetings and informal group conversations. The website Zoom is becoming popular for this. People, in the future, he says, are going to modify how they live and spend less money overall. All children are being homeschooled and people are finding this to be more efficient than classroom schooling. My oldest niece is able to meet with all of her teachers at the normal times, but via the internet.

I suspect that homeschooling is more efficient than the classroom, where so much time is wasted and the smarter children have to wait and sit through explanations of things they already understand, while the slower children are left behind. I am reminded of basketball practice. In a large group, a line will form and the kid at the front shoots at the hoop, then goes to the back of the line and waits for his turn to come up again. A child doing this alone shoots over and over again without having to wait. I imagine homeschooling is similar, and allows children to learn at the pace they need and focus on the material they need.

Perhaps these trends will continue after the pandemic and quarantines are over.

Back in St Augustine, my friend Lorin reports that St Augustine Beach is empty and traffic on Anastasia Island is about 20% of its normal amount. Most people in public are now wearing masks. Popular opinion is that this way of life will stick around for a long time. He is missing a vacation planned for Eleuthera at the moment.

I am still debating whether to return to the United States or stay in The Bahamas, or go to Panama for hurricane season and surf at Bocas Del Toro.

In the morning, the wind is strong and blowing directly opposite the incoming tide. I'm rowing out to the cut anyway, and the standing waves in the channel remind me of whitewater canoeing in West Virginia. The wind has more effect on *Little Flower* than the current, since most of her is out of the water, and, though the waves make it a challenge, I easily row through the cut against the incoming tide. Once outside, I gear up and get in the water.

The current pulls me back into the channel and I hold on to my dinghy's painter tight, since the wind is trying to pull her in the opposite direction. I swim down to the reef below and swiftly drift across, too fast to effectively hunt. Snapper and grouper sit still on the bottom as I speed across depressions, little caves, and reefs. Sometimes when I see a fish I want, I set the anchor, which I carry in my hand, and hang on, but I still can't move against the current. It's not producing dinner, but I'm having fun, so I do it over and over again, rowing outside and drifting back in underwater.

After a few drifts in the cut, I spear a small grunt in

the little cove by the point on Little Abaco. I then row all the way out to the small cays inside the bay. Here I get two small mangrove snapper in shallow water by laying still next to a little swim-through cave that the fish are passing through and spearing them as they emerge on my side, before they see me.

I swim away and continue hunting along these little cays, twice losing a fish and following the wounded fish as much as I can, but lose both. I see an octopus inside a little hole, outside of which is a pile of empty shells. This is the first octopus I have ever seen besides the ones in Sweetings Pond. I look, but do not attempt to spear the octopus; I have too much respect for these amazing animals.

While I am behind these cays, I keep an eye out for the blue hole the guy with the poached lobster told me about. I think I see one next to a calm grassy area, and I get in to inspect, carrying my spear in case I come across any prey. When I discover that it is just a circle of dark grass, I get back aboard and decide that I will fish one more point and then call it a day, and row across a windy gap between the two cays. But when I grab my spear, I notice that the new elastic is gone. The endcap is gone too, apparently it unscrewed, just like it did back by Scotland Cay. Somewhere on the bottom, probably in the grassy area, lays my new elastic. I have to find it.

I turn back to the grassy spot where I last was in the water with the spear and search long and hard, but to no avail. I return home with three small fish and again relegated to caveman-style spearfishing. I hope I can hide this fact from John, as I would be very embarrassed for him to find out that I have already lost the elastic he gave me.

In the morning, I return to the area on the 12-0 (the big surfboard) and paddle a long and very thorough search pattern while standing up, both of the area where I think it is and the area between there and the point where I noticed it was missing. I even search the area where I think it is a second time in a pattern perpendicular to my first search pattern. Since the air and water are calm, I can easily see the bottom as I paddle and drift across, but I never find the elastic and endcap.

After returning to the big boat, I have a mind to spearfish the cut as well as the other side of Crab Cay. I think it might be a good adventure to swim through the cut on the last of the outgoing tide, as close to slack tide as I can time it, then swim the length of Crab Cay, about a mile, while spearfishing.

In the northwest corner of the cut, the water is shallow and a forest of soft corals spring from the sand while little patches of hard coral provide oases of life. A wide variety of fish swim through here, and I am surprised at just how many fish there are. With no elastic on my spear, I am relegated to simply thrusting the primitive weapon at fish.

After a few fruitless attempts to spear moving snapper, a hogfish catches my eye. It swims behind a soft coral, stops, and changes color to blend in. Dark vertical stripes magically appear on its side, mimicking the coral. I sneak up and clumsily jab my spear at the fish with much force, but it darts away as soon as my shoulder movement gives away my intentions, the spear hits the hard bottom, and the impact nearly sprains my wrist.

I move on and swim along the outside of the island, towing the dinghy all the way to the end of the island, about a mile, where I climb back aboard and row another mile back to *Windflower.*

As of April 15, the US has 600,000 cases and 26,000 deaths from the coronavirus. Our president halts funding to the World Health Organization, and accuses them of mishandling the affair. Also in the news, our president is demanding that his name be printed on the stimulus checks, even if this causes a delay. Every tax-paying citizen of the USA has been promised a $1200 check.

During the day, on Little Abaco Island, large fires burn and send huge plumes of grey and black smoke billowing into the sky. I assume the fires are burning hurricane debris. During the majority of my stay here, the smoke has blown away from the anchorage, and has not been an issue. There was one day when I could smell it, and by the evening I was becoming intolerant of it, but it was gone the next day. I knew at this point that I would not want to stay here if the wind were to blow directly from the direction of the fires.

On April 16, the wind is predicted to veer and by evening will bring smoke directly into the anchorage. I fear that if the fires are burning, and I assume they will be, the smoke will become a real hazard in the anchorage. I decide to leave and choose Cave Cay as my next destination.

I sail off anchor and steer between the other vessels as I work my way out of the bay, quickly hitting 6.5 knots in 12-15 knots of breeze. We have the Sea of Abaco all to ourselves, with the exception of one small fishing boat that passes by, as we sail on a close reach. The sun is shining, the breeze is just the way I like it, and a fishing lure trails behind us, just in case I should be lucky.

As the breeze veers, we steer more and more away from our destination until it is 90 degrees to port, at which point I tack and sail towards West End Point and the narrow channel. The tide is middle and rising, perfect for crossing through the channel, which is six feet at low tide. We should barely make it through, but if we run aground, the rising tide will free us and I will turn around and go somewhere else, like Great Sale Cay. By this point in the adventure, I am crossing shallow areas at mid and rising tide, and I always have a backup plan. Anything less would be foolhardy.

The wind direction right now is not ideal for anchoring at Cave Cay, but if it veers as predicted, the anchorage will be acceptable. The following day I plan to move to the north side of the island an anchor off Little Cave Cay, since the wind is predicted to continue veering. Wind direction is always on my mind and always dictating where I go and how I anchor, and so far, in the Abacos especially, it changes daily as one front after another passes over. I am beginning to miss the all-around protection of Hatchet Bay.

The channel, as most are, is not visible except on the chart. Looking up, all I see is blue water under a partly-cloudy sky. Looking down at the chartplotter, I see very shallow water ahead with one narrow cut of deeper water where I might pass.

Sailing into the channel will put us almost directly downwind, and turning to port just inside the channel will necessitate a gybe, so I clip both preventers to the boom in preparation. I also start the engine, just in case something unexpected happens and I need to maneuver quickly or power off a sandbar.

The closer we get to the channel the more I realize just how narrow it is. It requires all of my attention to stay in the middle, and on top of this I have to let the sails out and tighten the preventer on the way in.

We pass through without incident, but the water on the inside is only between one and three feet deeper, so I have to remain vigilant. I also reduce sail to slow us down, since the wind has not yet veered as far as I hoped, and the anchorage is still exposed to it, but *Windflower* and I are in no hurry. We are in The Bahamas to sail, and we are sailing, so all is well.

The anchorage has a nice view of islands both near and far, with nothing manmade visible, but the wind blows 15-20 out of the east and across a mile and a half of shallow water before reaching us, producing a bit of chop. Luckily, *Windflower* is stable in chop and sits relatively still. I have two anchors set, since the wind is strengthening and veering and there is a rocky shore close by. The bottom is soft sand and grassy and I dive to set both anchors.

Location: 26.8614º N, 77.9082º W

This is a remote and lonely place, and grey clouds dominate the sky, adding to the loneliness. The island looks like a great place to explore, in more settled weather, with a shallow cove of bright blue water, a vertical rocky shore, and smaller rocks and cays that look like good places to spearfish. Even though it is windy and choppy, I can't resist the temptation of the rocky shore and I suit up, hoping to return with a fish for dinner.

The water is so cloudy that I can only see five feet at best. The bottom is covered in a fine silt and the choppy water has it all stirred up. I find a school of snapper, but my spearfishing is clumsy at best without elastic, and I can't get one. I return to the boat not only empty-handed but disenchanted with Cave Cay. The silty bottom means that the diving will likely be no good anywhere in the area. This is confirmed the next day, after moving to the north end of the island pair, where what looks like a sandy bottom from my boat turns out to be more silt. The visibility is very poor, and I cross the island off my mental list of places with decent diving.

Location: 26.8747º N, 77.9147º W

On the 17th of April, while I enjoy the solitude, if not the diving, at Little Cave Cay, the US has over 650,000 confirmed cases and just over 32,000 deaths from Covid-19, as the virus is now being called. Our president wants to start reopening the country, noting that the lockdown has caused a sharp rise in alcohol and drug abuse, heart disease, and other physical and mental illnesses. He proposes a three-phase schedule for reopening businesses, then schools, then lifting the social distancing protocols. But while he proposes May first as a date to start reopening, Dr. Fauci says that is too soon. New York has already issued stay-at-home orders until May 15.

Germany is easing restrictions, Austria has re-opened shops, Italy is opening some stores, Spain is opening some businesses, and Poland is lifting some restrictions. Meanwhile, France extends their lockdown to May 11, India to May 3, and the UK for 3 more weeks.

The news of the coming reopening of businesses, and

the continuous passing of fronts causing me to have to keep moving from place to place, are again making me think of heading back to the States soon. I wonder if I might be able to make it to Canada after all, assuming they open the border before July. I am also running out of islands as I work my way west, but I still want to explore Great Sale Cay and Double Breasted Cay.

I could stay at Little Cave Cay through the south wind, and the dolphin that swim around in the morning try to convince me to do so, but I am disenchanted with the island, due primarily to the poor visibility in the water. I am ready to leave, so I pull anchor.

We sail away on a broad reach in 17-20 knots of breeze, making 6.5-7.5 towards Little Sale Cay, where I plan to take shelter from the south wind and hope for some decent spearfishing.

Before reaching the long and skinny island, I first spot a series of rocks standing tall in the blue water and stretching in a line that leads to Little Sale Cay, which is oriented east-west. The wind is just south of west, so the island provides adequate protection, although the wind-swell wraps around the island and makes for a bit of roll in the anchorage.

As I arrive at the little island, tropicbirds fly overhead, always a welcome sight. Cliffs and caves make up what of the island I can see, and part of it is nearly cut through by the water. Someday this will be two islands, split at this low point. This and one other place look like it might provide dinghy access to the island, but even so it would be difficult to go ashore here. There is nothing resembling a beach. The only sign of man is a lone black pole on the west end of the island that rises a few meters into the air, and perhaps once held a light.

I motor around, find a suitable spot to anchor, and set two.

Location: 27.0452º N, 78.1704º W

As soon as the anchors are set, I row to shore and attempt to find dinner, but this is another fruitless effort. While I see many conch, I am not in the mood. I want fish, but don't even see any worth jabbing my primitive spear at.

However, fish is on the menu, because John and Kathi show up on *Makani*, and they give me a big mackerel fillet, which is perhaps the best fish I have yet eaten. They are heading out in the evening, after the thunderstorms pass, and will sail to Ft Pierce. Their cat dictates that they should not make longer passages.

I am thinking about trying for Double Breasted Cay, but I am not confident that it is deep enough for me to safely anchor in one of its sloughs (a narrow strip of water between two islands), where I will need to be to find shelter from the coming southwest winds. I talk to John about it, and he tells me that he thinks I can do it.

I decide to go for it in the morning. I'll leave at 4:00am and catch slack water at high tide around 6:30am. I set my alarm for 3:00am and go to sleep early.

The anchorage I hope for is accessible only by first passing through a shallow slough, subject to tidal current, then passing around a large sandbar in a tidal cut, and finally into another narrow slough between two cays. The comments on the chart say to only attempt this at slack water at high tide, because the current in the cut would set you either onto the sandbar or the rocks on the other side when entering the cut from the first slough. "Good light and visual navigation needed" is printed on the chart. I am sure to have neither good light nor visibility at 6:00am, but I trust the chartplotter and the Navionics app on my phone. Between the two of them, I feel confident enough to give it a try.

I wake up at 2:30am, well before the alarm goes off, and am up for an early start. The sky is without moon or clouds, so the stars shine in all their glory. I put the bimini down so I can take them all in as I sail. Although the stars are bright, the night is dark enough that I cannot see the rocky island only 300 yards away.

In my continuing effort to conserve fuel, I pull up the first anchor by hand. I have to let out a lot of the Vulcan's anchor line in order to reach the Fortress, and I am surprised at how much line I have out. Pulling up one anchor by hand is a lot of work, but pulling up two is more than twice as much work, because the second anchor must be pulled up while tired from pulling up the first.

By the time the Fortress is in, I am worn out and start the engine to motor up onto the Vulcan. I still have 47 gallons in the tank and ten more in jerry-cans, so I feel like I am being overcautious by not using the engine to motor up to the anchors. Besides, there is no reason, I realize, to sail off anchor, because the wind is too light to make it to Double Breasted Cay before high tide without the motor. I will need it anyway. Oddly enough, I always have to convince myself of the need to start the engine before doing so. I want to be the type of sailor who sails without the engine, and I take pride in sailing on and off anchor, even though there are no witnesses.

Sailing away from Little Sale Cay in the dark is a beautiful experience. The stars are out in full force and I stare up at them, using them as landmarks to steer by, taking in their beauty, and fully appreciating the present moment, aware of being in The Bahamas under a starry sky and sailing my extraordinary sailboat and home.

I am, at this point of the adventure, trying to sail without using the autopilot, since my main unit is down and I am not sure how much longer the backup unit will last. It has been making funny noises lately and I fear its time is running out. I both want to preserve what time it has left and I want the practice of sailing without it. Trimming the sails without an autopilot would be a lot easier if *Windflower* was still tiller-steered, as she had originally been, and once again I feel like the steering wheel's long-term appointment is in jeopardy.

I use the bright spreader lights while pulling up the anchors, but now that we are underway, all is dark. I feel for the main halyard, reach back to turn into the wind, and pull with all my might.

At the beginning of my time in The Bahamas, I was never able to pull the main all the way up without using the winch, but on this dark morning, I do, and I do it without the autopilot steering. I reach back a couple of times to steer, then continue pulling. Of course, the light wind makes this easier, but I count it as an improvement in my physique, yet another way that sailing in the tropical islands is making me healthier.

With the main up, I sit at the helm and rest for a bit before opening up the furling-line clutch and pulling on the leeward jib sheet. The genoa rolls out and takes its shape with a noise like a deep bass drum. *Windflower* accelerates another knot and I back off the throttle. *Little Flower* is following along behind us and I have to keep the speed below 6 knots to prevent her from filling with water.

Next up is the staysail, and I slide over to the windward bench while holding the wheel with my right hand and release the staysail downhaul, then pull on the halyard. It doesn't move.

Dang, I think, *it's caught on something.* The culprit is usually the old-fashioned and unused rope clutch on the mast. I lock off the wheel and carefully creep to the mast in the darkness, but now my eyes are adjusted and I push up the lever on the clutch on the mast and the halyard is freed. Carefully and crouched, I return to the cockpit. I really should be tethered, but I am getting complacent about tethering on these short interisland sails. It seems less dangerous here, but is it really? I look back and I can't even see Little Sale Cay. If I fell overboard here, I'd have to swim back to the island, where, assuming I found it, I may or may not be able to climb ashore, and then I'd be on an uninhabited island with no water and no food.

Back in the cockpit, I adjust the wheel to get us back on

course, lock it again, and pull up the staysail, which is small and easy to raise.

Once its sheet is pulled taught and cleated on the winch, I go below for a flashlight and use it to check the sails. The main is back-winding at the luff a bit, so I move the traveler to windward. The staysail is flat, so I let some sheet out, and take some in on the genoa.

The flashlight is bright, more so than necessary, and it takes my eyes a minute to adjust back to the nearly complete darkness. When they do, I am rewarded with a shooting star, and I smile while sitting at the helm, looking at the stars and nothing else.

Although I have no need of the autopilot right now, I turn it on anyway to test it, since it has been making funny noises. It steers for a few minutes, then the alarm goes off and the screen reads "motor stalled." This is not a good sign. I set it again, and after a few short minutes, it stops working again. I turn it off and consider my situation. I will need to either fix the autopilot, get the sheet-to-tiller self-steering working, or sail back to Florida in conditions that allow me to sail on a close reach at least some of the way, so I can lock off the wheel and rest. I'll need winds out of the west, ideally, but west winds always come with the passing of a front and thus foul weather.

I'm anxious for the sun to rise as we sail northwest. It's only a 10-mile sail and it is still completely dark. I can only enter at slack high tide, which should be at 6:00am, and I'll need good light to really be safe, which I certainly won't have. I'm willing to try it in less-than-ideal light, but weaving through the shallows in the dark would be an unwise move. The other problem is that if I run aground at high tide, I will be stuck for good, as the tide will only get lower.

I look at the horizon to my left and see a slight glow. That must be the sun coming up, I think.

I look around for boats and see none. The Bahamas are usually abuzz with boating traffic, even at 5:00am. Sport-fishers from Florida should be coming in for a week of fishing, spending money, and general debauchery. Sailboats should be slowly moving about, some going home and others arriving for two months of cruising before hurricane season. The Bahamas must be suffering gravely from the economic consequences of the pandemic.

Looking around the horizon again, an orange light, oddly shaped like a sail, stands tall on the horizon to my right and behind us. I've never seen a light quite like it, and I wonder what it could be. It's big, whatever it is, and it appears to be getting closer, fast.

I've let us drift downwind while looking at the mysterious light, and I look ahead again to correct the course.

The light's color reminds me of the moon, but it's on the wrong horizon; it should rise in the east, like the sun. I look back at the faint light on the other horizon, to my left, and it has not changed in the last hour, as a sunrise should. But what else could it be but the sun? I have a moment of confusion.

The world spins 180 degrees in my head as I realize that the light on my left is probably coming from South Florida, to the *west*. I look back to the right, which is the eastern sky, and a thin crescent moon is rising just over the horizon, oddly shaped like an orange sail. Just to the left of the moon is the faint glow of the real sunrise. For the second time in my sailing of *Windflower*, I have mistaken the moon for a boat.

I've always thought of the beach in Florida as being to the east, since it always is if you are in Florida, where I've lived for the past 23 years. This is how I've always oriented myself, by thinking about where the beach is, and recognizing that as east. But out here, the beach in Florida is to the west, which is a hard concept for me to grasp.

The sky slowly lights up in a barrage of warm colors, and as the low clouds on the horizon reflect all the hues between orange and magenta, Double Breasted Cay becomes visible ahead.

The water is still too dark to see through as I drop the sails and very slowly motor toward the entrance to the narrow channel. It is after 6:00, so I expect the tide to be slack, but I can see little standing wavelets on my side of a gap between islets to my right, indicating that water is flowing towards me through the gap and thus the tide is still flooding.

I put the transmission in neutral and wait to see if the current sweeps us back, but I detect no current, so I shift her back into forward gear and very slowly motor into the first slough, with the dark rocks of Double Breasted just feet to my right and Sand Cay to my left.

[*I should have had more patience. The fact that the tide was still flooding presented me with an advantage that I did not appreciate at the time. It was still too dark out to see through the water, and if I had waited longer for the tide to finish coming is, I would have had enough light to properly navigate the shallows ahead.*]

My chartplotter shows low-tide depths of 4-6 feet where we are, at the entrance to the slough, but I also am monitoring Navionics on my phone, which is more optimistic about the depths, and more recently updated. My sonar shows a minimum of 7' at one point, but then increases to 11' in the middle of the slough. As the sun slowly rises behind us, it illuminates a rocky bank disturbingly close to the right and a sandy beach not far to the left.

As we proceed, the sandy beach to the left becomes shallow water and the island on the right comes to a rocky point. This is where we will enter the channel where we might get pushed to the left by a strong current, and I'll have to take evasive action to stay off the sandbar.

I aim a bit right as we cross into the channel and accelerate as the current grabs the bow and tries to push it left. We shoot out into the dark and hopefully deep water of the channel in the low light of the early morning, where everything looks dark blue or black. The current pulls us to the left and I turn us that way, hoping to enter the other slough and the final anchorage by Sand Cay. I need to keep clear of the shallow sandbar on the left, but I can't tell the depth of the water in this light, and since we move with the current, everything is happening fast. The depth gauge is reading 9', then 8', 7' then quickly moves to 6' and even 5.6. I turn hard to starboard, back into the channel, I hope, and all the way around, pointing in the opposite direction. It's just too shallow, mission aborted.

We motor back to the entrance to the first slough, and I carefully enter as the current tries to set us onto the sandbar again, but once in the slough, I feel safe. The tide is nearly slack, and the current in here is minimal. I drive around in a circle, drawing a line on the chart representing 10' depth, then motor to the center, facing the current, put her in neutral, and proceed to the bow, where I drop the Vulcan near the top of the circle (the upstream end). I let out all the anchor line, then check our position, seeing it still within the circle, I drop the Fortress, then pull back in half the Vulcan's line while letting out the Fortress'. When we are in the center, I attach kellet weights to both lines and drop them on 10' of line each. We are here!

I really should have exercised more patience. Had I waited for better light, I would have avoided the harsh current and seen the deep-water route to the anchorage I was hoping to get to.

Location: 27.1976º N, 78.2861º W

After a short break to take in the beauty of my surroundings, I dive on both anchors, setting the Fortress in the sand where it lay while a barracuda swims by, checking out the newcomer. The bottom near the rocky bank is thick with grass and looks like conch habitat while the bottom everywhere else is white sand. The water is clear and cool.

The Vulcan sits on what looks like sand from above, but closer inspection shows it to be hard bottom. It is also a bit too close to the rocky bank, so I pick it up and walk along the bottom, carrying it to the center of the slough and deeper water, then set it in the soft sand.

Since strong wind is forecast to blow from the southwest, which would push us toward the rocky shore, I pull a third anchor out of the stern lazarette. It's only a very small Danforth, like a large dinghy anchor, but it has 300' of line. I row it all out and set the anchor in the shallow sandbar to the southwest, then return to the boat and pull the line tight. We lay to three anchors now, a first for me, and I feel safe.

By this time, the tide is going out at about 3 knots and we face the opposite direction as we did earlier, laying now to the Fortress. The sandbar begins to expose itself in a horseshoe shape as the water drains out into the Atlantic.

I want to end my time in The Bahamas in a beautiful setting, and Double Breasted Cay provides such. The water is clear and bright blue, little islands dot the horizon, a barracuda lurks under the boat hoping for handouts, and we are surrounded by what look like interesting places to snorkel.

I feel uncertain if I am going to like living in civilization after this experience, although I think some aspects of it will be nice, like being able to properly do laundry. But I've been living in such peace and quiet, close to nature, surrounded by natural beauty, for nearly four months. I certainly don't miss concrete and buildings, cars, noise, airplanes, and the crush of thousands of other people.

Living on my boat in the island has been healthy for me, of that I am sure. I certainly feel stronger than I have in years, but I also recognize mental benefits. My mind is clear, my confidence is as high as ever, I have little fear of anything, and I am at peace with myself and the world, even though the world seems to be going insane.

lying to three anchors at Double Breasted Cay

Windflower is oriented with the outgoing tide in the slough between Double Breasted Cay and Sand Cay. Walker's Cay is in the background.

On my second day at this magical island, compelled by the need to explore my surroundings, I row with the outgoing tide out and around the corner to the north side of the island, to the open water between us and the barrier reef. The water is calm and clear on the other side and I see what would be a nice anchorage in east through south winds and no north swell.

I row in the bright sunshine of the clear day past some small coral heads, then get in the water and drift by, spear in hand, but no fish are foolish enough to get within its short range. I see some beautiful fish, including a midnight parrotfish, which might be a first. But I only return with a conch, which I find particularly disgusting to clean and this emotion carries over into the meal and ruins it for me. Conch are, after all, giant snails, and thus slimy and gross.

I clean the conch on the edge of my boat, tossing the parts I deem waste into the water, while the barracuda underneath darts out and picks up my offerings. I'm surprised when a butterfly ray, which has a very short tail and no spine, glides onto the scene and displays itself in an aggressive manner to the barracuda, who disappears under the boat while the ray gets the rest of the scraps. I would have expected the opposite.

As the day wears on, the wind veers to the southwest and tries to push us into the rocks, and it would have if not for the little Danforth anchor, whose ½" nylon line is pulled so tight that it points in a straight line, 300' from the bow to the anchor, pulled, most likely, way beyond its intended working load. Yet it does its job faithfully and *Windflower* stays in the deep water of the slough and off the rocks, which seem awfully close before the wind veered, and now positively threaten.

While studying the chart on Navionics, looking for a

place to anchor after the southwest wind, for I am ready to be out of the tidal slough with its changing currents and rocky bank so close by, I notice a "?" symbol on the chart near the entrance to the slough. Investigation reveals it to be an uncharted rock that reaches the surface at low tide. The "?" symbol denotes that it was posted by a user. I could easily have hit this rock on the way in.

I begin to think that I acted foolishly for having sailed in here in the near darkness, and for not having studied the chart more carefully beforehand.

The barracuda is out in the morning, curious when I drop the ladder overboard and probably hoping for a snack. He swims back under the boat, but returns again when I drop the fenders over. I hooked him the day before, while fishing with conch as bait, but the big fish doesn't show any animosity towards me as I get in *Little Flower* and row to the sandbar to pull the small anchor from the fine white sand.

I pull the other two anchors at slack tide and motor out of the narrow tidal slough and into open water, moving very slowly and keeping exactly to the track that the chartplotter recorded on the way in. I anchor outside in between two large rocks, setting only the Vulcan. The rocks look like they might provide good snorkeling and perhaps lunch tomorrow, but the sun is nearly setting, so I only get in the water to set the anchor in the grassy bottom.

Location: 27.1885º N, 78.2712º W

Being anchored out in the open water feels liberating, without the strong and changing current and without the shallow water on two sides and the rocky bank right next to me. I am more relaxed out here; it was stressful to be depending on three anchors to stay in place and out of the shallows. Outside, with space all around and the rocky island half a mile away, I feel safe and stable. The change is good, as was the variety and protection that the tidal slough provided.

Soon after I anchor, three white tropicbirds come by to welcome me to this little-anchored spot. They fly about above *Windflower* with their long white tail-feathers trailing behind, chattering in their bird language, and then take off in three different directions. It is as if they are discussing their plans for the day, perhaps sharing information about different feeding locations, before getting started.

The tropicbirds come back after an hour or two, have another conversation, and again fly off in three different directions.

As the sun slowly climbs over the grey sea, the clouds fade, the world brightens, and the water becomes clear and blue and inviting. I get my gear together and slip into the water.

After giving the hull a brief cleaning and checking the anchor, I climb into the dinghy and set out for one of the two big rocks nearby. Since I will be fishing caveman-style, without elastic on the spear, I need to go after something easy.

I hunt around the two emergent rocks and the reef between them, then follow the reef further east. After chasing a grouper into a hole and never seeing it again, I find a lionfish. My desire to eat fish outweighs my fear of being stung by one of their 13 poisonous spines, so I row back to *Windflower* and get the three-pronged speartip, then return and spear three lionfish.

I am swimming in shallow water, about 5' deep, when a small school of large barjack, too big to spear, show up and swim very close to me, clearly checking me out. They turn and swim by me a second time. I can tell they are looking at me. It's a very strange thing to make eye contact with wild animals, and a reminder that they too are sentient beings.

Right after they pass the second time, a big nurse shark swims towards me from the direction the jack initially came. The shark turns away when it sees me and swims off toward the deeper water, and all the jacks immediately get in front of it. They are clearly escorting the shark, just like the barjack escorting the stingray at Little Galliot Cay, and they left their escort to investigate me, a potential threat.

Back at the big boat, I clean my catch and enjoy yet another fine meal of fresh fish while taking in the beauty of the tropical island setting. The water and sky are blue and nearly featureless, while the island is composed of stark brown rocks with a bit of green vegetation scattered about. I can neither see nor hear anything man-made, rather the beauty of nature fully embraces me. The clear water and the successful spearfishing have restored my good mood, and I am again happy to be in The Bahamas and ready to stay longer, although I am running out of islands to explore. I could stay where I am for one more day, but another front is coming and I will need to move again in two days.

Looking off towards Sand Cay, I notice an emergent rock that I haven't yet seen. It is low tide and I suppose this is the rock that the user labeled on the Navionics chart. I am again reminded of how careful we need to be when sailing around in The Bahamas, especially when off the beaten path. At any point, there could be an uncharted hazard just below the surface, waiting to gouge a hole in any passing boat. Good light really is a necessity out here.

I have no phone reception at Double Breasted Cay, but a friend reports, via the Garmin InReach, that the CDC estimates 2.5 million cases of covid-19 worldwide and 170,000 deaths, and 799,000 cases in the USA and 43,000 deaths. Discussions are underway about how and when to ease mitigation measures. South Florida plans to do so gradually but will tighten back up if cases rise. Japan and China both tried to ease restrictions but have already tightened back down.

The following day is calm and beautiful. The water is flat and its surface motionless and featureless, showing the grassy bottom ten feet down. The tropicbirds meet again in the sky above me, have their usual brief conversation, then part ways.

I read up on sheet-to-tiller self-steering in Andrew Evans' book and make some modifications to the system I have been setting up. I tie a snatch block to the base of a stanchion on each side of the boat just in front of the mast. I will run the staysail's sheet through the snatch block on the windward side of the boat and lead it back to the cockpit, where it will tie off to the short tiller I made.

The last time I raised the mainsail, and many times before, the sail's leechline got caught on a particular mast cleat, one that was unused. I set out to remove the offending cleat, but its bolts are frozen. I get out the cordless 4" grinder and cut it off. I am on a mission to make the raising of the mainsail as easy as possible, and any obstacles that cause me to have to go up on deck need to be eliminated. I want smooth, consistent, and reliable performance of all of *Windflower's* functions. I also remove the unused rope clutch for the staysail halyard on the mast.

My father sends me an update on the InReach. New cases and deaths are leveling off and decreasing in most states. Florida is reducing its stay-at-home restrictions, and Louisiana plans to do so May 1st. Higher risk groups are going to need to continue social distancing until a vaccine is made available or herd immunity occurs. He reports that the economy is a mess and that the oil and gas industry is about to collapse. Gasoline is down to $1.52 and the primary concern is for all the jobs suddenly lost and decreased state revenues which are dependent on taxes and royalties from oil and gas.

I suppose we are seeing the folly of an economy dependent on consumption. I wonder what a better system would look like. My father responds that there is a lot of discussion in the news media about exactly this, a better system coming out of the pandemic.

Our economy and our way of life are changing. What

has been an economy based on growth and consumption is bound to fail in an overpopulated world. Resources are being depleted and ecosystems destroyed. In a natural system, populations are controlled by predation, starvation, reduced fertility, aggression, and disease. If we continue on as before, this is what we will face, with the exception of predation, unless things go so bad that we began to eat each other, a grim possibility. Disease, war and starvation will be our population controls unless we consciously decide, as a world community, to reproduce less and to consume less, and to better protect our precious ecosystems. If we don't live in harmony with nature, nature will take no pity on us and we will end up living short and miserable lives on an inhospitable planet.

In order for our economies to survive, they need to be based on something besides over-consumption. They need to reward those who provide essential services, instead of just paying those workers the minimum possible while a select few are able to amass gluttonous stockpiles of money. I don't know what the specific solutions will be, but they must be put into play. For instance, it makes no sense to me why those who physically grow food, make clothing, or build houses make less than those who have figured ways of manipulating the monetary system. If someone does not provide a necessary good or service, they should not make money. Professions that strive to make money as the number one goal should not exist, rather they should strive to provide a necessary and quality service or produce a useful and quality product. When money is the number one goal, the highest priority, then the whole world suffers.

The most important aspect of any line of work is that it be honest, providing an honest product or service for an honest price, a necessary product or service, not one that is harmful or deceitful. Any job being considered should be analyzed under these criteria.

Making money without producing a good or providing a service is dishonest, it's like theft, or taxation without representation. Just because you can take something doesn't mean you should. We should all use our abilities and powers for good, not strictly for personal gain, and this takes discipline.

Today is hot and sunny, one of the first that feels like summer. The wind is very light and the water calm. *Windflower* drifts in the slight tidal current with her anchor rode slack. As I look down into the water, I am shocked to see a large coral head right behind us, too close for comfort. I am about to go spearfishing anyway, so I get in the water to investigate. Sure enough, it is a threat to the keel. I take off my fins and swim to the anchor, pick it up, and walk it out as far as I can, pull *Windflower* forward by the rode, and set the anchor.

This is yet another lesson about how uncharted rocks or coral heads could be anywhere. I vow to proceed with even more caution in the future.

Before rowing out, I spear a lionfish at the coral head by the boat, then I row to the third rock where I stopped the day before, where the barjack-escorted nurse shark swam by. Starting with a kill so early boosts my confidence, and lets me know that I will not return empty-handed.

I am limited to what fish I can go after without having elastic on my spear. Those that constantly move are impossible to get. But fish that instinctively try to hide are still on the menu. These include grouper, who always hide under a rock or in a cave, hogfish, who like to hide behind soft corals and alter their color to blend in, lionfish, who trust their poisonous spines to protect them and don't run away unless I miss, and bluestriped grunt, who hide under rocks, behind soft corals, or just on the bottom, where they lighten their colors to blend in to the sand.

For the lionfish, which I have come to think of as something like poisonous snakes, I use a three-pronged speartip, so they cannot slide down the spear and sting me. I also make sure to have a bucket in the dinghy, so I can keep them contained within and not accidentally sit on one when I climb aboard over the transom. The three-pronged speartip also allows me to slide them off the spear without having to handle them, as I do with the other tip that has a hinged barb that has to be held down and finessed back through the fish.

The lionfish are easy to spear, since they remain still when approached, and they have a fairly soft skin that the spear easily penetrates. Since they are an invasive exotic species, it feels like doing a community service to kill them. Some spearfishers just kill them and leave them for dead, since the lionfish actually do harm to the reef ecosystems.

For other fish, I prefer the speartip with the hinged barb, which holds the fish as long as it passes all the way through the fish's body.

Swimming along the rocky edge of the island, I see many fish. I spend some time following around hogfish, and jab my spear at more than one while they hide behind soft corals. But they are all too quick. I also see grunts, more large jacks, mutton snapper, and I get another lionfish.

I eventually reach the end of the island, and, like most of the other points I have encountered, it is full of fish. Two big mutton snapper swim by, but leave quickly when they see me.

As I swim close to the bank and look out in the deeper water, I notice the soft corals on the bottom bending sharply and vibrating, a clear sign of a strong outgoing current. I swim out once around a large rock, feel the current, and get back into the eddy up against the bank. I don't want to mess around in any strong current pulling out to sea, so I climb back in *Little Flower* and row up the island to a cut leading into the inner slough between the two long parallel islands that make up Double Breasted Cay.

The water in the slough is calm and still, without any hint of current. I row while looking for fish in the clear water, and notice that the bottom looks like silt, but I occasionally see small heads of coral.

Eventually I come to a large soft coral shaped like a menorah, and it appears to be animated, as if its entire shape is made up of fish. As I get closer and pass over it, fish scatter and I realize it is a big soft coral that was completely surrounded by fish. As I drift and look down, I spy many more fish and corals. This is a honey-hole for sure, and I drop the anchor and slip quietly into the water.

Fish crowd the area and swim all about. Most of the fish are bluestriped grunt, and many of these are larger than any others I have seen. Usually these fish are too small to justify spearing, but some of the individuals here are big enough to get my attention. I also see a few parrotfish, and one enormous starfish, or sea star, as biologists like to call them, since they are most certainly not fish.

Sea stars are strange animals whose vascular systems are full of seawater, instead of blood. The water vascular system is used to power the little tube feet that cover the bottom of the animal, which reach forward, attach via suction cups, and pull the sea star slowly along. Most sea stars eat by ejecting their stomach and enveloping their meal. When a sea star is injured, it drops off the injured arm and grows a new one. Usually the severed arm dies, but in some species, it grows a whole new body. Sea stars are animals, with males and females, and in the same phylum as sea urchins and sand dollars. That's right, sand dollars are live animals too.

My first choice is mangrove snapper, and I sit still on the bottom waiting for an opportunity, but they are all constantly moving, and not having any elastic on my spear, I give up on them after a few tries. I see some mutton snapper too, but they don't let me get close enough to even try. The grunt, however, sit still and try to hide from me. I spear three, one of which I hit right behind the eye. This fish dies instantly, and the others I grabbed with my left hand and held them out of the water while swimming back to the dinghy.

At this point, I have five fish and don't feel the need

to try for any more. I row up to another cut, which has a strong incoming current, and row hard to get outside. Rowing through the cut is like rowing up a river against the current. Outside, the water is calm and clear and I watch the bottom pass by as I row back to *Windflower*.

my last catch

The wind is forecast to strengthen and blow from the southeast tonight, so I need to move. Right next to us is Great Cay, and Well's Bay, which is on the western side of the island, looks like it could provide the protection I need.

High tide is not until after dark, but the depths between Double Breasted and Great Cays are adequate and I need good light for the short trip. I want to be able to see any rocks or coral heads that might be lurking just beneath the surface. I wait patiently for the tide to start coming back in before leaving and pull anchor at 5:00pm. I motor very slowly away from Double Breasted Cay and follow the route suggested by Navionics, for the most part.

Unfortunately, we are facing the sun on the way out and I can't see beneath the surface of the water at all. Most of the way is 12-15' and we move along at 5 knots when it is deep, but I throttle way back when the depth gets down into the single digits. I take us well outside of the little islands to stay in deeper water and luckily, we don't hit anything.

Passing all the little islets of Double Breasted Cay and the bright blue shallow water is a treat for the eyes. Dark brown rocks and little specks of land decorated with bits of greenery contrast with the turquoise water and the baby-blue sky. On the eastern edge of Grand Cay, perching just above the water, sits a cluster of pastel houses and grey wooden docks that connect land to sea.

The final approach to Well's Bay, which is to be my last anchorage in The Bahamas, takes me very close to the ominously named Burying Piece Rocks, all of which have strong tidal current ripping between them and coming my way. Each cut between the rocks has waves from the current like river rapids and the current pushes *Windflower's* bow hard to port while I steer to starboard to compensate.

The water running past the final rock, which I will turn around to enter the bay, looks to have the most current, and the charts show a shallow sandbar and a submerged rock very close downstream. I can't allow *Windflower* to get pushed to port when we pass by the rock, and the current looks fierce.

I throttle up and start steering to starboard early. The current hits us hard, but *Windflower* is already turned into it before we enter, and we pass across without being pushed aground, turn straight into the current, and slowly work our way into Well's Bay.

Dark green grass covers the bottom of most of the bay, so I motor around until I find a patch of sand as close to shore and Burying Piece Rocks as I can get while maintaining 10' depth.

Although the wind is coming from the north, we need protection from southeast through southwest for the night. It is forecast to blow up to 21 knots for the next day and a half.

I drop the Vulcan in a bright patch of sand surrounded by grass, let out 125' of rode, and get in the water to inspect.

Location: 27.2319º N, 78.3479º W

Underwater, I see that my patch of sand is actually flat rock with about an inch at most of silt on top. The Vulcan has dragged about 20' and found a little ridge to hold onto. But the patch of flat rock is surrounded by thick grass which rises above the rock depression, so I figure if the anchor drags, it would soon lodge into the grass. I test the grass with my spear and am able to easily push it deep into the bottom, so I leave the anchor alone.

Back onboard, I let out all the Vulcan's rode, drop the Fortress, then pull in half the Vulcan's rode. With two anchors out and no obstacles anywhere near us, I feel safe, even in strong winds. I go below and make a pot of chili.

While at Well's Bay in blissful solitude, I'm able to communicate with my sister, who lives in the Orlando, Florida, area. I ask about my three nieces. Since school is closed and they are all staying home and socially isolated, I am curious about how they were doing.

I am surprised that all three of my nieces are very disappointed at school being closed; I don't think this would have disappointed me at their age. The girls also see the good side of being able to spend more time with family

The oldest, who is in the 7th grade, has mixed feeling about school being cancelled. While she misses school and her friends, she is happy that exams are cancelled, but, like the little scholar she is, she also worries that the canceling of the exams might leave her unprepared for the 8th grade. Mostly, she is worried that things will never be the same and the quarantine will become the new normal. I have similar fears. She says her teachers told the class that this year would be historic and that teachers in the future would teach their students about the pandemic, but my niece thinks there would be little to say, except "Everyone was locked in their homes and too scared to leave, in fear they could catch the coronavirus." But while she is occasionally upset about it all, she knows others have it worse, like her sister in the fifth grade, and a friend who is a senior in high school.

The middle niece is devastated at the prospect of missing out on fifth-grade graduation and all the fun things that go along with it, like the student-teacher kickball game, the school play, reading buddies – all of which are cancelled. She finds the quarantine to be terribly boring, knowing every morning what the day will bring, riding the same route on her bicycle, playing the same games with her sisters. The worst thing, she says, is that she will never be able to say goodbye to her teachers and schoolmates as she is going to a new school the following year.

The youngest niece says that the worst thing about the quarantine is that it is "tearing apart my third grade like I do to mac-n-cheese."

Meanwhile, the quarantine is only preventing me from going ashore at Grand Cay, which isn't a big deal. I don't have any need to go ashore anyway, and I really don't know if I would be prevented from doing so if I tried. I am mostly unaffected by the quarantine, except that it has caused me to stay in The Bahamas for an extra month, and I will no longer be going to Canada in the summer, unless the borders open back up and I get all the work done to the boat quickly.

Well's Bay is a beautiful place. A long sandy beach lies on Grand Cay to the south, which we face. Green trees with their surviving branches covered in green growth look oddly misshapen, with no greenery between the branches, just empty space. Small islets and rocks to the southwest and west separate the bay from the Little Bahama Bank and shelter us from the waves produced by the southwest winds. Behind us sits Walker Cay, and to the north, the little Tom Brown's Cay. Seal Cay sits to the northeast and more rocks stretch from it to Grand Cay and its sandy beach. It all gives the impression that we are completely surrounded, yet the Atlantic Ocean is exposed to the northwest. I imagine it would be deadly rough in the bay with a north wind or a north swell running.

The Fortress holds us in position after we swing around in the night as the wind veers to the south. I didn't even set this anchor the day before, I just dropped it and made sure the chain didn't lay on top of it. The Fortress set itself in the thick grass. It and the Vulcan make a fine team.

In the morning, I sit in the cockpit drinking coffee in a peaceful state of mind. The air is clean and smells of nothing, and the contrast to breathing the mainland air, all full of dust and pollen and exhaust and everything else, is immense. My nostrils feel like wide open caverns, allowing free passage to the life-giving air, which for much of my life has been noticeably restricted.

Even so, I find myself looking forward to experiencing a bit of civilization, and I am not sure why. Perhaps I just want more contrast; perhaps The Bahamas has already become normal. I certainly am ready to do laundry, and I occasionally think about going to Café 11 on the beach and eating a big brunch with my lifeguard friends after a long ocean swim. The thought of a hot shower sometimes pops into my head. But these are all just luxuries that were common in my terrestrial life, and I am growing used to living without them, so I worry that returning to Florida will be anticlimactic and only interesting for the first coffee and the first hot shower, and then will quickly become overwhelming in its noise and hustle and the crowds of people.

I have certainly been in my element in the islands, deep within nature, fishing, swimming, surfing, diving, sailing, and writing. Meeting people was a new pleasure, since it had not been in my nature to do so before, but I accomplished the feat of changing myself and becoming more outgoing, introducing myself to strangers and smiling and making friends, and I like it.

People often ask if I am lonely sailing by myself, and the fact that I was going out of my way to meet other sailors might suggest that I was lonely, but I never felt so. The only time I get lonely is when I want to be with other people, but can't. This primarily happens on land when I am surrounded by other people, but have nobody to be with. When at sea, and no other people are anywhere nearby, there is no room for loneliness. Solitude takes its place.

The worst loneliness, for me, requires the possibility of intimacy, and the inability to obtain it. I am much more apt to get lonely when in society, when intimacy is unobtainable. Of course, I'd like to have a woman in my life, but I also know the time would soon come that I would want to sail away, alone, again. Being alone all the time, and separated from everyone, is much easier for me. Even so, I feel almost ready to return to society, if only for a few months.

Out here, I am happy to be alone, and the lack of other people makes it easy. I appreciate the peace and quiet and never having to compromise or suggest something only because I think my partner might want to do it. I like not having to confer with anyone over all the decisions. In fact, if I was not alone, I very likely would have gone straight to Florida when the alternator broke way back in December. I would have worked on the boat there for a month or more, and would have arrived in The Bahamas right before the quarantine started. I would have missed out.

Since I was alone on the boat, responsible only for myself, I was able to risk the passage and was rewarded with four months in the islands. I was able to make all the decisions for the entire journey, there was never an argument, and nobody ever broke my train of thought when I was gazing at the stars or simply enjoying the silence.

It is a funny dichotomy, I prefer being alone most of the time, but meeting other people is always a highlight.

As I sit in the cockpit, gazing at the peaceful surroundings, I reminisce on the highlights of my Bahamas 2020 adventure.

Surfing was certainly a highlight. I was able to surf a whole lot more on this journey, compared with the last time I was in The Bahamas, and I got more good waves in these four months than I did in the previous three years in Florida. All the days at Surfer's Beach, the friendly people I met there, the long lefts, the clear water, getting barreled on the shallow sandbar, will forever remain as fond memories. The short session I had at Egg Reef stands out as well. That reef, being nearly 2 miles offshore, feels like surfing in the open ocean, and the water there was clearer than any I've surfed in. I caught good waves at Elbow Cay, but the quarantine cut my surfing time short. I look forward to returning to the Abacos and exploring all the reefs that appear to go unsurfed.

Diving at Little Galliot Cay was a favorite. I'll never forget swimming through the cut between Little Galliot Cay and Big Farmer's Cay, in the deep and clear water, coral all over the bottom, the schools of fish, and the snapper I speared that almost got away and I had to spear a second time.

The sheer number of islands and reefs in The Bahamas is staggering and so great that one could not see them all in a lifetime. The next time I am here, I hope to dive more on the barrier reefs outside the islands, as well as the reefs in Exuma Sound.

Spearfishing at Hatchet Bay was a real treat, especially with all the new friends I made there. The depth was just enough to feel like freediving, but not dangerously deep. All the fallen rocks provided incredible habitat, as well as swim-through caverns. And the variety of life was endlessly intriguing.

The next time I visit the Bahamas, I intend to bring much more fishing gear. I'll bring a better fishing rod, a good spear, and I'll have a freezer to store fish when I catch more than I can eat in one sitting.

I also look forward to meeting more Bahamians next time. They were all so friendly and generous, always offering a ride when I was walking, or advice about where to go. But once

I got to the Abacos, the quarantine made it nearly impossible to meet anyone new, especially locals.

On April 24, the wind shifts in the night while blowing 20-25 knots and I get up more than once to check the anchor lines. While walking from the bow back to the cockpit, I happen to look down into the water and see something amazing. Flashing and hypnotic globes of light catch my attention and I stop walking and stare down into the black water at the light show within. The water is thick with lights, some the size of an egg, others as big as a large grapefruit, all at varying depths, flashing, fading, flashing, fading. The lights turn on and persist for a matter of seconds, then quickly fade. At any one moment, over a dozen lights can be seen in my small field of view. They must be everywhere, a mass gathering of luminous creatures who converse in flashes of light.

I imagine they are ctenophores, relatives of jellyfish. I have seen these in dense schools in many places in The Bahamas. They look like little footballs of clear jello, roughly the size of a large egg or smaller, and do not sting. Ctenophores are carnivorous, like jellyfish, but swim by beating cilia (like little hairs) that run down their bodies in rows, and are known to be bioluminescent.

In the morning, the wind blows from a new direction, chopping up the water and giving us a different view of the same place. The sky is cloudy and grey, and I imagine what the bay would look like on a calm sunny day. No doubt I would be exploring the underwater world around all the emergent rocks, diving beneath the surface, hunting grouper and snapper, and towing *Little Flower* behind. But in the windy, choppy, and cloudy weather, I feel no desire to get in the water. On the contrary, I feel my time in The Bahamas is coming to an end.

Throughout the day, thunderstorms roll by, some in the distance, others close, and some pass right over us. When the rain falls hard and thick, I stand on the deck and take a real shower, with soap and shampoo, for the first time since the Abaco Inn. I feel so clean, and am reminded of the luxuries of land and civilization, and I know the time to leave is coming soon.

I study a new weather report, taken from the Garmin InReach, and make a chart in a notebook. I pull up three weather reports: my location at Great Cay, 50nm east of Cape Canaveral, and 5nm east of St Augustine. I make three columns on the page, one for each location, and write the wind speed and direction, as well as the chance of heavy rain, for the times of day for the next three days, running vertically down the page. This way I can predict the conditions for a three-day passage to St Augustine.

While studying the weather, I realize that if I leave today, I will have a 30% chance of heavy rain tonight, a calm day for crossing the Gulf Stream, and a nice sail from Canaveral north to St Augustine. If I don't leave today, I will have to wait at least a week for another weather window. I make the decision to leave, it is time.

The wind this evening should be southwest to south-southwest between 10 and 18 knots, which should put me on a nice beam reach. Tomorrow, while crossing the Gulf Stream, it should be coming from behind at between 10 and 15 knots. Approaching St Augustine on Sunday, the breeze should be veering from southwest to west-northwest between 8 and 15 knots. It all looks like fine sailing, except that tonight there is a 30% chance of heavy rain, which doesn't sound like a big deal.

The tide is going out in the morning and high tide is not until 6pm. I want to let the thunderstorms pass by before leaving and I want to leave on a rising tide, since I am unfamiliar with the channel leading out, to the north, into the Atlantic Ocean.

I made a list of preparations for the passage yesterday, and have already started. Now I finish the tasks on the list:

Computer in plastic bag (I keep a large Ziplock bag in the

computer bag)

Charge all batteries (rechargeable flashlight, spotlight, cordless tools)

Lock all lockers (all have sliding bolts inside the doors)
V8 in lazarette
Prepares snacks, put in cockpit
Review route and obstacles
Foul weather gear ready
Lights ready
Handheld VHF outside
Watch on
Red pillow outside
Ditch bag ready and accessible
Binoculars in lazarette
Harness on
Seat cushions below
Deck organized
Flashlights outside
Headlamp outside
Sheet-to-tiller ready

In the future, I will add "check that all sheets are routed properly"

When the list is complete and the tide coming back in, I put on gloves and move to the bow, where I pull up both the kellet weights and stow them in the anchor locker. I then start the motor and pull up the Vulcan and tie it to a cleat. Finally, the Fortress comes up and we are underway. The Bahamas adventure is coming to an end, but the crossing adventure is only just beginning.

WELL'S BAY TO ST AUGUSTINE

Black sea mogul field
Wet sailor hands on wheel
Dynamic world free of light
Lit by heavenly fire fight
Rolling rumble booming free
Bass deep as angry sea
Wind unsure of its direction
Sails not trimmed to perfection
Sailboat built in seventy-two
Cuts the waves as old boats do
In these conditions she takes pride
Clearly she rather enjoys the ride
And at the helm wet sailor holds
Fast to the wheel with hands so cold
Staring off through black night
Holding down bit of fright
Alone at sea to nourish soul
Or electrify the sailor whole
Push a man to the very limit
Of mind and body when he is in it
And that perhaps is why we go
To sea alone so we can know
Just what it is that we can do
And what in life is really true
How far uphill can we push the ball

Like climbing a tree however tall
And just where lies our final limit
To love the world is to live within it

As we motor across Well's Bay at 2:00pm, I see five sailboat masts in the distance to the south, heading across the Little Bahama Bank, most likely sailing to Ft Pierce. While it makes me feel more confident about my decision to leave today, I briefly wonder if going to Ft Pierce is a better idea than going all the way to St Augustine, but I quickly dismiss the idea. There are still thunderstorms coming, and while I will be sailing across the Gulf Stream tomorrow, these boats will be crossing tonight and might have thunderstorms in the stream, a bad idea.

Besides, I have no desire to go to Ft Pierce, which would add considerable time and distance to the overall trip to St Augustine.

Following the suggested route on the charts, we motor slowly across the bay, then turn north to go between Tom Browns Cay and Seal Cay, two small and uninhabited islands. Tom Browns is a thin brown line of rock just above the water, while Seal Cay sports a sandy beach and palm trees. We pass between the two, then bare to starboard to avoid the big barrier reef to the west where waves break over shallow coral.

Outside the reef the chart labels Walker's Dive, Lobster Ledge, Shark Canyon, and Larry's Sharks. These last two names may have contributed to my decision not to spearfish at Well's Bay.

The white lines of waves breaking on the reef pass by on our left and then drift off behind, and the depth increases quickly through the hundreds of feet and beyond the reach of the sonar. Underwater, behind us is a plateau, the Little Bahama Bank, beneath us is a steep mountainside, and ahead is the abyss. St Augustine is 220nm away at 325 degrees.

We motor into the great Atlantic Ocean and the water is clear and blue. A bird flies over us and heads toward Seal Cay. A south swell rolls across the deep water and pushes us along, raising the transom, letting it down and raising the bow, endlessly repeating. The same waves that pass beneath *Windflower* continue on to either Florida, where I hope surfers will catch them, or to the reef I can still see to port, where they break in white lines.

While I expect wind from the southwest at 15-17 knots, which would be a fine beam reach, there is no wind and the sails remain down. Perhaps, I think, the thunderstorms have taken all the wind for themselves, but I'm sure it will come back and we will sail. Motoring all the way home would be no fun, but technically I could do this. If we motored at 5 knots in still water and 8 knots in the Gulf Stream, we could cover the 220nm in about 34 hours, and I have plenty of fuel for that.

Before the wind comes, a dolphin 300 yards to port leaps out of the ocean, coming our way, and smiling, as they always do. It leaps again, much closer this time, then I see it next to the boat, and more join in. The dolphin are small and decorated with white spots. They swim fast and leap often, and one has a pink belly. They must be Atlantic spotted dolphin, I think.

I turn on the autopilot and move to the bow, where I hold on to the furled jib and stare down into the water at the marine mammals, bowriding and jockeying for position. They ride the wake, dip out of sight, return, switch sides, roll, break the surface to breathe, and sometimes leap. They must be enjoying the ride; they certainly approached fast, excited to find a boat, leaping and looking at *Windflower*, confirming that what they hear in the distance is in fact a sailboat and thus a creator of waves.

This is surely a good omen, I muse, as I watch the animals play in the bow wake.

Since arriving in The Bahamas, all of my journeys have been smooth and I feel like my sailing skills have improved significantly. I have gotten to know *Windflower* much better and we have developed an amicable relationship. I've learned how to better prepare her for passages, become more efficient at hoisting, trimming, furling and reefing her sails, improved my skills at balancing her sailplan, and generally gotten to know her much better. Five months ago, when we were docked in the Chesapeake Bay, I was still timid sailing her, but now I have the increased confidence that comes from having sailed her over 1500nm.

The dolphin leave, but come back later for another ride, or perhaps these are different dolphin. It's hard to say, but they brighten my spirits just the same. It's a fine day to be on the ocean, wind or no wind, and I am happy to be returning to St Augustine, which I have not seen in six months. This is the longest I've been away in 23 years. I wonder what it will be like to return, and if I will be anxious with all the people, traffic, and noise; or will I appreciate its beauty and charm like I did when I first discovered the historic waterfront town?

A little bird flies by, not a sea bird, but a land bird. It circles us, then flies across twice, and finally chooses a spot and lands on deck. It's a small green and yellow bird, a yellow-rumped warbler, perhaps. The bird leaves, then returns with two of its friends and they all rest for a while before flying away.

How is it possible that such small and delicate birds could be out here, flying across the ocean, and in no distress, resting only for a few minutes before continuing? When the bird first landed, I expected it to stay. I thought it must be lost at sea and would ride with me until land was in sight, and we would become friends. But the birds all flew away as if impatient to get to wherever they were going, full of energy, healthy, and stopping by *Windflower* out of opportunity rather than need.

I feel a bit of breeze and check the anemometer, which reads 8 knots. If it rises above 10 I'll set the sails. I need to keep moving at 5 knots or more, because we need to be in St Augustine before Sunday evening, when the winds will veer to the north. Fifteen minutes later, the breeze is up to 9 and in another ten minutes it reads 10. I put the engine in idle and raise the mainsail, then unfurl the genoa.

The breeze continues to strengthen and veer and we have to alter course to starboard to continue sailing, for the wind is coming from the west, not the southwest as I hoped. Ahead and to port, the ocean becomes hazy and textured with jagged lines. A stronger breeze is surely coming and I furl in some of the genoa before it hits.

The breeze indeed hits, and with a vengeance. The anemometer jumps to 20 and *Windflower* heels to starboard. Our course alters even more to the north, and beyond to NNE. We are no longer heading towards Florida, but rather to Cape Hatteras or New England.

The new breeze comes not alone, but with waves, and they crash into the south swell, tackling each other like football players and throwing each other into the air like mad wrestlers. What was a calm ocean only moments ago has become chaotic and wild.

The water rises and falls, leaps and sprays in the wind. Waves who were formerly on a predictable and stable course now collide and refract, unsure where they are going. *Windflower* cuts through, but also takes waves on the beam, and our progress to windward is minimal, as is our speed.

I reef the mainsail while the autopilot steers, then retake the helm. Our course continues its progress to starboard, and I make the call to tack. I prepare the windward jibsheet, then turn the wheel to port. Since the genoa is on the headstay and the inner forestay is still rigged, I have to furl the genoa to tack, and, with bare hands, I pull hard on the wet furling line while turning into the wind.

Windflower turns in the confused waves and slows, and continues turning for longer than I expect. We were not as close to the wind as I thought, and *Windflower* stops turning before we tack, and the sails luff. We are "in irons," facing the wind and nearly stopped, an embarrassing position to be in and quite undesirable, especially in these conditions.

Our speed drops below 2 knots and we drift back onto a close reach while the waves and wind have their way with us. To get moving again, I steer us a bit more down and let the traveler down as well, but in the confused sea state, we don't accelerate like I hoped. Once we get moving again, I put the traveler back up and get us onto a close reach, then turn the wheel again, a bit more aggressively this time, and we tack. I let most of the genoa back out, but not all.

Once on a close reach on the new tack, I see that we are headed towards the barrier reef only 5nm way. We have tacked through 160 degrees, and thus are not making any reasonable progress to windward.

Something doesn't seem right with the genoa, it's leach is too curved. Is the lazy sheet holding it back? No, it's free and slack. What is it then? Aha! It's the line that held the Ocean Cruising Club burgee that I took down this morning. I tied the line back to the lifelines and I must have let the jib sheet get under it in the process. I clip in, set the autopilot, and creep to the leeward rail. I try to untie the line, but it's under pressure and I start to feel unsafe. Wait, I think, this is why I carry a knife. I pull out my sharp pocketknife, flick it open with one hand, cut the offending line, and the sheet springs up. I carefully creep back to the cockpit and retake the helm.

We sail on a close reach with spray occasionally wetting everything with warm saltwater, but we are heading for the reef now, only four miles away. I need to I tack again, and hope that the shifting wind is to blame for our poor progress to windward. I go through the process again, pulling on the furling line with wet hands, hard, as we turn to starboard, then letting the sail back out on the new tack.

But the results are the same, our new course is 160 degrees in the other direction. Normally, in calmer conditions, we could tack through 100 or 110 degrees, but it must be the confused sea state that has us tacking so poorly, or perhaps I have overlooked some problem, something not set up properly, one of the many lines not as it should be.

Whatever the problem, I am not willing to continue beating into the wind and making almost no progress to windward. I start the engine and check for lines in the water, then furl the genoa yet again. This is the strongest wind I have furled the genoa in, and not only is it taxing on my strength and my hands, but the sail furls tighter than it has before, and there is not quite enough furling line, so some of the sail remains out, which is embarrassing. Now I understand why there should be extra turns of furling line on the roller furler. I drop the main, check again for lines in the water, and put the engine in gear. We motor directly into the wind and the waves at 4.5 knots as the sky slowly darkens.

Little Flower, firmly strapped to the deck and cushioned with fenders, is askew. She has slipped off one of the fenders and is not only loose, but grinding into the deck. I have to fix this, so I set the autopilot, clip my tether to the jackline, and creep forward. I have to untie one of the lines that strap her down, lift her stern and push the fender back in, all while getting sprayed while *Windflower* crashes through the waves.

Once the fender is in, I re-tie the line, pulling it as tight as I can. I have her tied down better this time than I did on the passage to The Bahamas, but I clearly need to improve the system.

Back in the cockpit, I think I hear a rumbling from the west. Dark clouds are coming at us from that direction, and the 30% chance of heavy rain I now recognize as very real thunderstorms. I had hoped that they all passed by earlier in the day, but there is no denying the dark clouds and the rumble of distant thunder. As the sky darkens, distinct but faint flashes signify lightning to the west. I hope the storms pass by without incident, and I am reminded that the reason *Windflower* has electronics from 2016 is that she was struck by lightning.

The unfavorable wind backs and weakens after the sun sets and I decide to put the sails back up. With *Windflower* pointed into the wind, I pull on the main halyard, and nothing happens. The sail remains where it is and the halyard gives no resistance to my pull. Something is terribly wrong and I go below and turn on the spreader lights, which light up the entire deck and all the rigging below the spreaders about halfway up the mast.

The main halyard is dangling ten feet off the deck, just out of reach, and tangled in the lazy-jacks. The wind is only 12 knots, but the seas are still lumpy and confused. I think about climbing onto the boom, but dismiss the idea as too dangerous. The wind is just aft the beam, so I leave the halyard alone and unfurl the genoa, shut off the engine, and sit at the helm. I clip my long tether to the port jackline.

It's dark now and the western horizon flashes with light, yet I hear no thunder. It must be very far away, the storm, and we sail under the genoa alone through the lively sea, which remains invisible until a distant flash of light reflects off its dynamic surface.

The dark cloud to the west slowly engulfs more of the sky, and I watch it carefully, monitoring its movement and hoping that we will pass in front of it, but I know that this is not going to be the case. The cloud will soon cover the sky above us, bringing rain and lightning and more wind. It's not likely to be a pleasant night.

I watch the anemometer closely as the wind speed increases into the upper teens. When it begins gusting to 20, I furl more of the genoa, leaving only half of it out. The dark cloud is close now, and the loud thunder booms soon after the lightning, which are no longer diffuse flashes in the upper atmosphere clouds, but rather distinct bolts that connect sky and ocean. The thunder gets even louder, as if it is trying to scare me. A bolt off to port lights up the world with an explosion I can feel in my chest and three more flashes quickly follow.

The night is now black and flashes of light reveal snapshots of larger waves and airborne spray. I check the wind speed and it is now consistently above 20, but I feel more wind and the number rises to 25, then 27. Needing a boost of confidence, I clip my second tether, the shorter one, to the starboard jackline. Doubly clipped in, I feel better immediately.

The rain comes next and I pull the yellow raincoat from the lazarette, quickly put it on, and fasten all the snaps, thankful that I didn't have to go below to fetch it. The storm also brings waves and though I can't see them, I feel them lift the stern and we accelerate before each wave passes.

I hear it coming, then feel the pressure of more wind. *Windflower* turns herself more downwind and I keep the new course. The anemometer reads 30. A wave picks us up and we ride and our speed hits 8 knots, a boat speed I have not yet seen. I steer with the wave and we surf for a matter of seconds before it passes. Another lifts us and we surf again. The wind remains at 30 and the rain pelts me from behind while I steer with feet braced.

The lightning is all around us now, not threateningly close, but flashing and booming on all sides, bolts of unmeasurable energy connecting ocean and sky. The adventure level is high. I smile through gritted teeth while steering *Windflower* in the rain. The storm won't last forever, I remind myself. It will pass at some point, and I will take a nap. At least there is no traffic out here, in fact, I have not seen one boat since I left Well's Bay.

A flash of lightning illuminates the foredeck and again *Little Flower* has slipped off one of her fenders. This adds to the sense of chaos, but I can't fix it until the storm has passed.

The wind continues to blow, varying between 25 and 30, the lightning and thunder keep up their show. I remain at the wheel, focused on steering and reacting to the waves and gusts, trying not to look at *Little Flower* askew on the foredeck in the intermittent flashes of light.

After an hour or two, I can't tell, the wind steadily decreases and the rain lets up. I carefully make my way to *Little Flower* and fix her fenders and straps a second time.

The sky lightens and a star shows itself for a moment, then a cloud covers it, but minutes later another hole opens in the sky and more stars shine through. I steer by them as I stare up at the heavens.

Another dark cloud flashes diffusely and silently off to the west, but where we are, the wind is ideal for sailing, and I aim to get the main up. I go below and dig out a reaching and grabbing tool, with a handle on one end and a jaw on the other. It extends my reach about two feet. While below, I notice the old skateboard helmet hanging from a handhold. I've been carrying this helmet around for as long as I've been sailing, but hve never put it on, and now is just the time.

I stand on the rolling and pitching deck under the glare of the spreader lights with my long tether clipped to the starboard jackline and the old grey skateboard helmet protecting my head. The lights are bright and all I can see is the boat, but I know just outside my field of vision is the vast and indifferent Atlantic Ocean, which would swallow me up without pause if I fell in, although the tether should prevent that. I wouldn't be on deck without it.

My left arm is wrapped around the boom, which, although sheeted tight, swings back and forth about two feet in either direction while I hang on. In my right hand is the reaching tool and with it I try to reach and grab the halyard. I can see its shackle hanging open as it swings around. The halyard is no longer wrapped around one or two lazy-jack lines, now it's tangled in more lines that I can figure from my perspective, looking up into the bright lights at the swinging line while standing on a sailboat moving through unsettled seas.

I lurch back and forth with the boom, the line swings all about, and the reaching tool snaps its plastic jaws at the line. I have a moment of doubt and wonder if I shouldn't just go sit down in the cockpit and deal with this in the morning. I could just stop now.

I imagine myself falling backwards, catching the life-lines just below the waist and flipping overboard backwards. The tether catches me after I hit the water and holds firm while I am dragged alongside the boat, which is under sail and auto-pilot. As I struggle to keep my head above water, I think *you could have just left the halyard for tomorrow....*

But I remain standing and lurching, snapping the jaws of the grabbing tool at the halyard that swings just out of reach, like the coin-operated game with the stuffed animals in the glass case and the jaws that never close around the toy you want, or any other toy.

Finally I get the halyard in the jaws of the tool, but now what? Both hands are occupied.

I wait for the boat to lean to port and the boom swings that way and I rest my body against it as I let go with my left hand and transfer the tool from right to left and the halyard from tool to right hand. I've got it! But now what?

The halyard has been swinging around for hours and has wrapped itself around every line possible. I can see the last line it wrapped around and I loop it under one of the lazy-jack lines. One down.

Peering up into the bright spreader lights, I see a miasma of light and lines, and I don't feel so good anymore, but I mentally crush the threatening nausea. *I don't get seasick anymore*, I tell myself.

The next line to go around is another lazy jack, and then another, and I am making progress. The boat continues to pitch and roll and the boom swings back and forth, and I hang on with my arm. My left hand still holds the reaching tool, and I tell myself that I should have put it in the cockpit. I think I might just toss it in there, but I think better. I need to respect the tool that kept me from having to climb onto the boom, and I could use a break anyway.

I tie the halyard to a lazy-jack and return to the cockpit, where I set down the reaching tool and myself. I feel an immediate sense of exhaustion. And I lean back and close my eyes for a moment and melt into the bench as *Windflower* sails herself.

Moments later I feel better and return to the deck and the boom and the tangled halyard. The more I untangle it, the harder it is to see what needs to happen next, since the wraps are getting progressively higher up. Eventually I realize that it's around the boom topping lift (the line that runs from the top of the mast to the end of the boom) and to get the halyard around this, I need to take the halyard to the cockpit and outside the bimini and to the stern, where I might be able to loop it around the topping lift.

Finally, the job is done and I tie the halyard back to the sail, return to the cockpit and start raising the main. But as I pull the main up, there is noticeably more friction than normal. I crank hard for several minutes, denying the obviously increased friction. I want to believe that I've untangled the halyard, but deep down, I know there is still an issue. I leave in one reef, but by the time I have it up, I am thoroughly exhausted and need to sit down and shut my eyes again.

After a quick nap, I feel much better, and the conditions are better too. We are now sailing on a beam reach in 12-15 knots, fine conditions indeed. The sky ahead is clear enough that I can see the stars and I steer by them, one of my favorite things to do. I don't know the names of the stars I look at, or what constellation they are in, but I use my peripheral vision to keep the scene ahead consistent, and I keep one particular star in between the mast and the shrouds, occasionally glancing down at the heading on the chartplotter, then at the boat speed and the wind speed. We sail at 6 knots in 12-15 of breeze, it's no longer raining, and all is well, in fact, for the moment, it is a beautiful night.

I see no boats on the horizon or on the AIS, so I set the

autopilot and the countdown timer on my watch and lay back on the curved teak helm seat. When I rest my head against the lifelines and turnbuckles, I discover a great benefit to the skateboard helmet, which I forgot I was wearing. With it on, I can comfortably lean my head against anything. I fall asleep before I realize I'm trying to.

I wake 20 minutes later and look around. Off to the west, the dark cloud is moving forward. I hope it will pass ahead of us, but I can't be sure. Diffuse flashes of light and barely audible rumbles of thunder tell the tale of another thunderstorm that we might have to deal with.

Two ships show up on the AIS, but I can't see either of them. I check their statistics and see that they are both Carnival cruise ships, and both report speeds of zero. They are not moving. Within the hour, four more ships show up, all Carnival and all stationary. The depth here is over a thousand feet, so they aren't anchored, they're just sitting on the ocean, in international waters, waiting for better times. I've never seen boats do this.

I imagine they have no passengers and nowhere to go. With all the ships they own, the cruise lines must not have nearly enough berths for their ships, and I suppose they have been ordered to remain at sea until further notice. I wonder what is happening onboard one of the behemoths right now.

There must be countless empty rooms, restaurants devoid of the smells of food, ovens and stoves cool, swimming pools empty, movie theaters and stages quiet and dark. Someone probably sits at the helm reading a book or watching a movie on an iPad. Maybe some of the crew are in one of the theaters watching something on the big screen. Maybe one crew can play piano and is performing for the others as they raid the endless bar. Maybe they are all melancholy and worried about the future of their employment. Maybe some are sick and others isolate themselves in their rooms.

I wonder if the crew have taken the best rooms for themselves, having stayed only in tiny rooms with no windows, and now enjoy huge staterooms bigger than the houses they live in at home. Would the captain even know?

For the last two hours, the storm off to the left has been getting closer, and there's little doubt now that it will soon be on top of us. The wind is also backing and the speed is slowly increasing. As much work as it was to get the mainsail up, I now need to drop it again, and so it comes down and rests in the lazy-jacks. When we pass ahead of the first stationary cruise ship, I take another nap, feeling like this is my last chance to get some rest before the next thunderstorm.

It's gently raining when I wake up, and the dark cloud has moved closer. I want to know how close it is, so I switch the chartplotter to radar. But when I try to activate the radar, I find that I can't turn it on. The touchscreen, which is wet, does not respond to my fingers. This is one of the reasons to have radar, so we can see how far away and how thick thunderstorms are. Sometimes dark clouds are not heavy storms and thus don't show up on the radar, but storms with heavy rain do show up. It's a shame that now that I really need it, I cannot turn the radar on and will simply have to take whatever comes our way.

The wind comes and is accompanied by heavy rain and choppy waves, again from aft and slightly port. We ride the storm out as we did the last one, surfing downwind at 8 knots when the wind blows 30, and running on a deep broad reach at 7 to 7.5 when the wind blows 25. It is an identical thunderstorm to the last one. To a certain extent, I enjoy the excitement, but the storm is frightening, with lightning and thunder, wind and waves. It's as if the ocean is reminding me that it doesn't care if I live or die tonight.

The mighty *Windflower* takes it in stride and seems not to mind a bit. I only worry about the rigging, which was new in 2003, seventeen years ago, and the saying comes to mind that a ship can take more than her crew when sailing to windward, but the crew can take more than the ship when sailing downwind, as we are tonight. I hope I am not pushing *Windflower* too hard, but I don't even want to try furling the genoa any more. I can't see it, but I think about half of it is out. I think I might be better off with the genoa completely furled and just the staysail up, but I have left it down, thinking I would only use it for sheet-to-tiller self-steering, and since the wind direction and speed have been changing so much, I haven't tried this yet.

The storm drags on and on. It seems to last much longer than the first thunderstorm, but I can't be sure. I have no idea what time it is, or what time it was when the storm began, or how long the last storm was. I exist only in the present moment, because the present moment is demanding all my attention; time has little significance; action and reaction are more important.

It's raining hard now, my hood is up over the skateboard helmet, and I am thankful for the protection that the bimini provides. I think back to the time I was sailing *Sobrius* through a thunderstorm at night without a bimini. That was so much worse, mainly because I could not see at all due to the hard rain pelting me in the face and filling my eye sockets with water. The memory makes this seem easier, and really, I have no choice but to sit at the helm and steer, turning more downwind when the wind increases, riding the waves, making sure to keep the sail full and not turn beyond straight downwind. I'm also glad not to have the mainsail up; it's much easier, I have learned, to steer downwind without the main.

At some point in the long and difficult night, I realize that all of the lightning is off to starboard, in the eastern sky, and this means that the bulk of the storm has passed. I study the sky to the west, looking for any sign of more storms. Finding none, a sense of relief falls through me. The wind is decreasing, ever so slowly, from 25-30 down to 20-25, which makes quite a difference. The heavy rain becomes a light rain and the sky no longer seems angry, like it is running out of fuel.

As the conditions improve, I catch a glimpse of a point

of light in the otherwise black sky. It disappears, then later is revealed again, and others come out too, and before long I am steering by the stars. The wind calms to the mid-teens and I take a much-needed nap, resting my helmeted head against the steel railing and whatever else is behind me.

When I wake, stars dominate the sky and what clouds are left pass by like cars on a lonely road late at night. I look around, check the AIS, course, wind speed, and take another nap. The next time I wake, the sky is brighter and the sun is making its presence known to this side of the world. I sit up to watch the spectacle, and as slow as the big hand on a clock, the sky changes from grey to purple, then magenta and red and orange, yellow and blue, altering and moving across the clouds on the horizon, and finally the great ball of flame pierces the horizon and rises above the ocean. The thunderstorms are gone and the sun is here radiating happiness to illuminate a better day.

As soon as the sun rises, it moves behind clouds and the colors fade to grey and the magnificent display is completely over. Happiness becomes melancholy. The breeze blows only 5 knots out of the west and we motor on, approaching the Gulf Stream. I'll take it, these conditions, without complaint. After last night, I need a rest and I lay back for a nap, the first of many on this calm and peaceful, although grey and cloudy, day.

So far, the passage has been a far cry from the ideal sailing I had hoped for. Regardless, I am thankful that today is calm. Not only do I need the rest, but today we will cross the Gulf Stream, and to do so in thunderstorms would be very unpleasant.

At 11:30am, St Augustine is 138nm away at 319 degrees and Great Cay is 87nm behind us. I think we can make it to St Augustine by 2:00pm tomorrow if I can maintain focus and hold us on a straight course, and assuming we get some wind before too long. At the moment, the sails are down and the engine and propeller push us along at 5.5 knots. I lay back for another nap, as there is nothing in sight except water and sky.

An hour later, our speed is 6.5 knots. We are in the Gulf Stream at last, 60nm east of Cape Canaveral.

I expected wind in the mid-teens from the southwest today, but so far we only have 6-7 knots, and still we motor. I continue napping, and am in and out of sleep so much that I can't count how many naps I've taken. It's all a blur. All I know is where we are and what the conditions are. Everything else is irrelevant. Yesterday has exhausted me, and today I am trying to recover, by napping 20 minutes at a time, over and over again, as we cross the vast and lonely sea, strangely devoid of shipping traffic.

At 1:20pm, the south breeze arrives at 10 knots. I hoist the main and unfurl the genoa and we make 7 knots, helped along by the current which must be about 1.5 knots, as well as the engine. We motor-sail because the apparent wind is only 3 knots.

I enjoy the ride, then at 2:00 I lay down and immediately start dreaming. It's as if the dream starts as soon as I close my eyes, before I am asleep. But the sleep comes at the dream's heels. I nap until 3:00, waking each time after only 10 or 15 minutes. When I rise, the sails are slatting, even though the breeze blows at 9 knots; our speed is also 9 knots, so the apparent wind is zero. I take the sails down and leave the engine to do its job.

At 4:30pm, with gloved hands, I raise the main and unfurl the genoa. The skin on my hands is raw and sore, probably from all the line handling in the rain last night. The mainsail, as it often does, rises with much resistance. I check on it at the mast and find the leechline to be caught on a cleat. I curse the line out loud, then realize that I am angry. I'm glad no one is here to witness my lack of emotional control, and I remind myself that I am in the Gulf Stream in calm conditions, so a hung-up leech line is of no consequence. I suppose I need more sleep.

The breeze is fine and we sail on a beam reach. I shut off the noisy engine and we still make 9 knots. The current must be about 3 knots in our favor. The seas are calm but the sky is still grey and cloudy. Clear and beautiful water stares back up at me, bright sapphire blue, while the sky, in strange contrast, is grey.

At 6:30pm, we are north of the cape and 40nm east of the Canaveral Peninsula. The world is brighter than it was an hour ago. The clouds have moved on to the west revealing blue sky and bright yellow sun that feels warm on my skin and dries the deck and cockpit, which have been wet since yesterday. I take the bimini down, then lay back at the helm and stare up at the blue sky before dozing off yet again.

After an hour of short naps, the AIS detects a ship 20nm away. *Oasis of the Seas*, a cruise ship 360m long and 60m wide is anchored 20nm off the coast of Florida in 120' of water.

At 6:30pm, I shut off the engine and we sail again in perfect conditions: calm seas, 10-12 knots of breeze from ESE.

At 12:40am, we pass the fully lit-up *Harmony of the Seas*, another cruise ship at anchor. I wonder why all the lights are on and if there are passengers aboard, but there is no way to tell from two miles away. We are now 25nm east of Daytona. We are making 7 knots on a broad reach, and I drop the main, leaving the genoa to do the work alone. Our speed drops to 6.5 knots and the ride is fine indeed.

Soon after, the wind veers to just north of west and I raise the main again. My hands are still sore and it hurts to pull on the lines, even wearing gloves. We sail on a close reach and make 5.5 knots. I lock off the wheel and scan the horizon. There are no ships in sight, and the AIS agrees. I lay back to look at the stars. Right away, a meteor streaks across the sky leaving a long green trail of light that glows and disappears. I see two more before dozing off.

At 5:00 Sunday morning we are only 12nm away from the St Augustine Inlet. The breeze has backed to the west and we sail on a beam reach, perhaps the most pleasant point of sail. I make coffee while the sun rises and select chicken soup for breakfast. I don't know why I want chicken soup instead of my normal breakfast of oatmeal, but there certainly is no reason not to have chicken soup. I eat it from the pot while sitting in the cockpit watching Matanzas Inlet pass by. Ahead I can see small boats, probably the good citizens of St Augustine out fishing on this Sunday morning.

We continue sailing on a close reach, due north, until we are perpendicular to the inlet. Rick, from Sail Ready, texts and says he will meet me at the Oasis Boatyard to catch my lines. Rick is going to replace my standing rigging and he has arranged a slip for me, as well as a haul-out. I tell him I think we will be there between 10:00 and 11:00am.

I start the engine, drop the main, furl the genoa, check for lines in the water, and put her in gear. We motor towards the red and white safe-water buoy outside the inlet, and our speed increases as the tidal current pulls us in to the town I still think of as home.

I have a moment of anxiety about sailing my 40' boat, which suddenly seems big, into the notorious St Augustine inlet, through all the traffic I will surely encounter inside, up the narrow San Sebastian River, and docking at an unfamiliar marina. But then I remember all the narrow channels I traversed in The Bahamas, and all the currents I negotiated, the rocks and reefs I avoided, and I realize that motoring into St Augustine is child's play in comparison. On top of that, here I have Tow Boat US to come rescue me if I should run aground or have any other problem. In The Bahamas, I was on my own whatever happened. No, there is no need to worry about anything here in Florida.

Carefully and slowly I follow the channel markers, occasionally repeating the phrase "red right return" in my head. Shallow sandbars that have destroyed more than a few boats line the inlet on both sides, I know, yet they remain invisible in these calm conditions. When there is swell, waves break on both sides of the inlet, close to the boat traffic, and it is an ominous sight indeed.

The strength of the current increases as Vilano Beach and the houses of Porpoise Point pass by to starboard. To port a rock jetty holds the water back from the lonely beach of the state park. We pass Salt Run, where I used to moor *Sobrius*, and the Conch House Marina where my band I-Vibes played Reggae Sunday gigs. The houses and docks of Davis Shores passes by to port, and the Vilano causeway, over which I have driven many times, spans the Intracoastal to starboard.

Downtown comes into view, first the fort and its slanted coquina walls and ancient cannons aiming out at long-forgotten foes, then the historic buildings, and all the sailboats in the north mooring field, boats I admired from land for many years.

I call the Bridge of Lions and request passage on the next opening, then *Windflower* and I motor around in circles, like tourists looking at the city from the water.

The bridge opens at 10:30 and we pass through while cars and their drivers and passengers all wait, as I have done countless times. I ring the bronze bell that hangs from the solar panel arch after clearing the bridge and continue on past the City Marina and the south mooring field. A red sailboat catches my eye, one that I recognize. I recognize her by the red hull that I painted, the solar panels that I installed, the red jib that I hoisted, and of course the unmistakable lines of the Dufour Arpege. I forgot *Sobrius*, my previous sailboat, might be here, but I remember that Mark, the buyer, said he might keep her in St Augustine.

While boat traffic was absent on the ocean, here on the intracoastal it is thick and I watch the oncoming vessels carefully. One crosses my bow and heads into the mooring field to starboard while another passes to port. A dinghy is coming straight at me from Fish Island Marina. We are on a collision course, yet I don't alter my course since I am restricted by draft, but then I recognize the driver as Captain Josh, a friend who was at Eleuthera captaining a big catamaran at the same time I was there.

Josh waves and says "Welcome home," studies *Windflower's* lines, and congratulates me both on my choice of vessel and my successful passage. I tell him that I just arrived from Grand Cay, in The Bahamas, and he says "I know, I've been following you." This is one reason I love social media, the ability to share my adventures with others. Instead of trying to explain to people what I've been up to, now when I come home, they know already, since they have seen my pictures and read my posts.

We continue on and turn to starboard and up the San Sebastian River, new territory for me, and certainly for *Windflower*. At the Oasis, Rick and his wife Sarah step out onto the only empty slip at the end of a T-dock. I slowly motor past, turn around and very slowly approach the dock. I toss a line to Rick and Sarah takes the bow line, and all is well as *Windflower* comes to a rest after 4 months of hard work.

It's a wonderful thing to have someone meet you at the dock after making a passage, to recognize your passage and understand what you went through, to validate the achievement, and to catch your lines. Rick even has a keycard for me so I can get in and out of the marina.

The Bahamas was so nice, and I clearly don't like being cold, that I think I might stay here through the summer and return to The Bahamas as soon as hurricane season in over in November or December. I remember thinking, when I was sailing south from Massachusetts and then again from Chesapeake Bay, that there is nothing good about sailing in the cold. It's just miserable. I like warm weather, good surf, spearfishing, friendly people, and sunshine. Another season in the tropical islands might be good practice anyway, before attempting Newfoundland.

Being back in St Augustine was wonderful. I met old friends right away, was offered jobs, the use a truck, guest houses, and bicycles.

I walked into town, in my old neighborhood of Lincolnville, and got a bacon cheeseburger at the Blue Hen. There I ran into my friends Jay and Stephanie, and I joined them walking to the house of more friends where we ate by their pool. The hamburger might have been the best I ever had.

In the morning, I walked through town, deserted because all of the stores are closed due to the pandemic. I passed through the city marina, where I saw boats I recognized from The Bahamas: *Second Sojourn, Calliope,* and a Tartan 42. I was reminded of walking through town late at night, after a gig, when everything was closed and I was carrying gear back to my truck, and very few people were on the streets. But this is in the daytime, and I've never seen St Augustine deserted like this, but I have to admit, I liked it. Walking through town with almost nobody else around was a peaceful and unique experience.

I returned to St Augustine, my home town, after having achieved a major goal and life dream. I sold my house, quit my job, bought a bigger boat, moved onto it, sailed it from New England to The Bahamas, enjoyed four months of adventure, and wrote about it.

I learned that I can handle a 40' boat alone, that I love spearfishing and eating fresh fish, that I don't have to dive deep to enjoy the underwater world, that I do not like sailing in cold weather, that a bimini is a must-have, that I prefer a tiller to a wheel, that I want a windvane autopilot, that it is easy to make friends while cruising, and that making friends enhances the experience.

I reconnected with my love of surfing. I learned that a sailboat is an ideal place to live during a pandemic, that I can be alone for four months and not get lonely, that every island has much to offer and many places to dive and explore underwater, that hitchhiking is easy and safe in The Bahamas, and that the locals are friendly and willing to help.

I learned to ask for help when I need it. I learned that sailing downwind is easier under headsail alone, with the main down. I learned that the skateboard helmet is great for sleeping in on deck, that foul weather gear, snacks, binoculars, a VHF, the spotlight, and a headlight need to be in the cockpit somewhere with easy access while sailing on a passage. I learned that you can't trust the charts about minimum depths in anchorages, it's better to know the tide and its range.

While we live in a world that discourages chasing our dreams, I want to be a voice for the opposition. I say dream big, dream smart, and chase your dreams to the end. This is the only way to achieve greatness. This is the only way to achieve satisfaction. This is the only way to live, wild and free, doing exactly what you want and nothing else.

Implicit in the sky
and speed of wind
the day will pass by
at work and mend
for the weather is king
and will dictate
what the day will bring
and choose my fate
On a calmer day
I'd row to a reef

CHASING THE NOMADIC DREAM

descend in play
tropical fish to seek
But when conditions
are not so kind
I find a mission
within my mind

EPILOGUE

It is now late November, 2020. *Windflower* and I are still at the Oasis Marina and Boatyard, where I have been working on her since our arrival in late April.

I hauled out specifically to fix the bottom of the keel, which I did, and to replace the standing rigging and mast step, which Rick and Sarah Gardner did. But as refits go, all the tasks multiplied.

In effort to fix the leaking hatches, I injected epoxy in the small cracks between the wood trim they sit on and the deck. This led to varnishing the wood trim, and that led to varnishing all the exterior teak, a difficult two-month job.

I decided to replace *Windflower's* cutlass bearing, and this led to a new propshaft. It was recommended that I replace a couple parts on the engine, and in that effort, I discovered that it is nearly impossible to find parts for the Westerbeke 40. I ended up replacing the engine with a Beta 38, and of course, that meant a new propeller as well.

I also installed a Hydrovane windvane autopilot, installed new chainplates and bolts, replaced the boom, repaired bulkheads, added new deck hardware, rebuilt the seahood, replaced the holding tank, and completed countless other tasks in my effort to both make *Windflower* a comfortable home and the stout and seaworthy vessel she was meant to be.

I intend to return to The Bahamas and spend the winter there, and then go to Newfoundland in the summer. But the covid-19 pandemic is making this difficult. At present, travelling to The Bahamas requires getting a covid test, applying to the Bahamas Health Department for permission to visit, then arriving in The Bahamas within five days of having taken the test, and clearing customs at one of the designated offices. After clearing customs, there is a five-day quarantine, followed by another covid test, and after this one is permitted to cruise within a given area. Moving to another island group requires permission and another test after arriving. This all makes travel there difficult, but I imagine the spearfishing will be very good this year!

Canada's border is still closed. If it remains closed next summer, I will consider sailing to the Azores instead, and possibly mainland Portugal afterwards.

The dreaded "second wave" of covid-19, as predicted by the scientists, is currently ravaging the United States, and much of the world. The United States now has 11.5 million cases and has had 250,000 deaths. Globally, there are 57,407,792 cases and 1,368,818 deaths. Yesterday, the boatyard shut down because one of the employees tested positive. In June, 19 lifeguards here, and one of which I swam with, tested positive. Soon after, my parents got it, and I spent two weeks in Louisiana looking after them. Thankfully, they recovered, but those were two miserable weeks for them and two scary weeks for me.

I am still chasing my nomadic dream, and so far, I have greatly enjoyed it, although the last six months have not been nomadic at all. Rather they have been living mostly on the hard, and working very hard. But this is all part of what it takes to live on a sailboat, and soon I will be cruising again.

In the last six months, I have learned a lot, mostly about my boat, and boats in general. There is no denying the benefit of working on one's boat, and doing as much of the work oneself as possible. I now know a lot more about diesel engines, electrical systems, and all the intricacies of my boat than I did in April.

I have also reaped the rewards of living an honest and generous life in St Augustine for the last 23 years. After arriving, I was given a truck to use by my friend Todd, and I drove it for nearly five months until he needed it back. In that time. I was then offered the use of another truck by my friend Dave, which I can use on weekends or evenings, since it is his work truck. My friends Mark and Tanja let me stay in their guest house for a week, and my friend Danielle let me stay in her guest house for three weeks, and I house-sat for her in her main house for two weeks. This all allowed me to avoid living on my boat, on the hard, during the hottest part of the summer. My friend Noah lets me keep a surfboard at his apartment, which is oceanfront, and he also let me use a bicycle, which has been a great help. And finally, my friend Jay is letting me use his woodshop, which is just down the street. This has allowed me to make quite a few custom pieces for the boat, and has made me the envy of a few other boaters here.

All of these people have helped me, I assume, because they like me, and this, I assume again, is because I have lived my life seeking good karma over personal fortune, and I have learned that the former is vastly more valuable than the latter.

The nomadic dream is still alive, and I am still chasing it. The dream relies on my own motivation and hard work, specifically writing books. But it also relies on people like you, who have bought and read my books, so I thank you, for you are the driving force behind my ability to live the life I have designed for myself.

Watch for my sailing and diving videos on YouTube, listen to my podcast "Offshore Sailing and Cruising with Paul Trammell," and keep an eye out for more books in the future. I'm currently working on a novel about treasure-hunting. Everything I do can be found at my website paultrammell.com

Happy sailing, and peace out!

ACKNOWLEDGE-MENTS

I would like to thank the following people: Dr. Christopher Ruhland for taking the time out of his busy academic schedule to edit this book; Cristina Vidal Artaud for her help editing the first chapter and for helping me sail from Mattapoisett to the Chesapeake Bay; Albert also for that sail; everyone at the Mattapoisett Boatyard for their kindness and help with *Windflower*; Mark Nunes for taking care of *Windflower* before me, and for selling her to me; Tad Morse for brokering the deal and for selling me *Little Flower*; my parents for their support; everyone at the York River Yacht Haven for their kindness and help; Rick and Sarah Gardner for setting me up at the Oasis Boatyard and catching my lines on arrival; everyone at the Oasis Boatyard for their help, kindness, and for sharing their knowledge.

BOOKS BY THIS AUTHOR

Alcoholics Not Anonymous, A Modern Way To Quit Drinking

Do you need to quit drinking now? This book will guide you through a modern and successful method that will get you sober, happy, and healthy. This is a short and concise book without filler. It is an accurate description of a method to permanently quit drinking alcohol or using other addictive drugs. Alcohol is a very addictive and destructive drug, yet it is commonly accepted and legal. A huge percentage of people are addicted to alcohol, so there is no longer any need to stay anonymous about having a drinking problem. By being not-anonymous, your chances of success are greatly improved. In this book, I outline a method to step away and stay away from drinking.

Becoming A Sailor, A Singlehand Sailing Adventure

"Fear is here for us to face, and adventure waits on the other side. "

This is a tale of chasing a dream. The story is told beginning with the vision and desire to sail on the ocean, through the training and education, buying a boat, gaining experience, and finally embarking on a 1000-nautical-mile journey home, singlehanded.

Journey To The Ragged Islands, Sailing Solo Through The Bahamas

Come along for the ride with Paul Trammell in his solo quest for adventure in The Bahamas. In this dramatic and immersive nonfiction, firsthand account of a singlehand sailing voyage, Paul sails alone on a 30' Dufour Arpege from Jacksonville, Florida to the central and southern Bahamas. Searching for uninhabited islands, blue holes, serenity, surf, and natural beauty, the author encounters all this, as well as foul weather, sharks, a near-death experience, beautiful sunsets, enchanting islands, a hermit, friendly sailors, coral reefs, whales, eels, and an old friend.

The reader will feel the power of the ocean and the exhilaration of the wind in the sails, the hand on the tiller, and the spray in the face. We will travel to the bottom of the ocean in blue holes and poke our heads into caves that lead to the depths the earth. We will ride waves alone on an offshore reef. We will face beasts who are considering whether or not to eat us. We will meditate in a stone hermitage on top of the highest hill in The Bahamas. We will face our fears and reap the rewards in the currency of adventure.

Dead Flowers On Wednesday

A small-time band embarks on their first tour in effort to chase their musical dreams. After a bizarre run-in with a violent motorcycle gang, the tour starts off fun and innocent enough, for a reggae band anyway. But things change as they abandon their inhibitions and get suckered into a bit of criminal activity. This leads the band into a downward spiral of violence and crime. Eventually they hit rock bottom and some pull themselves out, while others aren't so lucky.

Printed in Great Britain
by Amazon